Schools Council
Research Studies

Education of
Travelling
Children

Christopher Reiss

Macmillan

First published 1975

SBN 333 17468 2

Published by
MACMILLAN EDUCATION LTD
London and Basingstoke

Associated companies and representatives
throughout the world

Printed in Great Britain by
Hazell Watson & Viney Ltd
Aylesbury, Bucks

Schools Council
Research Studies

Education of
Travelling
Children

The report of the Schools Council Education of Travelling Children Project, based at West Midlands College of Education, Walsall, on the background and educational difficulties of Gypsy, canal-boat and fairground children, current approaches and successful practice in schools, and recommendations for development

Foreword

The Schools Council Project on the Education of Travelling Children was set up in January 1971 under the direction of Christopher Reiss and based at the West Midlands College of Education. The project continued for eighteen months; its brief was to inquire into the background of Gypsy, canal-boat and fairground children, their current educational difficulties and the educational approaches that are most successful with them.

This research study includes the results of questionnaires to local authorities and headteachers, and a survey of successful practice in schools visited by the project. Though data presented are for the years 1970–72 and great strides have been made since then in extending provision to travellers, the picture today remains essentially the same as described in this report. It is inevitable, when dealing with an area of education undergoing very rapid development, that delays between writing and publication result in a failure to keep abreast of the current situation. However, it is hoped that the range of provision described in this report corresponds accurately with current practice. Two main sections of the report are an account of the characteristics of travellers and the project director's recommendations for classroom activities and for the overall development of traveller education nationally. (The views expressed in the report represent those of the project and are not to be taken as necessarily being those of the Schools Council.)

The Plowden Report, *Children and their Primary Schools* (HMSO, 1967), named these children as 'probably the most deprived group in the country'. Under the implementation of the 1968 Caravan Sites Act, Part 2, an increasing number of children of travelling parents will be able to attend school as permanent sites are established. It is hoped that this report will be an aid to teachers and educational administrators faced with the problems of providing education for these children whose educationally inimical backgrounds and nomadic way of life may seem insuperable barriers.

Contents

1 Introduction

The project: context and aims

The setting up in January 1971 of the Schools Council Project on the Education of Travelling Children was a timely response to the rediscovery that most Gypsy and other nomadic children were receiving irregular or, in many cases, no schooling. The 1968 Caravan Sites Act, Part 2, was in the early stages of implementation, and it was thought that this would result in an immediate and widespread provision of Gypsy caravan sites by the local authorities of England and Wales. Permanent sites make access to school much easier, and it was considered that there was an urgent need for information and advice to teachers and local education authorities who would have to cope with the influx of school-age children from the new sites.

It was intended that the Gypsies should be the main study, but circus and fairground showmen's children and the children of bargees were to be included as a minor aspect of the project because there was very little knowledge of their educational predicament.

There was a topical and increasingly vociferous public concern about the educational privation of the travellers (that is, Gypsies and related groups), partly generated by the Gypsy Council formed in 1967, the National Gypsy Education Council (1969), and the National Council for Civil Liberties.* On the local level numerous support groups were being formed, and several voluntary educational projects were already operating—for instance at Redbridge, at Outwood in Surrey, and in Walsall. The social and political climate at local council and resident level continued to be controversial and in certain cases explosive. The travellers were conscious of the forces operating on them and of the major process of adaptation which they faced; if not fully desirous of schooling for their children, they were becoming more conscious of their lack of literacy and education.

* Confusion exists over the nature of the Gypsy Council (a civil rights organization sometimes called the National Gypsy Council) and the National Gypsy Education Council (a charitable voluntary body frequently abbreviated to NGEC). These confusions have been exacerbated by conflicts in both organizations which have recently led to the creation of the Romany Guild and the Advisory Committee for the Education of Romanies and other Travellers (ACERT)—concerned with civil rights and education respectively.

E.T.C.—I*

This new atmosphere had formed at the same time as the educational world was undergoing considerable structural change: the forming of comprehensive secondary schools, the raising of the school-leaving age to sixteen (RoSLA), the creation of open-plan primary schools, and of the middle school, the expansion of nursery schools and of the pre-school playgroup movement, and the setting up of educational priority area programmes (EPAs). There were also new preoccupations with educational aims and objectives, curriculum, materials and methods, teacher training, and a review of the role of school. The concepts of social and cultural deprivation and the education of minority groups were topical issues. Compensatory programmes were being studied in depth by the Schools Council Compensatory Education Research and Development Project based at the University of Swansea. Much was being written on these subjects in many countries.[1]

Some of the issues were being debated from socio-political and ethical standpoints; the terms 'compensatory', 'deprivation', 'disadvantage', 'restricted language', and so on, were under fire from many quarters. Interestingly, it has been Basil Bernstein himself who has led the socio-linguistic attack on traditional views about deprivation and language impoverishment on this side of the Atlantic—'interestingly' because his original notion of 'restricted and elaborated codes' has been one of the pillars, admittedly based upon a misinterpretation of Bernstein's actual statements, of the deprivation theories.[2] But the most telling attack has been mounted by W. Labov, whose in-depth study of non-standard English and social values prevalent among Harlem Negro adolescents in New York leads him to conclude that:

The notion of verbal 'deprivation' is a part of the modern mythology of educational psychology, typical of the unfounded notions which tend to expand rapidly in our educational system. . . . But the myth of verbal deprivation is particularly dangerous because it diverts attention from the real defects of our educational system to imaginary defects of the child. . . .[3]

Though unaware of Labov's work at the time of the initial writing of this report, the present writer had had increasing apprehension about the almost universal view expressed by teachers that travellers and their children were suffering from acute verbal deprivation which was, in many cases, seen as an insurmountable obstacle to educational progress. Labov's work, though in the Harlem context, provides a vital perspective to many of the conclusions of this report and to our notions about the disadvantaged child in general. The topicality of this project also derives from more general fields than socio-linguistics.

There was and still is much talk of majority culture being imposed on minorities, of the negative self-imagery developing among such minorities and of the abnormally high numbers of West Indian children, for instance, who were in special schools. There was talk of 'de-schooling', and a whole new jargon was being developed. The position of the Gypsy and the traveller was beginning to arouse much interest. The Council of Europe in 1969 passed a resolution that the education of travellers should be viewed with grave concern and subject to united international action.[4]

There was more interest than ever before in the world's distinctive minority groups, such as the American Indian, the migrant Mexican labourer, the Maori, the Aborigine, the Lapp, the Bedouin and the American black man. The ubiquitous European Gypsies and travellers, the fairground and circus showmen, and the bargees of Europe could be looked upon as another fascinating area for action and research. The days of concentration on the 'normal' child were over.[5]

It was beyond the scope and capacity of this project to attempt a comparative international study of nomad education. There was, anyway, a shortage of domestic national studies on such a subject. However, it is hoped that this report will provide one more localized study for some future major international review.

The purpose of the project was to aid teachers of travelling children by providing information about social background, cultures and educational needs of travellers and about the approaches, methods of organization and teaching materials that had proved to be most successful in schools which had already experienced the attendance of travelling children in significant numbers. It became increasingly clear once the project was under way that teachers welcomed it and confirmed that they were working in isolation and needed to know about methods being employed elsewhere. Though opinion was divided, particularly on whether assimilation or separatism should be the dominant approach, the majority of teachers expressed doubts about what they had or had not achieved already, and the potential power of education to alleviate a problem which was political and social in nature. Their reservations about the relevance of conventional schooling to nomadic families were mixed with the feeling that it might not be in the best interests of the children to continue to follow the life style of their parents in a changing world.

As the project progressed, it became obvious that these more theoretical considerations would have to be a major preoccupation of the report and that certain sections of the report should be addressed to educational administrators rather than to practising classroom teachers.

Methods of study

The methods of study used for the project were determined by five main factors:

(*a*) The project was run as a one-man team and operated for eighteen months.

(*b*) Only an atypical minority of the project's subjects were in schools; it was considered equally important to study the majority, whose non-attendance might be a symptom of factors of wider over-all significance than, for instance, classroom methods suitable for the small number of attenders.

(*c*) There was, and remains, a paucity of reliable literature and data on travellers—and even less on their education. This necessitated substantial grassroots field-work. Academic research was thought to be inappropriate, considering the small number of children involved and the limited and short-lived experience of traveller schooling. Traditional test procedures, besides creating problems in cultural fairness, would merely have confirmed what was already known—low levels of educational attainment even among the children regularly in schools. In these circumstances, judicious observation was of greater value and validity.

(*d*) There was a great need for a theoretical reappraisal of the educational needs of traveller children and of the feasible and suitable ways of meeting these needs. This necessitated as much thought and discussion of untried methods as reportage on those already operating with varying success.

(*e*) One of the first findings of the project was that the travellers are an essentially heterogeneous community. This determined a wider approach and the working out of a flexible and diverse set of recommendations rather than a cure-all solution. Although some of the suggestions made in the final chapter of this report are specific, they are collectively very tentative in nature, as will be seen from the flow chart on pages 162–3.

Before the beginning of the project, a survey of LEAs was conducted by the Schools Council during the autumn term of 1970 to ascertain the numbers and locations of maintained and direct grant schools in England and Wales with travelling pupils, and to elicit basic information about such schools and the background of the children. This survey was followed by a more detailed questionnaire to headteachers at 125 schools mentioned by the LEAs to have had the longest and most interesting experience. Information was requested about attendance, category of traveller (for instance, whether Gypsy, Irish Tinker, bargee, from a fairground or circus family, and so on), educational attainment on first entry and subsequent progress, the major difficulties of the schools and the travelling pupils and how to overcome them. Questions were also included which gave a picture of the parental attitudes of traveller and settled (gauje) families, of the views of the teaching profession about the ideal methods of providing for traveller children, and of the liaison between schools receiving the same children at different parts of the year. The dispatch of the questionnaire took place during the spring term of 1971.

The third stage of the project was a programme of visits to about forty schools which seemed to have the most to offer in terms of experience and methods. The choice was also determined by the advisability of sampling not only the different geographical regions but also the age range of the school, urban and rural locations, size of traveller intake and its proportion to the total roll, designation of children (Gypsy, bargee, fairground, and whether settled or nomadic), and diversity of educational provision. This programme of visits proved valuable in initiating an indispensable dialogue with teachers, and forms the basis of opinion expressed in this report. It confirmed that a degree of experience and successful teaching existed, but in almost complete isolation in schools throughout the country, and that teachers felt the need for communication and for information about what was taking place elsewhere. On these visits every opportunity was taken to meet traveller parents, educational welfare officers (EWOs), LEA officers, and managers of caravan sites.

Parallel to the three surveys described above, a similar study was devoted to the traveller families outside the education system. Visits were made to sites and unauthorized encampments, and discussions about educational problems and needs were held with parents and children. The causes of non-attendance were analysed, and observations were made during this field-work which very often proved more valuable than extant literature on travellers, especially for the preparation of the background study.

By approaching the whole problem of traveller education from the different and opposite ends of the spectrum—from inside the school and from inside the Gypsy family whose children were not attending school—it was possible to gain a much wider perspective and to come to grips with the root problems of cultural heritage, nomadism and the human factors of which non-attendance is a symptom.

Mixing with travellers proved rewarding not only because initial suspicion was invariably replaced by courtesy and hospitality, but also because the role of investigator was frequently superseded by that of impromptu teacher once it was realized that a 'school man' was present. A strong impression was gained, which was to be reinforced by information supplied by workers in voluntary educational projects with Gypsies, that many travellers want education and particularly the skills of reading and writing for their children. However, this does not always involve school attendance as an essential prerequisite.

The project was based at the West Midlands College of Education in Walsall, and the project director was able to continue a personal contact that had already been established as well as a voluntary teaching association with some of the numerous local traveller families. This field-work, which combined action and research, actually at grassroots on the roadside, gave first-hand insight into many of the problems that are often unfamiliar to teachers of traveller children in normal schools. Merely to have reviewed the current education and existing classroom practice with the atypically 'easy' children from private and local authority sites would have been questionable. It would have been the soft option and, significantly, one which would have tended to produce conclusions dominated by the concept of disadvantage which pervaded so many of the answers given on the question-naire to headteachers. Instead, a different picture emerges, which leads to conclusions that may seem to be at variance or even in conflict with those of the majority in the teaching profession.

An attempt has also been made to report on the feelings and views of the travellers themselves. It is not always fair to expect travellers to express opinions on such hypothetical subjects as the most appropriate education for their children, for they do not know the range of options. Travellers are skilled in giving answers which will please the questioner, but it is hoped that a more accurate picture of their opinions has been obtained by means of persistent discussion and by winning their confidence. There is certainly no consensus of opinion within the travelling community about education, for the travellers are deeply divided on the issue. However, judging by the experience of the project, travellers have a great deal to offer the teachers of their children, for there is a not unexpected tradition of homespun wisdom within the community.

This report

Chapter 2 deals with the historical setting and development of education in the three main groups of travellers. The dearth of previous studies makes this an unfortunately short and callow chapter.

Chapter 3 contains the main findings of the research and inquiry stage of the project based on the LEA survey, the headteachers' questionnaire and the visits to schools. It deals with the problem of estimating the number of travelling children inside and outside the school system, the patterns of attend-ance, the schools receiving them, the effect of current social legislation and its future implications, opinion within the teaching profession about the best methods of schooling these children and, lastly, a review of current edu-cational theory with respect to travellers.

Chapter 4 deals with the nature of travelling society. It defines the different groups, traces their origins and histories, their numbers and health and describes their conditions of life and their cultural heritage and language. It is concluded by a composite profile of the traveller child as a case for education.

Chapter 5 is a detailed review of the range of successful methods of organization in maintained schools observed during visits, and a report of the recent innovations established since the project completed its research phase (these include examples from both the maintained and independent sectors). Chapter 6 offers the practising teacher advice on teaching methods, classroom activities, materials and curriculum (both an integrated basic skills programme and a scheme oriented towards social studies with a traveller frame of reference).

The final chapter contains a summary of the main findings and conclusions of the project as well as recommendations for the future development of traveller education.

There are two appendices. Appendix A deals with the secret travelling languages of Anglo-Romany and Shelta (or Gammon) with a glossary of common words which teachers may hear from their traveller pupils. Appendix B gives details of a new scheme in the West Midlands for the centralization of educational records of Gypsy children to help in maintaining educational continuity in moving from school to school.

Summary of conclusions and recommendations

A detailed consideration of the conclusions and recommendations of this project can be found in Chapter 7, with a flow chart which, it is hoped, brings together all the threads of this report and indicates the logical relationship of what is said in the various chapters. Briefly, the following main points will strike the reader:

(a) The travellers are a distinctive social group with a common heritage and genealogy, often denied by casual observers; but they are heterogeneous in terms of mobility, contact with the school system and in their social standing within the host community.

(b) It is impractical, and probably unethical, to ignore their stigmatized image and threatened minority status when considering social and educational policies.

(c) There has been a degree of successful schooling of travellers, but the families involved have been more settled and desirous of education for their children. Consequently, established methods may be inappropriate with the nomadic, the unofficially encamped, and the new site tenants who have had little contact with schools or sites in the past.

(d) Mass non-attendance, which characterized the past and is only just beginning to diminish now because of new sites, public and official concern, and traveller awareness itself, should be seen as the symptom of a whole syndrome of causes and not as a culpable obstinacy exhibited by an anti-social group.

(e) In view of the lack of experience and fully evaluated successful methods, there should be at least a five-year period of experimental provision by LEAs, which can be assessed before an eventual—and at present notional—policy is decided upon.

(f) Traveller education is potentially a very exciting area because many of the innovatory measures that educationists are now recommending—as in the Halsey Report[6]—are so obviously relevant. There may be much that can be developed specifically for travellers which will later have application to other groups of children.

(g) Though travellers often reveal classic symptoms of severe social and cultural deprivation, they cannot easily be placed within the general spectrum of the disadvantaged. Their unique and fascinating case presents a very real challenge to teachers and educationists.

(h) Education alone, however responsive and flexible the systems in meeting travellers' needs, will not solve their problems. Ultimately the travellers hold the keys. It must be stated that it is believed that there is every reason for optimism on this point, with one large proviso: travellers and teachers are both to a large extent at the mercy of political and social policy. The major area for concern, therefore, is not basically an educational one.

Notes and references

1 For detailed bibliography see *Compensatory Education: an Introduction*, Occasional Publication no. 1, Schools Council Compensatory Education Research and Development Project, Swansea (1968); also *Compensatory Early Childhood Education: a Selective Working Bibliography* (The Hague: Bernard van Leer Foundation, 1971); or the standard American text on deprivation, which has extensive bibliographies: Jerome Hellmuth, ed., *Disadvantaged Child*, 3 vols (New York: Brunner Mazel, 1967, 1968, 1970).

2 B. B. Bernstein, 'Education cannot compensate for society', *New Society*, no. 387 (1970), pp. 344–7; and Bernstein, 'Social class, language and socialization' in *Language and Social Context*, ed P. P. Giglioli (Penguin, 1972).

3 W. Labov, 'The logic of nonstandard English', in *Language and Social Context*, pp. 179–80. See also W. Labov, et al., *A Study of the Non-Standard English of Negro and Puerto Rican Speakers in New York City*, Final Report, Cooperative Research Project no. 3288, vols 1 and 2 (Washington, DC: Office of Education, 1968), and H. Ginsburg, *The Myth of the Deprived Child* (Englewood Cliffs, N J: Prentice-Hall, 1972).

4 See also D. Wiklund, *Report to the Council of Europe Consultative Assembly*, Document 2629 (1969).

5 There is a reasonable body of literature, some of it in translation (see Bibliography), but much of it is superficial or deals with sedentary groups and those who have abandoned nomadism and moved into the inner-city centres—the American Indian, for instance. The best documentation is from the education of the migrant Mexican agricultural workers in the USA. Swedish and Dutch studies of Gypsies and travellers are rather more advanced than elsewhere, but centre on the settled and are geared to long-term rehabilitation programmes.

6 A. H. Halsey, *Educational Priority*, vol. 1: *EPA Problems and Policies* (HMSO, 1972).

2 The historical setting

The educational history of the Gypsies, showmen and bargees of England and Wales is characteristic of the world-wide phenomenon of educational neglect among nomadic peoples. Migrant groups, with their traditional self-sufficiency, distinctive cultures and life styles, have viewed formal education with apprehension, for they fear that the sedentary majority may use it as an instrument to enforce settlement and conformity. They provide within their community their own system of child rearing and training in the skills of economic and social subsistence, a training which they feel to be beyond the capacity of normal schoolteachers. Attendance at school thus deprives the nomadic child of valuable educative upbringing at home, and is frequently seen by parents as dangerous experience during which the child may lose his physical resistance to the rigours of nomadic life.[1] While most educationists would stress the higher aims of education in terms, for example, of civilizing and spiritual development, the nomad has his own heritage and philosophy of life. Predictably, he feels his way of life to be superior to that of the settled society, which he has not so much rejected as refused to join.

Almost universally the educational systems of the settled community have been conceived exclusively in terms of compulsory school attendance. The nomad's mobility makes static attendance impractical and also enables him to evade the enforcers of attendance. Nomadism seems to be incompatible with education, at least in this narrow view.

Since the introduction of compulsory schooling in England and Wales in the 1870s, our travellers have proved to be the most intractable of groups to incorporate within the educational system.[2] True to international form, the Gypsies, fairground showmen and bargees have become the bane of attendance officers and educational administrators. Their non-attendance has intermittently been claimed as a national scandal, from as early as the impassioned pleas in the 1880s of George Smith of Coalville[3] to the more restrained language of the Plowden Report in 1967. The total numbers of school-age children in the three main groups under study have been the subject of pretty wild guesswork, and there seems to have been no adequate census of the different groups, as they notoriously fail to register on normal national censuses. However, the claim that between 5 and 10% of them attended school is surprisingly common. How the populations of the three groups have changed over the last hundred years and when the showmen's children started to go to school with any regularity (perhaps not until the 1930s) are interesting academic questions; but in view of the priorities of the project, which concerned the present plight of the Gypsies, these are questions that it was not possible to investigate in depth. Whereas there is no reason to feel that the non-attendance of the Gypsies has changed dramatically, the bargees were certainly a severe problem in the 1920s.[4] They probably continued to be so well into the 1950s, when the decline of the commercial use of the canal system was already taking its toll, but by the mid-1960s they had disappeared as a group and ceased to be an attendance problem.

The attendance of travelling children at school was the subject of repeated legislation prior to the current 1944 Education Act. Children of parents with no fixed abode who follow itinerant trades are required by law to attend only for two hundred sessions (half days) per year—roughly half the normal school time (see pages 115–17). Initially this special dispensation applied only to bargee children, and originated in the Canals Boats Act of 1877 (6 and 12). The clause was retained in the 1921 Education Act (50), in the 1933 Children and Young Persons Act (10) as well as in the current 1944 Education Act (39·3), which widened its application to many other migrant groups.[5] Today this clause is rarely invoked and perhaps wisely so, for it seems never to have been an effective measure in ensuring even partial attendance, though it is still used in certain parts of Scotland and is not unknown in Kent. The more relaxed and less punitive methods now used by the Educational Welfare Officers, as opposed to the feared 'School Board' attendance officers, may obscure the fact that the clause was used more frequently in the fifties and early sixties. In this not too distant past the attendance officer acted unconsciously—and sometimes consciously—as an eviction agency, for it was known that a family would move rather than have its children forced into school or face the fine for non-attendance.[6]

Taken individually, the educational histories of the three groups provide distinctive perspectives on the nomadism/education dilemma, one that has been partially solved only in the case of the fairground and circus showmen's children.

Canal-boat children

In the past, the lack of schooling of the children from the canal boats caused more concern than that of the other groups. This may have been due to their employment by the large carrying companies involved in the canal trade, which meant that such companies as the British Waterways Board and Inland Waterways Association were in no small way held to be responsible for the welfare of their employees' families. Working in canal boats also came under the various factory and public health laws, and there was much public as well as official indignation at the lurid descriptions of living conditions in boat cabins that filled many pages in the reports of inspectors.[7]

The educational experience of the boater children seems to have been negligible, spasmodic attendances in maintained schools near to the canal stopping places and loading wharfs. Few of them learned to read or write. Attempts, some of them quite recent, were made to provide alternative schooling and religious training: the boat schools at Brentford, for instance, and the floating barge classroom usually at Southall. These all tended to be brief and minor experiments, as did an extreme solution of compulsory boarding during the 1950s in the Wood Hall Hostel in Birmingham, though similar hostels had been tried before. This latter experiment was remembered with considerable resentment by former inmates met during a visit to a Coventry school. On a visit to Groningen in the north-east of Holland, a large residential school for bargees was observed.[8]

This picture seems not to have changed much until the gradual run-down of the canals as a commercial network and their final eclipse more than a decade ago. A handful of families still operate working boats, but few have children and they are only on short-run traffic. Today, the bargees are virtually extinct. Through the Inland Waterways Board and the co-operation of local authorities, nearly all the families have now been housed, though a few in the older generation have been given moorings in the old canal basins and remain in the long-boats. Some ex-bargees have found employment as lock-keepers and lengthmen involved in maintenance work on the canals, but these are indeed the lucky few. The majority have had to find jobs inland where their traditional skills have little value. If they in fact succeed in settling to a regular form of employment, it is likely to be of the most menial kind because of their lack of education. Distaste for the monotony and lack of individual freedom and independence in such jobs makes many of the men almost unemployable. More serious is the inevitable decline in general morale, which has been caused by the destruction of their former way of life and the dislocation of their cultural heritage, that no longer has roots in their daily occupations. Involuntary adaptation is almost universally a contributory cause of inadequacy, and the completely new life which the boater community has been forced to adopt has had far-reaching and deleterious effects.

For the generations of school-age children since the collapse of the boaters' raison d'être, attendance at school has become an established fact, though standards of attainment are predictably low. The protectiveness and affectionate warmth of the family appear to be as strong as they ever were, but the children exhibit the same depressive lack of purpose as their parents. The ghettos of ex-bargee families are familiar sights in areas close to the canal stopping places. In these communities nostalgia for the once rich and vigorous life and heritage is strong, and there is nothing at present to replace it.

Fairground and circus showmen

A quite different and less troubled picture can be drawn of the educational history of the showmen. Though both fairground and circus trades are suffering a post-war decline in popularity, neither group has been affected as dramatically as the boaters. The circus has become even more centralized under the big family operators and increasingly draws its individual shows from an international pool. Circuses are more static than fairs (though recently two small independent travelling circuses have been established and appear to be flourishing), and television coverage has added a source of income. The fairground families' life style has altered little since the flourishing inter-war period, when social acceptance increased and a network of permanent winter-quarter sites was established. Neither group has had to face the same stigma as the Gypsies and bargees, for whose children it has been a traditional problem in school.

For many years affluent circus and fairground families have sent their children to expensive private boarding schools. This practice has spread among some of the middle-income families, especially for their children from ten to fourteen. As circus families need their children for acts, they make special educational provision for them, partly through private schooling and tutoring. In this respect the position of the children is similar to that of other child actors in the entertainment world. The fairground children who are not sent to boarding schools usually go regularly to maintained schools when the family is settled from October to March, though there may be a move to continue fairs into November and start them earlier in the spring. These children attend maintained schools serving the catchment area in which the winter-quarter site is placed. The children continue to go to these schools whenever the family is close enough for them to be driven to school, and this may continue during the season if the families are on a local circuit. When travelling a wider circuit, many families are punctilious about sending the children to schools in whichever town they may be, even if it is for only a few days. Other families opt out of the educational system during the season, but even here it seems that at least two hundred sessions per year are achieved. One factor which should be mentioned, however, is that these children are usually absent during examination times. There is also a tendency for withdrawal, especially by the boys, around the age of thirteen, when right of passage into the adult world and full participation in the fair itself is achieved.

Fairground parents have a much more positive and favourable attitude to education than the other groups under study. Unlike the others, they have developed a powerful leadership pattern and have had a strong central association—the Showmen's Guild, which was formed in 1889 and has gradually grown in power ever since.[9] Winter-quarter sites and exemption from a great deal of the inhibiting legislation affecting Gypsy caravan dwellers are major successes of the Guild. It publishes the *Showmen's Guild Year Book* (obtainable only by members of the Guild), in which all the rules and regulations of membership and fairground operation are detailed. The Guild has also fostered the value of education among its members, and the fairground magazine *World's Fair* reveals the inner strength and close autonomy of the group. Their family structure shows a remarkable similarity to that of the Gypsies (described in Chapter 4 of this report), and it is a well-established fact that many Gypsies in the past joined the showmen's group and have become assimilated into it. There is considerable uneasiness between the two groups, though some kinship links are reluctantly admitted and many Gypsies wear the Showmen's Guild lapel badge even though they have little current contact with fairgrounds.

Although there are improvements that could be made—such as greater communication between schools and between LEAs receiving the same children at different times of the year—it was concluded that in general the education of the showmen's children is satisfactory. The schooling that most of their children receive adequately complements the training they receive in fairground operation within the family. The small, family-owned show still remains the basic economic unit of the community and will probably continue to sustain it for many years to come.

It is not easy to assess from what period the relatively satisfactory educational position of the showmen's children began. In the early decades after the Guild was established the group continued to be hounded by attendance officers, and reports about the overcrowded life in showmen's vans continued to be a preoccupation of inspectors. At least by the 1930s, however, attendance had become an established pattern in many families.[10]

In school, the fairground child quickly wins the respect, if not the admiration, of other children. Several schools were visited during the project that had both Gypsies and show children on the roll. The two groups of children contrasted strongly: many of the fairground children were, if anything, of above-average attainment and mixed with ease, whereas the Gypsies were far behind settled norms and presented considerable social problems within the school. The show child's skills in drawing and in mechanical operations were significant, and orally they participated freely and informatively. Because their educational position is far less serious than that of the Gypsies, they are featured only rarely in the remainder of this report.

Gypsies and other travellers

The educational plight of the Gypsies has changed little since the 1870s. In the subsequent hundred years the Gypsies have assumed a very different outward appearance and have probably been subjected to increasing social antagonism. As they have become more urban, they have also, with motorization, become more conspicuous, and yet they appear to enjoy continued freedom from the law while the settled house dweller has gradually become subjected to increased bureaucratic control. Even their apparent freedom from schooling may be cause for jealousy in some quarters.

Their population may have remained constant throughout the period, or possibly been subject to a marginal increase, which would have been much greater had there not always been a corresponding exodus from the roadside into houses, followed by partial assimilation into the settled host community. In spite of the current fluctuations in scrap metal prices the Gypsies have probably never been so prosperous. The subsistence economy of casual agricultural work, supplemented by the sale of traditional craft materials, never enabled families to accumulate wealth in the same way as do modern urban occupations. Attendance rates at rural schools in villages where the families were well known to headteachers and attendance officers were probably higher than are now possible; in the shifting situation in urban areas there are additional pressures on schools from population movements and immigrant settlements, and the Gypsy is less welcome.

Unlike the circus and fairground showmen, the Gypsy family is an almost totally independent unit economically. There is no central representative organization such as the Showmen's Guild, though the recent establishment of the gauje-led Gypsy Council and its even more newly formed break-away all-traveller Romany Guild (see pages 195–6) could be the first manifestations of a leadership structure and an ethnic consciousness. As yet, neither organization is nationally representative nor politically mature. As will be seen from Chapter 4 of this report, the Gypsies' family and kinship structures are still too hegemonic to enable any leader to have a following beyond the family. Both organizations are centred in London and the Home Counties, and though the Gypsy Council has a branch in the North, there is little support regionally and many travellers have no knowledge of the existence of either body.

Gypsies have had greater difficulties in finding places to camp since the war because of increasing pressures on land, particularly around the larger towns. Development in these areas has closed a number of traditional stopping places. The decline in demand for traditional Gypsy craft work has led them to turn increasingly to dealing in scrap metal near towns, and resulted in some areas in heavy concentrations of Gypsies sometimes in unsuitable places, where they sometimes cause extreme nuisance and annoyance to householders. This has led in many instances to continual harassing and moving on of Gypsies, despite repeated advice from successive governments that they should not be needlessly moved on from one unauthorized site to another. In addition, since the war, the Town and Country Planning Acts, the Caravan Sites and Control of Development Act 1960, together with numerous highway regulations and trade licensing provisions have made life more difficult for the Gypsy. In recognition of this fact the Caravan Sites Act 1968, which came into operation in April 1970, placed a duty on county, county borough and London borough councils to provide adequate accommodation for Gypsies in their areas. The duty of site provision in respect of London and county boroughs is limited to accommodation for 15 Gypsy caravans at a time. By the end of 1974 there were about one hundred local authority sites providing about 1400 pitches, and in addition there were some 25 to 30 temporary sites providing over 300 pitches. Although the acceleration in site provision under the 1968 Act is now well under way, it will be some time before the whole Gypsy population find legal pitches on which to park. In the meantime Gypsies will be forced to resort to unauthorized encampment and face, as a result, the prospect of a vicious circle of eviction. Before the war and the 1960 Caravan Sites Act, many more families than now rented pitches on private sites, and it may be true that fewer families are legally encamped five years after the Caravan Sites Act 1968 than a decade before.

The insecurity of unauthorized encampment is a major inhibitory factor on school attendance. The basic situation has not changed since the Plowden Report and *Gypsies and Other Travellers* (the Ministry of Housing and Local Government report on the 1965 census of travellers), both of which were published in 1967. Most traveller children do not attend school, and the ones who do tend not to make satisfactory progress. The influx into schools of the early 1960s, when the first official sites were set up after the Ministry of Housing and Local Government Circular No. 6/62, was followed by a decade of marginal increase in attendance, and it is only now that the second-phase influx is taking place with the opening of more sites. The seasonal absence from the months of March to October which dominated the past continues to a much reduced and less regular extent today. Unlike the fairground pattern of regular circuits, the Gypsies' migrations are unpredictable and tend to take place over the whole year.

The educational history of the Gypsies is therefore in contrast to that of the showmen and the bargees, for it has changed little since the late nineteenth century. It is obviously a myth that all Gypsies are illiterate and fail to attend schools. Some of the relatively settled families have produced lawyers, politicians, even university teachers, though only a handful and at the expense of their traditional life style. A small minority of children have been a familiar although seasonal feature on the registers of isolated rural schools through successive generations of the same families since the onset of compulsory schooling. Documented examples exist at Alkham in Kent, for instance, and at Kingsteignton, where the Devonian Smalls have attended regularly since 1903, when Moses, Reuben, May and Priscilla (the children of Joshua Small) followed in the steps of their cousins Caroline and Defiance Orchard who had enrolled before the turn of the century.[11]

The seasonal attendance pattern, the colourful Gypsy forenames and famous Romany surnames of Boswell, Lee, Smith, Price, Wood, Herne, Penfold or Pinfold and so on, make their recognition a relatively easy and worth-while task in many country and urban areas which have long been traditional Gypsy haunts and where the old registers have been preserved. Evidence of former attendance can be collected by interviewing older travellers who frequently have memories of spasmodic attendances, of brawls with gauje children, sometimes of harsh and discriminative treatment from teachers, and of very little learnt. Often these memories are embellished in the re-telling—the traditional oral art of the Gypsy. The relics of these attendances of short duration are often limited to a superficial literacy and the ability to write only the capital letters.

The present outbreak of voluntary and charitable educational projects is nothing new, for several historical precedents, largely evangelical in ethos, were established in the last century and the early part of this. George Smith mentions some of these that date back to the 1830s. A 'school' was established at Farnham in Dorset in the 1840s, and such short-lived attempts seem to have continued periodically until that mentioned in the *Journal of the Gypsy Lore Society* for 1934 at Hurtwood, Surrey.[12] In general, however, the pervading picture is of educational abstinence and official frustration— an educational neglect no less severe than that which characterized the bargees and the showmen of the past.

Notes and references

1 Professor F. Rehfisch, University of Hull (in conversation).

2 It is not often fully realized that there is no actual state educational system in England and Wales. The system as such is maintained by the local education authorities (LEAs) separately. The duty to provide education for the traveller—as for any other child—rests with the LEA in which the child resides, or jointly through the 'pool' system if the child resides in more than one area. Legally, it is the duty of parents 'of every child of compulsory school age to cause him to receive efficient full-time education suitable to his age, ability and aptitude, either by regular attendance at school or otherwise'. The Department of Education and Science (DES), formerly the Ministry of Education, exercises the responsibilities it has over the LEAs by its control of capital spending, by ensuring that parliamentary legislation on education is implemented, through the advisory inspectorate (HMIs) and by the issue of administrative memoranda and circulars.

The DES is not responsible for the building of maintained schools, and it has no powers to run these schools or to appoint teachers to them; these functions are solely in the hands of the LEAs. Throughout this report, therefore, schools in the public (i.e. 'state') sector are referred to as *maintained* schools (county, voluntary controlled and aided), whereas those which are private or charitable are called *independent* schools. This may cause some confusion, for there are several independent educational projects for Gypsies in the country which call themselves 'schools' but which are not recognized as such by the DES. However, in the interests of clarity and brevity such projects will be accorded their self-ascribed label even though it must be remembered that they are not legally schools.

3   George Smith of Coalville wrote numerous articles and books on bargees, the fairground showmen and Gypsies—viz., *Gypsy Life* (1880) and *Canal Adventures by Moonlight* (1881)—but some of his strongest remarks can be found in the Report of the Select Committee on Canals, *Parliamentary Papers*, Hansard, 1883 (252) XIII, Appendix 25, pp. 229–331.

4   See, for instance, H. Gordon, *Mental and Scholastic Tests Amongst Retarded Children*, Board of Education Pamphlet No. 44 (HMSO, 1923), section on canal-boat children.

5   M. M. Wells and P. S. Taylor, *The New Law of Education*, 6th edn (Butterworth, 1961), p. 49. This is more detailed than George Taylor and John B. Saunders, *The New Law of Education* 7th edn. (Butterworth, 1971), p. 46.

6   Mr David Smith (of the Centre for Environmental Studies project, and joint author of the sections on Gypsy children in the Plowden Report) in conversation. He also suggested that this would explain the fact that in the fifties and early sixties a casual visitor to a site would not see the school-age children because they were very carefully hidden, in case they were spotted by an attendance officer.

7   Report of the Select Committee on Canals, *Parliamentry Papers*, Hansard, 1883 (252) XIII, various pages; Report of the Select Committee on the Temporary Dwellings Bill 1887, *Parliamentry Papers*, Hansard, 1887 (279) XIII, especially submission by Dr Brydone, pp. 19–21; Report of the Select Committee of the House of Lords on the Moveable Dwellings Bill 1909–10, *Parliamentary Papers*, 1909 (HL 199) X, 1910 (HL 146) IX; Reports of the Inspectors of Factories for the half year ending 31st October 1875, *Parliamentary Papers*, 1876 (c 1434) XVI, particularly report by Robert Baker, pp. 126–33.

8   G. N. Conduct, 'Some aspects of the education of canal boat children in Birmingham', *Educational Review*, vol. 6, no. 3 (1954), pp. 198–201. Also a note in *Waterways Magazine*, July 1958.

9   Thomas Murphy, *History of the Showmen's Guild*, vols 1 and 2 (1938, 1948), privately published and obtainable from the Showmen's Guild; Duncan Dallas, *The Travelling People* (Macmillan, 1971).

10   Duncan Dallas, *The Travelling People*, p. 77.

11   Information supplied by the headteacher at Kingsteignton Church of England Primary School and Miss Mollie Clarke of Devon County Council Education Authority.

12   Enid Camm, 'Hurtwood School', *Journal of the Gypsy Lore Society*, third series, vol. XIII, part 4 (1934), notes and queries no. 21, pp. 221–2. This school operated from 1926 to 1934 and was established by the Surrey Education Authority. H. J. Francis and D. E. Yates, 'Borrow's Gypsies in a Journal of 1867–8', *Journal of the Gypsy Lore Society*, third series, vol. XIV, part 1 (1935), pp. 1–21.

3 Travelling children and schools: the inquiry stage of the project

This chapter is a report of the main findings of the research and inquiry stage of the project and a description of the current schooling of traveller children. The following topics are covered: the numbers of travelling children attending school; the numbers who do not attend; patterns of attendance; the schools involved and their traveller intake; traveller and gauje parental attitudes; opinions within the teaching profession about the major difficulties faced by traveller children in school and how to overcome them; the effects and implications of the 1968 Caravan Sites Act, Part 2; and finally, a review of educational theory and the schooling of travellers.

The statistical data presented here need considerable qualification and very careful interpretation. At one time there was a reluctance to include them at all, but in view of the absence of previous similar studies, the fact that they are probably the best figures at present available, and because future research may avoid the obvious mistakes and fill the many gaps, it was decided to give them a public airing. A further justification for presenting such fragmentary evidence is that the over-all conclusions in this report are to some extent at variance with the opinions expressed by the teaching profession. Traveller education raises important controversies, including those concerning problems of deprivation and assimilative versus separatist classroom strategies. This chapter of the report enables the voice of the teacher to be heard more clearly than anywhere else. It also presents an opportunity for a review of the situation as it was in 1970, having regard to the extremely fast development of traveller education.

How many travelling children attend school?

In order to assess how many traveller children attend schools it will be necessary to define much more precisely than is usual for children of the host community what is meant by attendance. Names on rolls tell us little about regularity, and the same names may be duplicated in several schools; perhaps even different names on different rolls refer to the same children.

The LEA survey and the questionnaire to headteachers were designed to enable suitable schools to be selected for closer study and not to construct a major statistical analysis of traveller attendance. Only the inclusion of a traveller category on the annual DES Form 7 returns would give an indication of accurate attendance patterns as they change over the next few years.

LEAs were asked to give approximate numbers of travelling children on the rolls of their schools at any one time during the eighteen months before the end of 1970. The figures therefore represent a potentially maximum view of attendance. They were asked to name the schools involved and to give a rough indication of the category of children concerned. The purpose was to gain an indication of approximately how many schools were affected and to what extent. Annual variations, very short influxes and complicated seasonal patterns of attendance were to be described generally, not specifically. By collating returns, the following over-all picture emerges:

(a) The total number of 'traveller' roll entries for the period was just under 3000 (including very short stays and probably considerable multiple attendance at different schools). Excluding the two factors in parenthesis, a truer figure would therefore be about half—i.e., 1500 children who attended with some regularity.

(b) The proportions of children from the seven categories requested— probably a more accurate assessment than the over-all figures—were as follows:

Gypsies (caravans/travelling)	60% (approximately 1700)
Gypsies (recently housed)	10% (approximately 250)
Irish Tinkers (caravans/travelling)	6% (approximately 175)
Irish Tinkers (recently housed)	1% (approximately 30)
Fairground and circus	just over 20% (approximately 625)
Canal boat (bargee)	—(only 7 mentioned)
Migrant labourer	2% (approximately 75)

Several reservations must be made clear: some twenty out of the total number of 162 LEAs did not reply, even though a very small proportion of their travellers were later found to be in schools. Of the forty LEAs that gave nil returns, a few did have travellers in school. It was discovered in the subsequent headteachers' questionnaire that some of the schools that were mentioned as having traveller pupils had not in fact had any for many years, whereas others had children who were not travellers by heritage—that is, the count included some children of servicemen and travelling salesmen. One or two LEAs included recent European immigrants—for instance, Polish and Italian miners. The figures for the canal-boat children are a gross underestimate, for at one school visited during the project there were twenty such children currently in attendance, though all but two were housed. The undercounting of bargee and ex-bargee children points to the fact that they are not sufficiently recognized as a group with special needs. The impression gained during the project was that there must be at least 500 such children, whose families have been housed so recently—probably this is the first or second generation—as not to have been assimilated properly into the settled community and whose educational backwardness is cause for greater recognition and concern.

The figures for the housed Gypsies and Irish Tinkers are probably again an underestimate. It is as difficult to recognize their children as it is to recognize those of the ex-bargee, and it was established in several cases that teachers were themselves unaware of the background of the children. Less is known about the Gypsy community that is housed or temporarily housed than about what may be the tip of the iceberg, the families dwelling in caravans and still travelling. The existence of this anonymous but frequently culturally-conscious ghetto community of housed Gypsies and Irish Tinkers is well established in certain areas—especially where they swell the numbers of Gypsy children attending local schools from neighbouring caravan sites. Educational problems as acute as those of the roadside traveller linger on for several generations. Though some families eventually become assimilated into the settled community, others retain their close economic and kinship links with roadside families and may remain in houses only for a short time. Often the children of the housed Gypsies marry back on to the road and set themselves up in caravans. The question whether a Gypsy ceases to be a Gypsy when he lives in a house is difficult, for legally he is one only when he is living an itinerant life in a movable dwelling (see page 49). The Centre for Environmental Studies has developed a very useful definition of Gypsy identity which is basically an ethnic one: self-ascription, acceptance as a member by other Gypsies and membership through descent from at least one parent.[1]

From an educational point of view it is important to understand that the housed Gypsy child very frequently exhibits problems identical to those of the travelling caravan dweller, and that housing may only be a temporary expedient. It is also possible for the family to be nomadic by resorting to a sequence of short stays in different houses, a habit not uncommon among some European Gypsies and Scottish travellers. There is also much evidence, not least from public houses serving Gypsy housed communities, that heritage and Anglo-Romany speech may be more richly and openly displayed by such families than by those having little time for such matters in the daily exigencies of caravan travelling, even though both groups are interlocked by kinship.

The figures for the children of migrant labourers, working for instance on remote stretches of motorway construction or in isolated dockyard development, are very small and do not directly concern us here. With

Britain's entry into the European Economic Community and the increasing mobility of labour, there may well develop major educational problems similar to those of immigrants or of service children, though neither of these is a travelling society.

The categories of children which most concern us here are those of the travelling Gypsies and Irish Tinkers. These are the children whose attendance is likely to have been most spasmodic and whose numbers are almost certainly subject to multiple counting because they appeared on the rolls of more than one school during the period covered by the LEA figures. That only eight headteachers of the 125 to whom the questionnaire was sent were able to state positively that they knew that their children had attended other schools during periods of absence, in no way denies the concept of multiple counting: travellers and their children are notoriously evasive and secretive about their former and future whereabouts. They fear that schools may be instrumental in enabling the law or a local authority to catch up with them for the purpose of exacting fines or collecting outstanding rent, or to follow up summonses or minor regulation infringements, and so on. This evasiveness comes naturally to the children—it is one of their travelling skills—and they may pretend not to know the names of previous schools attended, although ignorance of these is often genuine.

By taking all these factors into account—especially the multiple counting and the fact that the figures include migrant children who are not travellers by heritage—it is reasonable to suggest that approximately 1500 caravan-dwelling Gypsies and Irish Tinkers attended schools for at least part of the academic year 1969–70. The proportion of Irish was probably less than 10%. The figures for the circus and fairground children, subject to even greater incidence of multiple counting, are probably closer to 500 than to 625. However, an unknown proportion of their total school-age population were in private boarding schools, for which no data were collected. All data in this chapter are for the maintained system in England and Wales.

How many travelling children do not attend school?

The major focus here is on the travelling caravan dweller, for most of the other groups that are housed tend to be in school, though there may be high withdrawal rates at secondary level. The major question to be asked is whether it is possible to support or refute the Plowden Report claim that less than 10% of traveller children attend school.[2]

It is beyond the reach of present scholarship to hazard more than an informed guess at the total number of school-age travellers in England and Wales. With so much doubt about the total population of travellers (who can be estimated at 20 000 or 40 000 with equal impunity), it is only fair to suggest that there may be between 6000 and 12 000 traveller children, probably the higher figure being nearer the truth.[3] But this is as much an impression gained by judicious observation as by careful analysis of the 1965 census figures (see pages 65–7). Only two points can be made with any certainty: firstly, that school-age children represent at least a quarter of the entire traveller population (this being significantly higher than the 15·8% national proportion); and secondly, that there is no sound evidence that the traveller population has massively increased over the last decade, for all we can say is that we are counting better than in 1965. Whether the traveller population is in the process of doubling between 1965 and 1985, as is projected in the report of the 1965 census,[4] is again subject to too much uncertainty to judge.

If it is accepted that around 1500 travellers attended school during the academic year 1969–70, they could represent anything between 10 and 25% of the potential number, but this is to some extent a meaningless statement, for out of the 1500, only one third attended regularly throughout the year, another third may have attended for only half of it, and the remainder for only a short period or spasmodically. In other words, it is not possible to refute the Plowden Report's claim, though there is some justification in giving it credence. But the Plowden Report was published more than five years ago, and the LEA survey for this project is three years old; it is almost certain that in the intervening time there has been a gradual improvement in attendance due to the opening of new sites and the public and official interest generated in the meantime.

For schools and LEAs it does not matter very much anyway. Traveller children appear only as a local problem to them, and, working on the observation that each traveller family with children produces on average at least two school-age children, the opening of a new site for fifteen trailers is likely to produce only thirty potential attenders, divided between the three age-level schools at roughly ten per school.

Patterns of traveller attendance

In the questionnaire to headteachers there were several questions about attendance patterns: 'percentage of actual over possible' (i.e., for period on the roll). This was to be averaged out for all the travellers in the school. They were also asked whether attendance followed seasonal fluctuations, and whether the children were known to attend other schools during their absences. Replies were received from about one hundred schools, so the following figures may be taken as approximate percentages:

35 schools described the attendance of the children while on the roll as 'good'—i.e., over 85%;
27 reported it to be 'average'—i.e., 70–85%;

18 judged it 'poor'—less than 70%;
20 schools were unable to give a definite answer because it varied between years, between families and within the same families.

There is some confusion here, for the length of time a child is kept on a school roll varies, especially in the case of travellers, where LEA regulations may be waived. There were several cases of readmission of the same children during the same academic year.

On the question whether attendance was subject to seasonal absence, mostly from May to October, a surprisingly high percentage of schools claimed that it was:

65 headteachers reported regular seasonal absence—though a few suggested that there had been even higher seasonal absence during the previous few years;
18 denied that seasonal patterns existed;
17 could give no definite answer because of variations among their children.

Discussion with headteachers on the visits to about forty schools, and with several educational welfare officers confirmed that patterns of attendance varied greatly, due to seasonal migrations, not only for summer fruit picking but also for Christmas tree felling, turkey plucking, family reunions at festive times, horse fairs and race meetings. Regular movements were also accounted for because the scrap collected in the school catchment area was accumulated on a fortnightly or monthly basis and then transported for selling to another area where market prices were higher. With fairground and circus children the season of the fairs accounted for absences. In one case, a scrap-dealing Gypsy family regularly moved to a Dorset seaside resort where it operated a Punch and Judy show every summer—the children being diligently sent to school there for the few weeks before the end of the summer term and for the first weeks of the winter term. In this and several other cases attendance percentages for the period on the roll were in the high nineties; in one school the over-all yearly attendance rates were far higher than the norms of the settled society children in the school. However, these were exceptions, for even with children from permanent local authority sites, headteachers complained of absenteeism for such 'trivial' reasons as the beginnings and ends of terms, weeks (Mondays and Fridays were always poor days), the days either side of half terms, days when there was a school outing, a medical inspection, swimming, open days and prize givings, and even such excuses as good weather, bad weather, sibling illness, the arrival of a large load of rags or scrap on the site, and, significantly in more than one school, when their favourite teacher was absent. Headteachers who were most successful in reducing these casual absences insisted that there was no substitute to establishing a 'tea-drinking' relationship with parents in their own caravans, getting other members of staff to visit the site regularly, even to call past it every morning before nine o'clock, frequently to go and collect children if they were late. Where LEAs had provided special coach transport, teachers were sometimes offered the job of helping the coach driver. Liaison with site wardens was also suggested as an essential ingredient for good attendance. EWOs frequently spent an inordinate proportion of their time working the sites, and where a friendly but firm relationship had been established this invariably helped with attendance rates. However, both teachers and EWOs recognized that there were many instances when forcing the children into school caused considerable family inconvenience and at times positive damage. Many expressed doubts about an over-officious chasing up of non-attenders: it could be counter-productive. Some saw clearly that there was an essential conflict between the travellers' traditional life style and school attendance requirements, and made special allowances for this. A few mentioned Section 39·3 of the 1944 Education Act.

The attendance of the secondary-age children was described as the least satisfactory. Indeed, visits made to sites during the project, especially if timed during the early evening, resulted in the discovery of many more older school-age children than were previously given by official informants. Such children would be potential cases for evening home tuition or intensive summer schooling.

It must therefore be concluded that attendance patterns not only vary seasonally and with different age groups, but also are subject to considerable casual absenteeism and truancy with parental consent. A small minority of the headteachers at schools visited by the project suggested with discernment that their children were not necessarily being deprived of valuable educative experience when casually absent from school, and that such experience could be exploited in the classroom at a later date.

The schools involved and their traveller intake

Four main conclusions can be drawn from the LEA survey, concerning both the schools which have received traveller children and the traveller children themselves:

(a) Of the 650 schools mentioned, about 75% were at the primary level (infant and junior) and 25% were secondary (not very significant, for this follows national trends).

(b) The proportion of traveller pupils on rolls in primary and secondary schools, however, was much greater than the national average, well above 3 to 1 as opposed to the 5 to 3 reported for all children in the

DES *Statistics of Education 1971* (Volume 1). This factor was confirmed by evidence provided by the headteachers' questionnaire: the attendance of travellers at secondary level drops off considerably, and the number of children from nomadic families or those camped on unauthorized land who attend at secondary level is very small indeed. Most travellers reach adult status around the age of 12 or 13, and it is possible that the widespread introduction of middle schools will delay the drop-out by a year or so but reinforce secondary abstention at the senior school level. In Holland, it has become necessary to resort to making attendance at site schools compulsory for the age group 3 to 12.[5] The raising of the school-leaving age here has resulted in increasing the number of teen-age travellers avoiding compulsory attendance.

(c) The size of the traveller intake per school was the most significant point to be drawn from the LEA survey. Seventy per cent of affected schools had only between 1 and 4 travellers on their rolls, and a further 20% had between 5 and 9. Thus 90% of affected schools had fewer than 10 travellers to cope with. At least three schools, however, had around 40 traveller pupils, but of these a significant proportion were housed. Only 7% of schools with travellers had between 10 and 19 of them, though one can certainly expect this proportion to increase significantly as the sites network gradually develops, and as a higher proportion of children on sites are persuaded to attend regularly. Numbers revealed in special schools were small—around 1%.

It is thus important to put the problem in true perspective. Schools need not be too alarmed by the prospect of a new site opening, for it is most unlikely that numbers will exceed an average of 10 travellers per school, though of course it is possible that numbers could be much higher, especially with Irish Tinker families. Irish traveller families tend to be much larger than English or Welsh; however, their choice of Catholic schools may help to ease congestion in local schools where there is a mixed British-Irish site. In county areas where there may be large sites (50 rather than 15 trailers) and small rural schools the problem is of a different dimension; but these cases will be rare and can be remedied to some extent by dispersal of the site children into several schools in the area by a special transport arrangement. The existence of housed families in the neighbourhood of established sites, especially where it has been local authority policy to house site tenants where possible, may swell the numbers.

(d) Though the spread of the sites network may slightly alter school enrolment, the regional distribution of traveller children on school rolls follows, with only slight variation, the distribution of travellers generally as revealed by the 1965 census report.

Table 1 Comparison of 1971 distribution of school attendance
with 1965 distribution of traveller families

Region	No. of children on school rolls (percentage)	No. of traveller families in 1965 (percentage)*
Northern	5·5	2
Yorkshire and Humberside	11·5	6
North West	16·0	3
East Midlands	5·0	6
West Midlands	6·0	17
South East	44·5	43
South West	8·0	14
Wales	3·5	9
	100·0	100

* Source: *Gypsies and Other Travellers*[6]

This regional distribution does show some significant variations. Attendance appears relatively good in the North West, Yorkshire and Humberside and in the North East. It is particularly bad in the West Midlands and Wales.

It is possible that such conclusions are invalid because there have been migration and changes in distribution since 1965, but these are more likely to have been from rural to urban areas and not among regions. Observations made during the project supported the impressions gained from comparing the LEA survey and the 1965 census figures. Especially in the Black Country conurbation in the West Midlands, it is certain that, until very recently, a hard-line policy on eviction and a lack of positive attempts to encourage traveller attendance had resulted in almost non-existent schooling in one of the most densely traveller populated areas in the country.

Generally speaking, traveller children are widely distributed throughout the country near centres of urban populations, and, as with over-all national population distributions, just under half are to be found in the South East.

Traveller and gauje parental attitudes

The attendance of traveller children at a maintained school is usually met in the early stages with considerable apprehension by both traveller and gauje parents. The decline of this apprehension in time is related to the effectiveness of the headteacher and staff in reassuring gauje parents about hygienic and educational standards and in establishing a friendly relationship with site families. Tension subsides generally with time when a permanent site has been established; and antagonism between travellers and residents in most, though not all, cases is an attitude of mind rather than a genuine conflict based on actual grievance. In school, fights between traveller and gauje children are rarer than fights among the travellers—often reflections of family quarrels and feuds and sometimes posing a serious problem. Gauje parental fears about lowering of educational standards are less likely to occur when the travellers are segregated into a special class or withdrawn for substantial periods, especially if a special teacher has been appointed. The smaller the ratio of travellers to the total roll, the less is the apprehension among gauje parents, for they feel that the travellers will impinge less upon the time that teachers can devote to their children. Schools where there are already pupils with acute educational problems or pressures caused by immigrant intakes are likely to find it harder to cope with a further educationally backward group. This may lead to justifiable objections from teachers, travellers and the parents of the abler children in the school. Inner-city schools and schools serving suburbs in which a local authority site has been established in spite of strong resident opposition are equally likely to find parental objections to Gypsy children. In several instances, the mere threat of Gypsy attendance has caused local parents to protest, sometimes with extremes of emotion rarely met even when objections to immigrants are concerned. The schools which seem to have had the smallest problems with gauje parental disapproval are those in rural areas with a long history of Gypsy attendance, and middle-class and affluent commuter areas in which there is already a degree of liberal concern about the plight of Gypsy children, though some meet the prospect of Gypsies attending by transferring their children to private schools. However, in general, headteachers reported that where there had been apprehension this was soon replaced by indifference.

On the credit side were a few isolated examples of gauje parents taking a genuine interest in the welfare of the traveller children and volunteering assistance to the school.

Traveller parental attitudes were reported as varying dramatically, from 'keen and determined that their children should become literate' to 'definitely against the educational interests of school and child'; however, the pervading picture that headteachers painted was one of widespread indifference and lack of interest, which resulted in casual absenteeism of the kinds already described.

Headteachers' reports of the readiness of traveller parents to visit the school and discuss their children with teachers was directly linked to the extent to which there was a close contact with the site—where, in fact, to visit the headteacher or one member of staff was to reciprocate a home visit. Heads who did not make it a practice to visit the site tended to reply that the mothers came only when there was some complaint about free meals, clothing, injuries to children supposedly caused by gauje children, and so on. Whereas all reported that traveller parental attitudes varied between families, teachers who made it a practice to visit the encampment were much more favourably impressed by the travellers' concern for the educational welfare of their children. They pointed to the sacrifices made: care taken with dress and cleaning the children; the carrying of children hundreds of yards over seas of mud so that they should arrive with clean footwear; families who continued to deliver and collect their children in a lorry long after they had been evicted and had moved to a new location nearly ten miles away from the school. A few teachers reported that traveller parents had brought in examples of their craft work—wooden flowers, pegs, model wagons and so on—for exhibition in the school.

All these examples are exceptions to the general rule of traveller diffidence and apparent lack of interest in their children's actual educational progress. Headteachers reported that too often there was satisfaction with a low level of rudimentary literacy, and some even spoke of parents being jealous that their children were learning to read, when they themselves could not. A genuine interest in proficient literacy and progress in other subjects is rare, and some teachers felt that this was a contributory factor behind the children's poor performance.

The major concern of the traveller is that his children should be happy in school, be treated fairly, and not be subjected to 'dirty Gyppo' taunts from other children. They see their children's education in the light of their own brief and frequently unpleasant experience of school—Silvester Gordon Boswell, for instance, explains why his right fist is larger than his left:

We went to school there [Romford]—at Mauney Road School they called it. It was a big school. None of us was happy there, but we had to go all the same. Looking back on those days, the lads in our school were a rough lot, sons of coster parents and the like. The old master was a bad-tempered case. He had a King Edward beard, and spent most of the time giving the lads the cane. Not only on their hands: he would bend you over a desk and lay it on thick and heavy. He hadn't much patience with us at all.

And of course the Cock of the School had to have battle with the Gypsy boys, so we had to defend ourselves at all times. Not many days passed without a fight. If I won one, Brother Lewis would lose his and that made me look for the one that beat him and so it went on. My sisters would have their share of battles too. We got the 'Gypsy, Gypsy, live in a tent, can't afford to pay your rent!' This was one of the worst schools we were sent to. I think it was because it was so big, and so many children. We seemed for ever in trouble— all because we were Gypsies and looked different from the others. . . .

We then moved to Suffolk, to a little place called Wenhaston, and stayed on the common there, and went to school for a while.

Still my parents insisted that we must go to school and learn to read and write—and then we needn't go any more—that was the promise.[7]

A school tends to be judged as a good one because 'that nice Mr or Mrs X is there' rather than on its educational philosophy. There seems to be little evidence of a widespread disapproval of 'modern' teaching methods suggested in the Plowden Report,[8] though traditional and rote-fashion teaching may be anticipated or considered a more effective means of giving literacy than the emphasis on painting and drama which some travellers feel to be over-stressed. This is somewhat parodoxical, for the methods used by parents when training their children very often involve discovery and exploration so that self-reliance can be built up.

Many of the traveller parental attitudes can be attributed to protectiveness and concern about morality. Very few allow their children to go on school visits unless they have been personally approached and know that a trusted teacher will be accompanying the children. Although they may allow their children short day trips, outings involving staying overnight—camping, for instance—are unheard of. There is a fear about the general permissiveness of gauje society, based on television programmes and on experience of behaviour patterns of gaujes at evictions and during resident protest meetings. Parents fear that their children may be corrupted by school—by drugs, which are anathema to travellers, and by sexual licence. This protectiveness and the view that settled society is decadent is part of the nomad's belief in his superiority; and it is hardly surprising that when a traveller child has acquired a superficial level of literacy, his parents rarely oppose his wish to leave school and work in the family business.

Opinions within the teaching profession about the major difficulties faced by traveller children in school and how to overcome them

The views of headteachers expressed in the questionnaire and those of teachers in schools visited during the project leave little doubt as to opinion in the profession about the major difficulties of teaching traveller children.

(*a*) The major obstacles to satisfactory progress are the frequent lateness of the start of attendance, its lack of continuity and regularity, the likelihood of premature withdrawal at secondary level, and sometimes the difficulty in getting the children to attend at all.

(*b*) The extremely low levels of attainment at entry even among five-year-olds, who give the appearance of being two years behind settled norms in terms of general motor and perceptual development, mean that travellers start at a severe disadvantage. Many teachers claim that traveller children have very low IQ levels, and the tests that have been conducted tend to substantiate this, most scores being between 60 and 80, though cultural factors may be thought to invalidate the results. Where older children enter school for the first time, lack of previous education frequently presents an insurmountable barrier to catching up with gauje norms.

(c) Lack of education and particularly literacy in the home background is all too obvious, as are poor speech, linguistic restriction, the absence of 'cultural standards', limited cognitive experience, abnormally short concentration spans and an invariably low academic expectation.

(d) Learning capacity is severely reduced by problems of social adaptation to the school and classroom environment, resulting from the life style of caravan dwelling and nomadism and from belonging to a stigmatized and alienated minority group. Claustrophobia in buildings—the corollary to the freedom of the outdoor life—results in restlessness and inability to sit down for extended periods. Feelings of social insecurity and lack of ability to establish relationships with other children and teachers combine with these other factors to produce behaviour that is easily taken for maladjustment and necessitates a long-term process of socialization and orientation to school life before efficient learning can take place.

(e) Traveller children are at a great disadvantage because of their lack of skills normally well-developed in house-dwelling gauje children and the existence of certain traveller skills which have little relevance or value in the school situation, and which may even be considered as positively dangerous or sub-criminal traits—for example, evasiveness, family loyalty, robustness of solutions to quarrels among themselves, a keen eye for valuable waste products (in terms of the scrap market).

(f) Traveller children lack vocational motivation other than following into parental footsteps, as well as an appreciation of the value of educational attainment and qualifications. Education is not considered as a passport to better living.

(g) There is little willingness on the part of most traveller children to mix socially with gauje children or to participate in extra-curricular activities outside school times. They remain very much a gauche and clannish group within the school, but show uninhibited affection towards teachers they like.

(h) With some but not all traveller children there are problems of health, hygiene, infestation, unfamiliarity with toilets, running water and sitting at table and inadequate clothing. In wet winters some have a distinctive smell—not unfamiliar with other children where there is a lack of sanitation and washing facilities in the home. These problems and that of the already stigmatized Gypsy image single them out as 'different' from other children, and socially 'less desirable'.

On most of these factors there is little conflict of opinion among teachers, though it is admitted that general appearance varies between families. Programmes of socialization and training in the school can succeed, as can initial teaching in the basic skills to bring the children up to a sufficiently high level to be integrated into ordinary classes. However, because of the turn-over of tenancies and of nomadic patterns, a school is likely to continue to have educationally virginal children entering and joining other traveller children who have already been partially oriented to school life. Several of the children may have had substantial previous educational experience, and it is likely that most schools will have travellers with a wide range of ability. This makes it difficult to think only of short-term inductive reception classes followed by normal dispersal into classes with gauje children, for it is unlikely that a school will be dealing with a stable group of children. Headteachers were almost unanimous in stating that they were up against a long-term educational problem.

In many schools which had had travellers for a considerable period, teachers admitted that they had failed to assimilate the children into the school completely even though many were confident that in the classroom at least a casual visitor would be hard put to distinguish the travellers from the gaujes. The main failure was in making it possible for the two groups to mix socially. This is vividly shown by the headteachers' replies to the questionnaire.

Mixing in the classroom: This was described as 'good' by only 13 schools. 33 suggested that it was 'average', and 25 characterized it as 'poor'.

Mixing at breaktimes and in the playground: 9 schools reported this as 'good', 13 as 'average', and 44 as 'poor'.

Mixing out of school: Social mixing out of school was reported to be 'good' by 2 schools, as 'average' by 4 schools; 21 schools evaded the issue, and 73 gave an emphatic 'nil' to any mixing at all, many of which extended this 'nil' answer to the other two questions above.

This pattern of clannishness is similar to that which operates for immigrants in school and is a phenomenon which some teachers felt could not be eliminated by action within the school. An important difference can be noted when fairground children are involved, for they mix with 'flattie' (the fairground equivalent of gauje) children within the school with little problem, though out-of-school contact is limited. This difference also applied in schools where there were Gypsies and fairground pupils, the latter keeping well away from their Gypsy neighbours.

Replying to the question about the level of attainment on first entry into school, 51 headteachers indicated a 'nil' educational level on entry, 40 schools described it as 'low' and only 3 headteachers reported it to be 'normal'. Asked to state the satisfactoriness of subsequent progress in general educational attainment, 10 headteachers claimed that it was 'good', 50 that it was 'average and reasonable', but 40 stated that it was 'far from satisfactory'. Specific progress in literacy and numeracy seemed to follow a similar pattern.

Progress in the basic skills was reported as 'reasonable' by 30 schools, 'slow' by 56, and 14 gave no definite reply.

Though both questions and answers were vague and to some extent head-teachers were being asked to judge their schools' own success, the dialogue with teachers that ensued from the questionnaire and the visits to schools reinforced the impression given in the questionnaire replies that there was substantial school failure by most travelling children, even by those attending regularly.

Whereas it is true that many non-traveller children, perhaps a quarter,[9] also reveal serious learning difficulties in acquiring literacy, it must be stated that observations made of travellers regularly in school, who could be expected to have made strides in the direction of literacy, suggested that they were suffering from what can figuratively be described as an acute communal dyslexia. This is worrying not least because literacy is the one area where it can be confidently expected that the children have high motivation to learn. Such poor progress is obviously related to social background, lack of literacy in the home, poor attendance rates, and the quantity and quality of intensive tuition of individuals and small groups. It might also be that the traveller child has a more specific syndrome of learning difficulties with reading and writing: he may be occupationally long-sighted—with an eye for spotting possible scrap sources and unmetalled roads at a long distance. He may have learnt from parents various strategies for covering up illiteracy or even have developed an emotional blockage to learning the basic skills. Lack of teacher experience with reading readiness techniques at junior and secondary levels may be another crucial factor linked, of course, to the efficacy of learning situations created in school. Unless the child is enabled to develop a synthe-sized insight into the code system of written language, there is every likelihood that unskilled or misdirected remedial teaching of reading and writing may be useless. There is also a possibility that limited exposure to oral English and dialect interference from Anglo-Romany and Shelta may play a deleterious role, though we know very little about such problems.[10] Another factor may be even more important: most traveller children tackle tasks at home in which they can easily master the essential skills and reveal competence and adequacy. They are given little insight into the great difficulties of learning to read and write, and when they discover how little progress they seem to be making they tend to experience a traumatic sense of inadequacy and despair of ever mastering literacy. That they see the same failure in their traveller companions in the same class, surrounded as they are by gaujes who appear to have little difficulty in reading and writing, leads to a group sense of inferiority or a rejection of literacy as an unnecessary gauje accom-plishment.

Many headteachers and teachers recognize these problems, but, unless they have time and favourable staffing ratios, they know that they have little hope of meeting the educational needs and demands of their travellers. Some schools, however, were having significant success with literacy levels, and it is possible to make judgements about the factors which led to their success. Much depended on the type of family from which the traveller children came, their regularity of attendance and length of previous education. The charisma and ability of individual teachers played a major part. The devotion of time to individual tuition (either in normal classes or in special all-traveller withdrawal groups) was also crucial, as was the relationship between the teacher and her or his traveller pupils. Factors which seemed irrelevant were the actual methods of teaching reading and the schemes and readers used, though infant school pre-reading activities linked to traveller culture played an important role. Methods of classroom organization, streaming and grouping of children, traditional or progressive techniques, extent of child-centredness, and teaching materials appeared to be insignificant. There was a subjective feeling sometimes that progress in literacy was closely linked to the age of the teacher and to his or her length of experience: the older and longer, the better the progress. This is not merely to be interpreted as a question of teacher quality but may arise because traveller children frequently learn better when under an older and more respectable-looking teacher. Another point which cannot be ignored is the sex of the teacher: boys gravitate towards male teachers (a junior school headmaster, for instance); whereas traveller girls feel insecure with a man. In general, traveller children respond well when their teachers are married and have children, especially if they can all go to the site for a friendly visit.

Opinion within the teaching profession about the educational action most suitable for traveller children was varied: pre-school and nursery education was universally considered as an important potential measure to enable travellers to enter school on a developmental par with gauje children. Non-educational measures were also stressed: more and better permanent sites, a settlement programme, a policy of changing traveller occupations and vocations to bring them closer to settled norms, social work to alleviate 'problem families', an attempt to replace the waning Gypsy culture with an alternative and more educationally amenable ethos presumably closer to that of the teacher. Most teachers saw traveller children as socially and culturally deprived and disadvantaged. There seemed a widespread belief that the travellers had no culture or even subculture as such but merely a way of life—and one which met with general teacher disapproval. They saw their traveller pupils as linguistically impoverished and in dire need of compensatory education. There was no question that most teachers were very concerned about their traveller pupils, and several thought that education could play a role in preventing the children from having to follow in their parents' footsteps. They tended to view traveller society as anachronistic and

E.T.C.—2*

saw little future in it. Many teachers felt travellers to be anti-social and considered that it was in their interests, and in the interests of society generally, to intervene and force them to settle. Virtually all admitted that the educational problems of traveller children could only be partially met while the travelling life continued to exist in its present form.

More teachers saw schooling as a major force of social change among Gypsies at the primary level of the profession than at the secondary. Primary teachers saw more tangible success than secondary teachers, among whom there was much resignation to the facts that many travellers would prematurely drop out and that few seemed to have been much changed by their schooling. Yet few teachers saw the need for educational provision outside or in addition to the school itself, and in general they disapproved of the 'interference' of voluntary workers establishing summer schools and pre-school units in caravans on sites, though other teachers participated actively in these.

Most stressed the need for improving the educational provision within schools, extra staff and more accommodation being the most essential requirements. Asked to state what special provision they thought would be best suited to traveller children, headteachers revealed that opinions were deeply divided about the wisdom and effectiveness of special and separate traveller classes. Also opinions were strongly held, and it was obvious that such terms as 'integration', 'segregation', 'assimilation' and 'separatist' are highly emotive and that their use distracts attention from the real issues.

Thirty-four schools out of roughly one hundred had made some special provision in the form of induction–reception classes, regular remedial or withdrawal groups, extra intensive teaching or the appointment of special additional teachers with responsibility for the Gypsy children. An additional 15 schools had been able to make only marginal extra provision because of limitations in accommodation and staffing. Twenty-eight schools had used special strategies at one time but now resorted to conventional dispersal. Twenty-three schools had never made special provision for their traveller children. There was considerable conflict of opinion about the effectiveness of separate situations—some claiming that they were essential and completely justified by results, while others asserted that they were socially divisive and psychologically disturbing for the children. A major reservation held by those schools which had tried to make special provision without additional resources of man-power and accommodation was that the extra burden upon staff was damaging and such provision could only be made at some loss to the non-travelling children in the school.

Four conditions seemed to determine whether special provision was made: firstly, the length of previous educational experience of the travellers; next, the philosophy of the staff and headteacher; thirdly, the availability of extra resources; and lastly, the age level of the school. There was a general movement from separate reception situations to dispersal into normal classes as the children became socialized into the school routine. Special methods were less likely to have been needed in situations in which the travellers were already partially assimilated into the local community and had already had at least one generation of schooling. In general, infant schools favoured assimilation and socialization into normal classes—not surprisingly, for the infant school is to some extent dominated by socialization objectives, and the disparity between the educational attainment of travellers and gauje is not so noticeable at infant age. Junior schools tended to favour regular remedial withdrawal groups and sometimes all-age special traveller classes. Secondary schools tended to have existing remedial classes into which the traveller children with low educational attainment were directed and from which they moved back into normal classes for craft and non-academic subjects. Traveller children who were at least approaching the educational attainment norms of other children were dispersed in the normal manner at all levels of the system.

At the time of the questionnaire (early 1971), only three schools had special teachers or ancillary helpers solely for the traveller children; but between then and the conclusion of the project in August 1972, this picture changed dramatically, and there were increases both in appointments of special, sometimes peripatetic, teachers and in special accommodation units both in and outside school, on the site itself, for instance. Whether these developments were caused by a further phase in the implementation of the Caravan Sites Act, resulting in a new influx of unschooled children, or by a change of attitude within schools and LEAs about special methods and the educational needs of the child from unauthorized encampments is not clear. It might even be that the establishment of this Schools Council project caused authorities to review the success of existing measures. The National Gypsy Education Council, at that time under Lady Plowden's personal chairmanship, played an important role and was instrumental in instigating several LEA innovatory projects. Certainly it has gradually been realized that a conventional 'open-door' policy on admission of traveller children into schools fails, and that the attendance of traveller children in a school universally makes great demands upon the resources and staff involved. It has also been established that orthodox assimilative dispersal into normal classes is in many cases insufficient to meet the requirements of the children, and that there is a real need for some form of preparatory and bridging education before travellers, formerly outside the system, can take full advantage of schooling.

The over-all conclusions of the research and inquiry stage of this project based upon the LEA survey, the headteachers' questionnaire, the visits to schools and the dialogue with teachers, are the same as those stated in the 1967 Plowden Report:

They [travellers] are probably the most severely deprived children in the country. Most of them do not even go to school, and the potential abilities of those who do are stunted. [*Vol. 1, para. 155*]

Extreme as they are, the needs of gypsy children cannot be effectively met by measures of the kind we recommend for the more general problems of urban deprivation. They will require special attention and carefully planned action. [*Vol. 2, Appendix 12, p. 595*]

The effects and implications of the 1968 Caravan Sites Act, Part 2

It is not unusual for the effects of social legislation to be unpredictable and at times counter-productive: the 1968 Caravan Sites Act, Part 2 (namely, that which deals with Gypsy encampments) is proving no exception. Its passage through Parliament as a private member's bill proposed by Eric Lubbock (now Lord Avebury) was supported by all parties and by the local authorities' associations, and met with virtually no opposition. Its implementation by the local authorities has been extremely slow and has been bitterly opposed at local level. At the end of 1973 the Department of the Environment estimated that roughly one hundred sites providing about 1400 pitches had been opened, though this included several sites open long before the Act came into effect.

The framers of the Act hoped that a network of between 200 and 250 local authority Gypsy caravan sites would soon be created and would provide about 4000 individual hard-standings, which would be sufficient for the number of families thought to exist, based on the 1965 census figures. It was expected that most sites would be for 15 to 20 families (a slight miscalculation, for many families have more than one trailer-caravan), and that a few would be much larger. The Act's preamble stated that it was aimed at eliminating harassment and eviction, at eradicating the social nuisance of unauthorized encampments and at giving travellers a legal place to live.

Though there is no clause in the Act which implied it, there was, and still is, widespread belief that the provision of sites would result in a first-phase programme of settlement and an end to nomadism, followed by a second phase of movement into houses and assimilation into the settled host society. It was certainly thought by many that sites would enable all the children to go to school, and that it would be through the agency of education that the new generation of Gypsies would see that travelling was no longer relevant in contemporary society and would not continue the unsatisfactory life style of its parents—amid the litter and unseemly scrap dumped on the roadside. Sites would also bring the Gypsies under the law, and they would no longer be able to evade income tax, vehicle registration and insurance and so on.

Not everyone took this line; rather, they saw sites as providing the travellers with a network of legal camping areas where they could continue their mode of life, including nomadism and their itinerant occupations. They would have to adapt to site life and live less outside the law, and their children would attend school regularly. But it was thought that this would improve the standard and the quality of their life. Education would enable them to understand their position in society and help them to deal with bureaucracy. It would also give their children at least the choice of settling in houses.

Both viewpoints took it for granted that sites would be provided quickly and that, together with education, would be a social cure-all for the problems of the Gypsy. Whether such a solution would be short- or long-term varied between commentators. Those who saw the Act as an instrument of eventual destruction of travelling and the assimilation of the group into the mainstream of late twentieth-century life felt that Gypsies and travellers were an anti-social and outdated group. Those who wished to give them the choice of continuing their basic life style within the restriction of official sites obviously had a greater respect for the Gypsy heritage and represented the standpoint which favoured a pluralistic concept of society.

The purport of all present research, including this project's work and observations, suggests that a strong note of caution must be sounded at those who see the Act and education as a cure-all solution, whether it is approached from the majority assimilative view or the minority pluralistic one. There are many reasons for such caution. The main one is that, at the rate of present local authority implementation, it may be well into the next century before enough sites have been built. The second major reason is that there may have been a miscalculation about the strength of the Gypsy heritage and the feelings about the provision of sites among the travellers themselves.

The tones adopted in the Ministry of Housing and Local Government report, *Gypsies and Other Travellers*, and in the Plowden Report were as compassionate and as humanitarian as those of the Act itself, but the over-all attitude was based on the belief that the Gypsies were a depressed and disadvantaged group facing a new crisis brought about by urban and suburban development which had removed their traditional camping haunts.[11] The Gypsies were seen by many as a group facing extinction because of the increasingly organized nature of modern government and society generally. If the opponents of Gypsies viewed them as depraved and anti-social, their advocates and supporters saw them as exceptional cases within the general spectrum of deprivation and in dire need of social work and social action. Such views still dominate thought within the teaching profession and within council officialdom.

Several additional considerations must be taken into account. The first of these is the serious underestimation of the traveller population, which is discussed in detail in the next chapter. Second, there are indications that with a gradual population increase,[12] supplemented by a small but steady influx from Eire and a possible exodus of housed travellers on to the new sites, the number of families who will remain on unauthorized land may not be significantly reduced by the sites network for several years yet. In that time, the number of children outside the school system is likely to remain constant or even increase, although the number entering schools will grow. The raising of the school-leaving age has obviously already added to this trend. These predictions are based on present trends and might prove invalid if site provision accelerates further and LEAs adopt positive intervention policies on attendance and educational facilities.

There are additional reasons, however, for pessimism: tenants on the new sites tend to be small families, partly because this eases management problems and partly because selection policies favour the smaller family. There is almost certainly a bulge in the present under-five age group, and as medical supervision improves this trend will continue as infant mortality is reduced.

There is a further major paradox in the 1968 Act—the limitation imposed on the obligatory provision by London and county boroughs. These need only to provide 'adequate accommodation for 15 caravans'. County councils have no limitation and must provide for the needs of the travellers in their respective areas, which will include the excess county borough families driven out of the urban areas. These will become 'no-go' districts once pitches for fifteen caravans have been provided and designation under the Act granted. (It is not clear how local government reorganization will alter this, if at all.) Designation gives an authority greater powers of eviction than ever before: magistrates' courts can summarily impose £25 fines on travellers who set up camp without authority and adequate excuse; and an additional £5 fine for every subsequent day the family remains in the designated area. The courts are empowered to give a designated local authority the right to use whatever measures may be necessary to evict surplus families—and these may include, presumably, those created by a marriage between the grown-up children of tenants on the official site. By January 1973, only three county boroughs had been granted designation, and these have not yet put their powers into effect. County councils can also be granted designation, but it is hard to believe that it will be given until all the county boroughs within and nearby the county boundaries have provided for their fifteen caravans and have already been designated, for until this has taken place there is no way of estimating the actual needs of travellers in the county.

The statutory limits on county borough provision and the concept of designation may have a dramatic effect upon travellers. It may necessitate a major redistribution of families, the main result of which will be the de-urbanization of a community that, following the same directions as the settled community, has become increasingly urban ever since the decline of its agricultural occupations and the development of the scrap-metal industry. This will reverse a movement that has been taking place for up to fifty years, and it will almost certainly cause an economic crisis if families are forced into sites in remote rural districts where the transport overheads of scrap collection in the distant urban areas will be too high for economic subsistence. The other effect of an involuntary redistribution of families will be a dislocation of the wider 'extended' family and close kinship system that has been a major force of cohesion and survival within the travelling community.

The net effect of the Act may thus be the creation of a new group of economically inadequate families. There may be a severe decline in family morale, which may have catastrophic implications on the education of the children. If, as must be expected, the Gypsies attempt to resist this enforced redistribution away from the districts they most need to frequent for economic reasons, and attempt to continue unauthorized camping in designated areas, there will be a period of court action, evictions and harassment more acute than that which the Act was designed to stop. If this does take place, the Gypsy will feel even more persecuted and alienated than he already does, and this will result in his having an even greater fear of and disrespect for the settled community and its institutions—including its schools.

The local authority sites which have been developed so far, though they vary greatly in quality of amenities and in their topographical settings, have been of a surprisingly uniform design which takes little account of the heterogeneity of the travellers. There is virtually no provision of transit pitches or transit sites for the nomadic families. The needs of the minority of old-fashioned horse and wagon families have been largely ignored, and virtually no sites have grazing land for families who keep horses.

Partly because so few sites have been developed and partly because of the way in which sites are managed, the travellers who have gained access to them are a far from representative group. Sites have obviously attracted those families who most wish to settle, and in turn local authorities have avoided tenants not likely to settle. Parents wanting their children to go to school have opted for sites, and this is sometimes a very acceptable qualification for tenancy. Only a small minority of the families who move on are 'distress' families seeking the easier access to social-welfare benefits which is likely to be characteristic of a site. The majority of families choose to go to sites because they can afford the rents or are members of the older generation (another reason for the smaller number of school-age children on sites as opposed to unauthorized encampments). Local authority site managers reinforce self-selection processes because they favour the more 'respectable', affluent, and smaller families. They shy away from traditional Gypsies because they are 'dirty', though parodoxically they are closer to the romantic image of the Romany which some councils prefer to that of the modern 'flash' caravan traveller. Site managers prefer families who make a show of outward appearances: vehicles of a recent model and expensive caravans. They also accept length of residence in the area as a criterion of selection; and those families with long-standing local connexions have preference over outsiders wanting to resort to the area. This works against the Irish and the Scottish, who are anyway considered socially less desirable. In fact, the Irish and Scottish travellers may have been resorting to the area for many generations—may have been born in it; but their accents and reputations weigh against them. Site managers tend not to favour dealers in ferrous scrap metals and car-breakers who have to break their scrap on the site. Managers therefore choose travellers who can afford to rent yards locally and those who deal in non-ferrous metals and other 'clean' trades—perhaps a more justifiable criterion than supposed nationality.

Many of the sites opened are unsatisfactory from a health point of view—something about which many teachers become extremely concerned. Some sites are located on former corporation rubbish tips or other unsavoury ground. Power stations, railway lines, stagnant water, canals, poor drainage, operative tips, and other unwholesome artefacts are common neighbours. Few sites have play areas for the children or communal recreational facilities. They tend to be too compact, and the over-proximity of caravans gives rise to frequent quarrels between families. The local authority site, usually coated with tarmac, may be an improvement over the roadside verge encampment where parents restricted the play and movement of their children because of the dangers of fast-moving traffic, but such sites provide less space for play and exploration than the unauthorized waste-land camps. For some travellers the official site with its neat rows of evenly spaced trailers and the exclusion of the normal detritus of traveller occupations is a poor substitute and a less exciting place in which to live. Evictions and travelling to many different camping places meant that the children had plenty of new cognitive experience, and teachers sometimes comment that the roadside child seems to have more to talk about than his cousin on the site.

Most sites have regulations which erode the traditional heritage of travellers: restrictions on the keeping of animals; on the lighting of outdoor fires (the hub of traveller conversation and the meeting place for visitors and relatives, a place where children listened to gossip); the elimination of scrap sorting on the site and no provision of work areas, which are essential to the majority of travellers who do not rent private yards elsewhere. This last point is important, for already there is evidence that some families have had to move off permanent sites because they could not continue to make a living when they were forbidden to sort and break their scrap on the site. Communal toilet and washing facilities, rarely satisfactory among the settled community, create additional problems with travellers, for there are many taboos about cleanliness and there are sexual complications resulting from Gypsy tradi-tions. Some of the local authority sites have only minimal facilities—and would fail to reach the standards laid down for commercial sites—for example, they possess toilets and a tap but no sinks.

Not all sites are as unsatisfactory as this; some are by any standards luxurious, with individual family wash-houses and day rooms. Some have additional grazing land, playgrounds or community centres, and are placed in attractive surroundings. But these are in the minority, and teachers in many of the schools visited during the project were extremely disturbed about the poor quality of the sites and the unprepossessing environments in which their children lived.

In an educational report such as this it is neither the intention nor would it be permissible to make recommendations on social policy or to condemn certain aspects of social legislation. Yet the days when it was possible to discuss educational problems without taking into account social and political forces are over.[13] It is difficult to be optimistic about the effects which current implementation of the 1968 Act may have for education. The picture presented in the foregoing paragraphs is a realistic one, as anybody who travels the country observing sites and encampments will discover, and the educational and social dangers implicit in the situation *do* exist.

Review of educational theory and the schooling of travellers

In discussing educational theory, the main point at issue is whether travellers should be treated as belonging within the spectrum of general deprivation (in their case educational privation as well as social or cultural disadvantage) or whether they should be treated as a very special case unlike any other group of children. The Plowden Report was able to straddle the fence by claiming that they were 'probably the most deprived children' and yet could not be effectively catered for by the normal urban compensatory measures recommended. It stated that they would 'require special attention and carefully planned action', but did not specify what kind.

It was concluded at the end of the section on teacher opinion (see page 35) that there may be a great need for some form of bridging or inductive programme to enable travellers formerly outside the educational system to take full advantage of normal schooling.[14] Later in this report, various measures are described or suggested which would fulfil such a bridging operation. So far, however, the basic objectives of bringing the Gypsy child into the maintained system have not been questioned, though it has been noted that many teachers expressed doubts and reservations about this. Certainly no one would question that it is very wrong that traveller children should not have at least the same equality of opportunity that other children have, but as things stand equality can exist only if travellers stop being travellers. Any attempt to make a totally separate compulsory educational system for Gypsies and other travellers would founder because some of the travellers themselves would oppose it bitterly on the grounds of discrimination. It would not be recommended anyway because the segregrated Dutch system might be thought to create grave social alienation and isolation; besides, Dutch legislation has been passed in a different social context and in the light of a different educational philosophy.

It seems wiser to suggest that the maintained system should itself be adaptable to the special needs of traveller children. This it is, sometimes, under various clauses of the 1944 Act, for instance, section 56, which enables LEAs to provide education other than in school and education for less than the normal school year (see page 116).[15] Though many special measures are possible within the terms of existing legislation, it still remains for several LEAs and teachers to be convinced that the Gypsy warrants such consideration and favour; and there are three main justifications for such a view:

(a) The Gypsies are a very special minority group. Quite unlike other minority or immigrant groups, they are a *travelling society* with a distinctive heritage that owes little to the value systems of settled communities. They have entirely different vocational aims. They have not 'dropped out' of the host community, for they have never been part of its mainstream. They have their own family-centred educative system.

(b) The maintained educational system has singularly failed to attract or force the majority of travellers into attending schools. Secondary drop-out, casual absenteeism, continued nomadism even after a network of sites has been completed, will also certainly continue to prove that travellers and normal schooling procedures are subject to incompatible forces, which will frequently result in educational failure.

(c) The development of experimental educational strategies for such a minority group gives an ideal opportunity to test and modify innovatory educational practice which may be applicable to other groups of children, especially in view of some of the findings and recommendations of the Educational Priority Areas.[16]

Behind these arguments lies the hypothesis that although the travellers need educational support from the state in addition to what they provide for their children within the family setting, they are not a basically deprived or disadvantaged group. Nobody can be deprived of something he has rejected; so it is with the Gypsy and the life he chooses to live. Had none of his children opted to lead the same life through successive generations for the past five hundred years, there would be no Gypsies living in caravans today. Some of today's Gypsy families are inadequate and disadvantaged, but they are so in the Gypsies' terms as well as ours. Such families can and do fall back on state welfare support in dire necessity.

Certainly among some travellers—particularly the lower strata of Irish and Scottish—there are problems of alcoholism and habitual criminality (mainly for petty offences). These are problems in every section of society but some of the highest rates occur among formerly nomadic minority groups which have been forced to settle and change their traditional life styles—the American Indians, for instance. However, among traveller families in England and Wales, these problems are rare. It is significant that there are virtually no old Gypsy people in homes, very few Gypsy children in care, and little evidence of emotional maladjustment among Gypsy children.

Notes and references

1   Centre for Environmental Studies Gypsy Project, Draft Report (1972), chapter on Gypsy identity.

2   Central Advisory Council for Education (England), *Children and Their Primary Schools*, vol. 2 (HMSO, 1967), Appendix 12, p. 589, para 13.

3   Obtainable from National Gypsy Education Council. See Arthur Ivatts, *Report on NGEC Summer Schools* (1971), p. 23.

4   Ministry of Housing and Local Government, *Gypsies and Other Travellers* (HMSO, 1967), p. 9.

5   Information provided by P. H. J. M. Janssen, Inspector of Education for General Affairs during the project's visit to Holland in 1971. Also more complicated breakdown in Drs K. Sietaram, *Opvoeding van en Onderwijs aan Woonwagenkampkinderen* (Utrecht: University of Utrecht, 1968), p. 8.

6   *Gypsies and Other Travellers* (see n. 4), p. 6.

7   Silvester Gordon Boswell, *The Book of Boswell*, ed., John Seymour (Gollancz, 1970), pp. 36, 38.

8   *Children and Their Primary Schools* (see n. 2), vol. 2, Appendix 2, p. 598, para. 13.

9   Cf. Jessie Reid, 'The scope of the reading problem' in *Reading: Problems and Practices*, ed. Jessie Reid (Ward Lock Educational, 1972), pp. 37–43.

10   Schools Council Working Paper 29, *Teaching English to West Indian Children* (Evans/Methuen Educational, 1970). See also *Teacher's Manual* for the 'Dialect Kit' (E. J. Arnold, 1972), part of *Concept 7–9*, the teaching materials from the Schools Council's Teaching English to West Indian Children Project.

11   See especially *Gypsies and Other Travellers* (see n. 4.), pp. 65–8.

12   Ibid., p. 9.

13   *Report of the Conference on 'Social deprivation and change in education'*, Nuffield Teacher Enquiry Conference, University of York, April 1972, pp. 1–19.

14   See also *The Shadow on the Cheese*, ed. John Wallbridge (NGEC, 1972).

15   George Taylor and John B. Saunders, eds, *The New Law of Education*, 7th edn (Butterworth, 1971), p. 172.

16   A. H. Halsey, *Educational Priority*, Vol. 1: *EPA Problems and Policies*, (HMSO, 1972).

4 The nature of travelling society

Because the case made for special treatment for traveller children in this report rests upon its interpretation of the nature of traveller society, this chapter outlines the nature and background of travellers as they were observed during the project and in the light of previous studies. Its nine sections comprise a survey of previous studies; consideration of problems of terminology and definition; an account of origin and histories of the various travelling groups; categorization of travellers by extent of nomadism and settlement; a study of demography and health; accounts of regional and other differences in employment and life style; as well as of conditions of life (inside trailers, the immediate environment outside trailers and on sites and encampments); a sketch of their cultural heritage, customs and language; and, finally, a profile of the traveller child as a case for education.

Survey of previous studies[1]

The range of works on Gypsies, from the *Journal of the Gyspy Lore Society*, dating back to the 1880s, and the literature on travellers from John Hoyland's *Historical Survey of the Customs and Present State of the Gypsies* of 1816 (probably the first major work on Gypsies published in England) to Grattan Puxon and Dr Donald Kenrick's *The Destiny of Europe's Gypsies* (1972), is a tribute to the traveller's ability to intrigue but to confound the scholar. George Borrow and other sentimental writers, such as the Reverend George Hall in the latter half of the nineteenth century, were writing personal reminiscences about their dalliance on the fringe of the well-known 'gypsiries'. Smart and Crofton's *Dialect of the English Gypsies*, published in 1875, remains the best dictionary of Anglo-Romany, though there is now a real need for it to be up-dated and revised. George Smith of Coalville, the Simsons, Leland and many other writers of the nineteenth century provide contrasting but mainly distorted views likely to mislead readers rather than to illuminate them, as do Bercovici, Vesey-Fitzgerald, Jan Yoors, Croft-Cooke and Walter Starkie in the twentieth century. MacAlister has published a detailed discussion of Shelta, and gives a long wordlist in his *The Secret*

Languages of Ireland (1937), but it is mainly based on previous work by Sampson and not on original research. The first major political figure to take up the Gypsies' cause, Norman Dodds, M.P., produced *Gypsies, Didikois and Other Travellers* (posthumously published in 1966), but it is an idealistic mixture of polemics and personal reminiscence. Silvester Gordon Boswell has published an autobiography, *The Book of Boswell* (1970), edited by John Seymour, which may start a spate of much-needed writing by Gypsies themselves, though the works of Gypsy Petulengro before the war are stimulating. The books of Dominic Reeve give a useful though popularized guide to life on the roadside as it was rather than is. Perhaps the most interesting recent book has been *Gypsies: Wanderers of the World*, full of sumptuous colour photographs and journalistic reportage of Clifford Lee's journey from Liverpool to New Delhi, attempting to retrace the footsteps of his Romany ancestors, and descriptions of the many Gypsy communities he visited en route, published in book form by the National Geographic Society in 1970.

Taken as a body of literature it is entertaining and interesting but not very informative. Much of the material is now dated, but even the most recently published literature is either pretentious (for example, Duff's translation of Jean-Paul Clébert's *The Gypsies*—the standard Penguin) or seemingly out of touch with the realities of caravan dwelling and contemporary conditions among travellers. Grattan Puxon's *On the Road* (National Council for Civil Liberties) is in touch, but its tone of civil-rights outrage may be off-putting to many readers.

Perhaps of greater value to the reader wanting a quick insight into contemporary travellers are the official government reports. *The Report of the Commission on Itinerancy* (Dublin, 1963) is very much a report by officials. The 1967 Ministry of Housing and Local Government report of the 1965 census of travellers in England and Wales and an extended analysis of data collected in the census, *Gypsies and Other Travellers*, presents a humane, informative but now believed to be a rather superficial, description and suspect enumeration of travellers. The more detailed, but similiar, Scottish Development Department's *Scotland's Travelling People* (1971), contains the findings of an extended project and two censuses conducted in 1969.

These reports, especially the latter two, have the virtues of attempting to describe the real conditions of contemporary travelling life, and they avoid the romanticized notions of the 'true' or 'real' Gypsies and the cultural nostalgia that dominates so many of the previously mentioned works—with the exception of George Smith of Coalville, who saw it as a divine mission to eradicate the Gypsies' 'lying, plundering, dirty, filthy, cheating and crafty habits'.[2] However, these reports are limited because there are many pitfalls in relying too much upon normal sociological methods. To attempt to base an analysis of Gypsy and travelling communities on census and questionnaire data alone is very dangerous, and in fact the Scottish, and English and Welsh reports are on safer ground when their authors rely upon judicious observation. The recognition of gaps and unreliability in the English and Welsh report led the Centre for Environmental Studies to establish a project on travellers based upon extended field-work. There was close consultation between the Schools Council project and some members of the CES team, and draft chapters of their respective reports were exchanged. Some of the findings and conclusions of the reports complement and reinforce each other; and it is hoped that together they will contribute to traveller studies of the future by exposing the main areas about which so little is known.

The dangers of the questionnaire and statistical method of studying travellers is best illustrated by considering the two censuses conducted in Scotland in 1969. It must first be said that they were well planned and that account was taken of the pitfalls exposed by the earlier English and Welsh census. The results confirm that normal demographic analysis is extremely difficult in the case of travellers. The first count in March recorded 303 individual travelling families. The August census revealed 344—an increase of 41 families. However, an analysis of family data (names, ages and numbers of offspring and other adults in the household) resulted in the discovery that only 147 families recorded in March had been recounted in August. Between March and August, 197 families had materialized seemingly from nowhere; and 157 had disappeared or eluded the census team.[3]

There are many possible explanations for this remarkable discrepancy. Scottish travellers (a higher proportion of whom were in tents than in England and Wales) probably resort to winter housing and summer travelling more than do their counterparts south of the border. Some of the families counted in March may have travelled out of Scotland to England, Wales or Ireland; or they may have hidden in order to elude the census, or merely been overlooked. The same could be said about the August figure; though if traveller replies can be trusted a proportion confirmed that they had been in houses during March. An unknown number of families may not have been counted on either one or both occasions because they were actually travelling the roads that day. It must also be expected that several families, in traveller tradition, changed their names and gave different information about their offspring's ages, their number and so on. In short, as usual, the travellers managed to defy the attempt to study them. Perhaps the only way of making a reliable count of travellers (or rather, of caravans and tents) might be by aerial photography. Traveller camps and their trailer caravans are surprisingly easy to distinguish from chalet bungalows and chalet caravans on holiday or residential camps of the settled community, and it is even possible to distinguish between gauje and traveller trailers on mixed residential sites.

Nevertheless, the 1967 English and Welsh report and that for Scotland in 1971 have helped to establish traveller studies on a new sociological footing.

It was little wonder that the previous ephemeral literature, which lacked realistic description of the life style of ordinary travellers and helped to create the myth of the 'true' Gypsy, promoted the belief among teachers and other readers that contemporary travellers were nearing extinction, a racially diluted group which had come into the cities and were camped on major road verges waiting for the new sites that would be used as a stepping-stone to assimilation and house dwelling. The distorted emphasis on folk-lore, customs and culture based on European traditional Gypsy tribal rites, once given credence, resulted in widespread denial by teachers that their children possessed any semblance of culture—the outright denial, in fact, that they were Gypsies at all. Instead, they were 'itinerant scrap dealers', 'itinerant traders', 'scrap metal travellers', 'Welsh travelling scrap mer-chants', 'pickers', 'children who live in caravans' and 'social drop outs, more or less permanent', though one *aficionado* claimed that 'with the exception of one family of Romani the travellers were in the main Neidi and Didakais. There are no Tinkers or Mumpers.'

The report on travellers in England and Wales reinforced the view that the old Gypsy had died out, for, although it pointed out the derogatory nature of some of the terms described in the next section of this chapter, it did not deny their validity. Indeed, it claimed that:

Groups with no claim to Romany blood have also adopted the gypsy way of life and, in some cases, have followed it for several generations. This latter group are called *mumpers* . . .[4]

A detailed analysis of heritage was avoided, and the whole emphasis given in the report was factual and dealt with the external aspects of traveller life. The ultimate image of the Gypsy that comes across *is* that of an itinerant scrap dealer facing a social crisis.

It is probable that most of today's travellers have some Romany blood [cf. previous quotation]. And all, irrespective of the extent of their Romany blood, experience the same difficulties in carrying on their way of life in our society.[5]

The report itself was a policy recommendation, and its fruit was the Caravan Sites Act. The report has paradoxically helped to reduce the traveller to a social problem, part society's and part his own. Local authority officers, site managers and local councils are at present dominated by this attitude. It prevails with only a few notable exceptions among teachers.

Problems of terminology and definition

There is no question that many of the problems headteachers experienced in classifying their traveller children in the questionnaire arose because the terminology with respect to travellers is very confusing—and although it must be admitted that the questionnaire itself gave insufficient help, the resulting answers to the question of designation of child were sometimes extremely revealing.

The confusions do not arise merely because writers in the past have been imprecise. The terminology used for travellers is related to the host community's prejudice against the group, its stereotyping of it, the familiar scapegoat mechanism, and its proneness to 'divide' for the purpose of 'ruling'. It is also related to the traditional belief in ethnic or national purity, in racial purity and in their connexion—in the popular mind and in that of the nineteenth-century anthropologist—with cultural superiority and moral rectitude, as Thomas Acton has shown and as will be brought out in the report by the Centre for Environmental Studies.[6]

The travellers have themselves encouraged this, or have been forced into doing so because they have existed as outsiders under constant threat. Most writers have searched for the 'deepest' Romany words and grammar[7] and for the 'truest' Gypsies with the strongest culture and folklore which could support their thesis that the Gypsies came from northern India. Thus the travellers were given a defence against their stigmatized image and actual complaints against them made by the host community. They could always say that *they* were the 'real' Gypsies but that the people down the road were not and it was the latter who were unclean, deceitful and the cause of the trouble.[8]

This connexion between a 'good' Gypsy and a 'pure' Gypsy is based on two myths: first, that racial purity or blood determines moral and cultural behaviour;[9] and second, that the travelling population can be divided into two distinct groups—'real' and genetically 'debased' Romany stock.

It would be foolhardy to deny that some travellers intermarried with gaujes over the centuries more so than others. Whether there are any 'unadulterated' families is dubious, though there are still a few families who would claim this. Silvester Gordon Boswell presents his credentials in a family tree which he can trace back to the 1750s.[10] However, this is exceptional, and probably many other branches of the family have married non-Gypsies during this time. A hierarchy of Romany-ness probably does exist, at least *theoretically*, but it would have to include the Irish and Scottish travellers as well as Gypsy groups throughout Europe. It is almost impossible to prove pedigree, and families that are 'pure' would have achieved it by considerable close cousin marriages and might, therefore, be drawing on a dangerously restricted genetic pool—a point made by Gypsy Petulengro himself.[11] There is one further point that undermines the whole purity argument: nobody knows for certain the true origin of the Romany tribes. Was there one tribe or several? Did they all come from the same place? Was the Romany stock diluted *before* the influx into the British Isles? These points are dealt with later in this chapter (see pages 58 and 60), where it is indicated that in all probability there will never be answers to such questions; who, after all, can claim to be thoroughly 'Anglo-Saxon' or 'English'? At any rate, the search for pure lineage or for the creation of a hierarchy of Romany-ness are not pursuits which should in any way affect social or educational policy.

The problems of definition and terminology are also complicated by the existence of the restrictive legal definition of 'Gypsy' operating in England and Wales: 'Since a recent High Court ruling a *gypsy* is defined, for legal purposes, as a person without fixed abode who leads a nomadic life dwelling in tents or other shelters or caravans or other vehicles; i.e. as a class of person. . . .'[12]

This definition has already created anomalies—as, for example, when a recognized Gypsy loses a planning appeal to develop a private caravan site on the grounds that he was not a Gypsy because he had an address and had been settled for too long. Such a restrictive definition is of little value to sociologists and educators because it ignores the complex kinship and heritage patterns which cut across nomadic and sedentary life styles. The educational problems of housed and camp-site children have much in common, though nomadism introduces a major practical difficulty. Patterns of movement to and from houses and the roadside are complex. Legally, however, a person ceases to be a Gypsy as soon as he settles, although by acclaim, self-ascription, kinship links, and observable heritage there may be no question about his actual identity.

Gypsy
This spelling is preferred to 'Gipsy' by the literate traveller, and capitalized throughout this report because it is used in an ethnic sense. It is thought to be a contraction of 'Egyptian', the self-styled appellation used by the early Romany tribes reaching Western Europe and Britain in the fifteenth and sixteenth centuries. The European equivalents seem to be rather closer in etymology to 'Tinker': *Athinganōs* (Greek), *Cinghanes* (Turkish), *Gitanos* (Spanish), *Gitans* or *Tziganes* (French)—*Manouches*, a word very similar to the Bengali word for 'people', refers to a specific group in France—*Zigenare* (Swedish), *Zigeuner* (German and Dutch), *Zingari* (Italian). Perhaps the word 'itinerant' may be etymologically related too. Other countries have at least as many pejorative and cant alternatives for their 'mixed-blood' travellers. There are also native (non-Romany) nomadic groups, some with ancient origins and some of more modern origins who may have mixed with other travellers and Gypsies or with drop-outs from society. These native groups are called *tjötten* in Holland and *tattare* in Sweden. We, in this country, have a housed group of dealers in scrap metal and other waste products who in some areas are called 'tatters' or 'totters'. Such groups may have Gypsy commercial connexions but seem not to have married with them much—for instance, the 'tatters of Tipton in Staffordshire'.

The word 'Gypsy' is used by many writers as a synonym for 'Romany', but some may use 'Romany Gypsy' and 'Tinker Gypsy', which makes 'Gypsy' more generic as a term. Popular usage is similarly complex: sometimes flattering and sometimes abusive, occasionally drawing the distinction with 'Tinker' and at times used indiscriminately for all travelling groups (a fact much resented and hotly contested by fairground operators). The word also can be used adjectivally in such expressions as 'a Gypsy cure', 'a Gypsy curse', 'a Gypsy wife' (compare 'tinker's curse' and, in Scotland, 'tink(l)er wife'). Gypsiologists and some travellers prefer 'Romany', or 'Rom', 'Romanichal' to 'Gypsy' because of the popular denigration implied by the latter.[13]

There are regional differences in the word's usage and in its acceptability to travellers, the South West being the region where the most resistance exists. But it is interesting to note that even there, distinction is made between the word when used by outsiders and when used by a member of the group itself. This account of a conversation with an old woman in Somerset will illustrate the point.

Now don't yous go calling us that, young man. Gypsy is mumply old hedge-crawlers and dirty riff-raff. They give us a bad name. We's travellers.

She was then shown a large photograph of a traveller family group from the Black Country. She immediately called over a young grandson.

Look here. . . ! Them's a photer of our own people this man knows from miles away. Them's real old Gypsy folk. They's what we calls travelling Gypsies, see. Now [pointing to the father in the picture], that's my man's sister's son, and them's his children [naming them]. But she [the mother of the group], she's my mother's great-grand-niece, you see. Now there! But we's all Gypsies. All of us ———es. Now that's the truth of it, my dear love.

Her reason for not wanting her grandchildren to be called Gypsies in school was that too often it became 'dirty Gyppo' in the playground, and because she claimed that most gaujes did not understand what it meant.

The definition of 'Gypsy' preferred by the project and the one adopted elsewhere in this report is similar to that developed in a draft chapter of the report by the Centre for Environmental Studies already referred to: self-ascription, someone who is accepted by other members of the Gypsy community as a Gypsy, and has at least one natural parent who is a Gypsy. On rare occasions a non-Gypsy married to a Gypsy, who is accepted on all three counts, may be adopted and allowed to take on the identity, but his gauje nature is never forgotten. Children of mixed parenthood are granted Gypsy identity in nearly every case.

In this report, 'Gypsy' is used to distinguish the English and Welsh travellers who speak Anglo-Romany and have customs which can be related to a Romany past, from Irish and Scottish 'Tinkers', who possess a basically different heritage. There are Irish and Scottish 'Romanies', and evidence to date suggests that there has been so much intermarriage between the groups that, although the differences between the extremes are obvious, there are many families who can lay claim to both identities with equal justification. On a language level, Anglo-Romany is laced with Shelta (the secret language of the Irish Tinker) and the cant of Scottish travellers (also closely linked to Shelta). There are many families whose members can speak both languages. Nevertheless, such a broad distinction is justified and functional.

Didikoi(s)

'Didikois' is one of the most common terms used by the settled community to describe travellers whom they believe to be of mixed and impure Gypsy blood. Smart and Crofton in their 1875 dictionary suggest that the word is formed from '*dik-akei*', the half-breed Gypsy mispronouncing it 'did', thus signifying his 'debased' parentage,[14] though this may be thought rather far-fetched.[15] Whatever the origin, Gypsies tend to use it in two senses: firstly, when talking to aliens they refer to a half- or less than half-breed Gypsy; secondly, amongst themselves and friendly gaujes they admit its meaninglessness except as an abusive label. However, there is evidence to suggest that it may also be used as a synonym for 'Gypsy', though this may be dependent on regional deviation: the word is more common in Kent than in the Midlands. Thomas Acton suggests that multiple meanings co-exist, for he recorded the following variations of the well-known jingle, 'I'm the Romani Rai':

I'm the Romani Rai. I'm a true/real didicai.
I'm the Romani Rai. Just an old didicai.
They call me the Romani Rai, but I'm only an old didicai.[16]

When he pointed out this range of alternative meanings, the reply was that it was all the same song. This impression seemed to be confirmed in the course of research for this project, when a child in Wolverhampton sang each version in the reverse order to that presented above as the gradually changing refrain to the song. It is certainly not a word to be recommended to teachers.

Posh-rat

This is another denigrating term, the Anglo-Romany for half-breed (*posh*= half, *rat(t)*=blood). The bilingual pun and insult is too obvious to miss, and reinforces the pejorative connotation. This word is not very common nowadays and is, one hopes, dying out.

Needy (neidi, etc.), pikie, mumper or mumpli (sometimes adjectival), hedge-crawler

All these and many other often regionally limited terms are more extreme than posh-rat or didikois in suggesting even lower levels in the theoretical hierarchy of Romany-ness to which this report gives little credence.

Gauje (or gorgio)
The pronunciations vary, but perhaps the most common version heard is that which rhymes with 'orgy'. Smart and Crofton give several variants: 'gorjo', 'gorjer', as well as the French and Turkish versions from Dr Alexandre Paspati's *Etudes sur les Tchinghianes* (Constantinople, 1870)—*gadjó* (m) *gadji* (f) and *gadjé* (pl).[17] Such declensions can still be detected among some Gypsies in England and Wales, but so can non-declining and variant forms, such as 'gorgia' (as in 'Borgia'), often depending on dominant regional accent.

There is no confusion about the word's implication of gentile and non-traveller. Irish Tinkers may use 'buffer'. Scottish travellers may use 'flattie', as do the fairground showmen, but 'country people' is a more common equivalent. There are more derogatory words which all travellers use—but those are their privilege. 'Gauje' can usually be adopted by teachers once a good relationship has been established.

Tinker
This is the most awkward of all the terms applied to travellers and the one whose careless use is most likely to cause resentment from the people themselves. Unlike 'didikois' and 'mumper', it is a term that cannot easily be avoided.

'Tinker', or its Scottish variants 'Tink' or 'Tinkler', is normally applied to the Scottish and Irish travellers, only a very few of whom appear to have a strong Romany heritage. While there may be vestigial Romany traits resulting from mixed marriages many generations ago which can be detected in the small percentage of Anglo-Romany words in Shelta and Scottish Tinkers' cant, most writers make a clear distinction between the English and Welsh *Gypsies* and the Irish and Scottish travellers or *Tinkers*.[18] This point is discussed in greater detail later in this chapter, where it is suggested that such a broad distinction has sufficient validity to justify its adoption throughout this report.

However, the term has been widely used both in popular and in official circles to describe all travellers in England and Wales other than a small and usually unspecified group of 'true Gypsies'. This indiscriminate use is based on a myth which it is hoped has already been exploded by the definition and discussion of 'Gypsy' in the foregoing pages. English Gypsies are universally resentful if they are called Tinkers by officials and in local newspapers. Opinions among the Irish and Scottish travellers about being called Tinkers is mixed, but less hostility to the term may well exist among the Irish, some of whom are proud of its association with copper- and tin-smithery, seen as an élite occupation among itinerant groups. Nowadays the term has lost its occupational connotations, for it may be applied to tarmac layers, horse-dealers, scrap-metal workers or antique furniture dealers. Like the Gypsy, the Tinker gains his identity through the three main determinants of self-ascription, common acceptance and descent through at least one parent. His heritage is observably different from that of the Gypsy, though his life style and role in society are almost identical.

This raises some complicated questions. Are there no English or Welsh Tinkers? Are all Scottish and Irish travellers Tinkers and not Gypsies? To what extent are all the groups genealogically connected? For how long does a Scottish or Irish Tinker have to stay in England before his Tinker identity is lost? What are the possible political and social consequences of making an ethnic distinction between Gypsy and Tinker? Might it, for instance, rein-force existing discriminative practice against the Irish and Scottish? Having attempted to destroy the thesis of the 'true' Gypsy, has not another fallacious thesis been presented—that of the 'ordinary' Gypsy and the 'ordinary' Tinker, and one that exploits the accidental distribution of the Tinkers into Ireland and Scotland?

There is justification in asking each of these questions, but of course no neat definition can ipso facto answer them all. Nevertheless, it is possible to give some of the answers. Virtually no evidence was found in England and Wales of an ancient and indigenous nomadic group displaying such marginal Romany heritage as the Irish and Scottish Tinkers. There are admittedly a very small minority of Irish and Scottish Romany Gypsy families—or at least Gypsies travelling in Ireland and Scotland whose dominant second language is Anglo-Romany rather than Shelta. Some are visitors from Eng-land and Wales, others were born here but have strong Irish or Scottish accents. Yet, even within the same family, it is sometimes the case that the accents of the children depend upon where they spent their early years. Intermarriage among all these groups can be detected, but they are pro-portionately rare. In general, whenever a marriage between persons from the two groups took place, the new nuclear family created joined one of the groups and dissociated themselves from the other. This was sometimes observed as a cause in eventual marital breakdown.

Many Scottish and Irish Tinker families have been making excursions into England and Wales for generations, and some have even stayed here for surprisingly long periods, but they tend to visit their 'ancestral' countries regularly, sometimes even seasonally. They lose their identity only if they marry into the Gypsy community and become totally assimilated into it—for instance, in the case of some of the Raffertys or Finneys, though these were probably Irish Romany families in the first instance. The situation is extremely complicated, and there are many Irish Tinker families travelling the roads of England and Wales who by no stretch of the imagination can be called 'immigrants', for their children, perhaps even they themselves, were born here. Some would even claim to be at least as 'indigenous' as some of the Gypsies, say, of Wales, who have moved into the Black Country. Yet their accents are retained and Shelta is their dominant secret language. They would also claim to be Tinkers, not Gypsies. Yet there is much to be said for dropping both terms altogether and using only 'traveller'—a course of action strongly recommended to teachers within classroom and school situations. Nevertheless, the differences between the two groups are very clear and are acknowledged to be of great importance by the people themselves.

Broadly speaking, all would call themselves 'travellers', but none would wish to be called 'mumpers' or 'posh-rats' and so on. 'Didikois' is a confused term subject to regional variation in meaning; it is best left as an in-group nickname. 'Gypsy' and 'Tinker' are now used so widely that however unfortunate their connotations of stigma, it was felt that they would have to be adopted in this report.

These problems of definition and terminology have been concentrated upon because there is so much confusion about travellers and how to describe them. Besides the terms dealt with already, there is the official jargon: 'itinerant', 'migrant' and 'nomad'. There are also the words that frequently crop up in ancient as well as in recent legislation: 'hawker', 'pedlar' and 'tatter'. These obviously refer to particular trades which are practised by house dwellers as well as by travellers. Official and public confusion sometimes arises because the travellers are confused with vagrants or 'vagabonds' (archaic), or even tramps. In fact, the vagrant and the traveller community are poles apart, for the former are unquestionably society's drop-outs. Curiously, it is the Irish Tinker who is most likely to help the tramp or 'dosser' by offering him the cab of a lorry to sleep in, food and clothing, perhaps even a small wage, in return for casual labouring. A Tinker family may return several times to the same town and pick up the same dosser on each occasion. Some examples of this reveal little humanity on the part of the Tinker, for the dosser is used as a general skivvy, sleeping under the lorry and not in the cab. But several examples exist of a Tinker family adopting a chronic alcoholic and rehabilitating him as a special member of the group with a separate trailer and van.

Throughout this report the dominant term used is 'traveller'. It is the safest of all the labels because it is acceptable to all the groups. It has only two minor drawbacks: it is obviously euphemistic, and it is sometimes contradictory in that it is often applied to families who are virtually sedentary. Though there comes a time when some Gypsies and Tinkers can no longer be literally called 'travellers', the term is used in a generic sense throughout this report.

The problem of euphemism is one which the travellers themselves must meet. It is hard for them to do this while all the other names are so stigmatized. Eventually, the avoidance of 'Gypsy' and 'Tinker' may lead to denial of actual identity and a lack of faith in heritage. Silvester Gordon Boswell, who has grandchildren who are housed, makes this point strongly and movingly at the conclusion of his autobiography:

Yes, Lewis's little children will tell you he's a Gypsy. He's a Romany, a real Romany man. That what his little Lewis will say. Little Duggie does the same. Little Jimmy—'What are you, Jimmy?'

'I'm a Gypsy!'

And then probably these children will turn round and say to me when I tell them to keep quiet or something in the yard, or not ride their bicycle, they say: 'Gypsy—Gypsy—Gypsy Gypsy!'

Oh I like it—go on—carry on—keep it up! I like them to keep the word in the name—that is, with me. I tease them for it, to bring it out of them.

And then eventually they'll find out what a Gypsy means.[19]

This is a common parental attitude, and one also found in a very few schools where teachers recognized that their traveller children were being denied their true identity and were in danger of developing negative self-images, especially within the school environment.

Origins and histories of the various travelling groups

It has been argued in the previous section that the travellers in England and Wales can be divided into two main groups. The first are the Gypsies, native to England and Wales, who possess a vestigial but significant Romany heritage and who exhibit to a varying degree Romany ancestry. They speak Anglo-Romany, as a secret, 'in-group' language. They represent at least 80% of all the travellers in England and Wales. In addition, as has been suggested, there is an unknown number of housed Gypsies whom some observers think could easily outnumber those actually travelling and living in caravans. Secondly, there are the Irish and Scottish travellers or Tinkers, many of whom have been regularly journeying in England and Wales for generations, even centuries. They are probably well under 15% of the travelling population. Although they may easily be distinguished by accent and different background and although Romany heritage and ancestry have left traces in their histories, the dominant influence derives from an indigenous Celtic nomadic tradition. Shelta (or Gammon), spoken by the Irish, and Scottish 'Tinkers' cant' are closely related and appear to have a common origin. The Scottish travellers are much rarer than the Irish—3 or 4% of the total travelling population of England and Wales.

A very few visiting European Gypsies are recorded in various places— for instance, for a few months on the Redbridge site at Hainault in 1971. Dr D. Kenrick, then Secretary of the Gypsy Council, sent the project reports of semi-settled, housed Kalderesh communities in London and Birmingham, and of Lovari in Bristol. The group on the Redbridge site appeared to be Lovari from Germany and Holland, but their actual base was Yugoslavia. They are obviously internationally nomadic, and they deal mainly in carpets and gold ornaments.

There may be a very few travelling families caravanning who have neither Gypsy nor Tinker connexions; one, an engineer, has recently been prosecuted for being a 'Gypsy'. But other than this, even though they were sought after, none was seen during the course of the project. However, three or four caravan-dwelling families who were definitely gauje were met—'problem families' who had been placed on a permanent site as a temporary measure by a local authority. One was at the Bromsgrove RDC site, others were in Hertfordshire and Surrey, and among these there were probably some of traveller stock. There were several individuals living beside traveller families, nearly always single males and mostly dossers. In unauthorized encampments no family was seen which was genealogically isolated from other families on the site, from housed Gypsies or Tinkers in the neighbourhood, or from accepted travellers on nearby sites or camps. On one site owned privately by a Gypsy, one caravan was occupied by an ex-canal lengthman (the site bordered on a canal and a boatyard), and another was the holiday home of a retired academic and his wife. This man was allowed to stay on the site because 'he paid his rent' and was a personal friend. Another family on the site was denigrated as being non-Gypsy, but other travellers on a nearby site confirmed a blood relationship to them, and even said that the site owner was related.

Contrary to the majority views of teachers and local authority officers, the existence of an even moderately significant proportion of non-Gypsy, non-Tinker groups of itinerant scrap dealers who are drop-outs from settled society was not in any way substantiated by the work of the project. Rather, it was found that the belief in the existence of numbers of such vagrants is based on a combination of prejudice, lack of close observation and a tendency to see the whole question of identity in the light of ethnic purity. The government report, which accepted the existence of mumpers (non-Gypsies) and anyway treated all travellers, irrespective of background, as a social problem, rather than as a society with a distinct heritage and value system quite different from that of the settled community, also had its share of influence on popular opinion. Sometimes this view was held in spite of the incontestably Gypsy names of families on the site and the fact that all the families on the site 'appeared' to be or were actually known to be interrelated.

The family and kinship groupings were discovered to be even more intricate than was first expected. Schools were visited in many parts of England and Wales and in Perthshire. Travellers were met in Hull and surrounding areas of the East Riding, in Manchester and Wigan, in Nottinghamshire, throughout the West Midlands, at Brynmawr in Monmouthshire, in Somerset and Devon, Bedfordshire, in London and generally throughout the Home Counties deep into Kent. Although the primary purpose of these visits was to see the school, the teachers and their traveller pupils, there was sufficient time to undertake what proved to be a fascinating study in kinship among a nomadic people. A batch of photographs was accumulated, mainly of children in or passing through the West Midlands, note was made of family names and a minimum of data about first names of parents and children sufficient to establish kinship relations if they existed. This was incidental to the work of the project, and it is not possible to record it all because of lack of time and of skill. Besides, to establish precise relationships necessitates more trust than can be gained on a one-day casual visit. However, it became absolutely clear that the travellers of England and Wales consist of a complex network of interrelated families with extremely far-reaching kinship patterns which link together all the Gypsies. Similar patterns exist among most of the Irish and Scottish, and the three major groups are also interlocked to a minor extent. All three groups have extensive contact with house-dwelling Gypsy or Tinker families, who are subject to the same kinship structure. Most of the families admitted that both now and in the past there had been marriage into and from the host gauje community; that indeed a branch of the family were no longer travellers and some had even been lost from the Gypsy or Tinker community altogether.

Thus the Boswells, Lees, Prices, Smiths, Hernes, Woods, Penfolds, Hugheses, Chapmans, Joneses, Gaskins, Lovells, Taylors, Brazills and others spread throughout England and Wales and are to a lesser degree related to all the other families, including the Scottish and Irish. The picture is similar to that of a small geographically isolated settled community in which intermarriage and first- and second-cousin pairings are common. The basic difference is that this is a nomadic people and so kinship is spread nationwide. Several families mentioned European and Canadian or Australian relatives, some had American cousins—so there is an international structure too.

It is not surprising to find that these same names recur throughout literature on British Gypsies—from the writings of Hoyland to those of Silvester Gordon Boswell. The Gypsy community, for all its admixture of gauje blood, has retained its traditions and its family-based life style. It is no longer possible to identify Gypsies physically by dark complexion, black hair and dark eyes or by other facial features (though the East Riding Smiths come close to a traditional image and many families have genetic throwbacks who are extremely swarthy). The Kent Smiths tend to be blond, as do many of the Prices, but the latter frequently hide this by make-up and hair dyeing. Families involved in fortune telling and traditional craft-work may also exaggerate their Romany looks for good reason. Mannerism and posture (the latter especially amongst the older women) may be highly distinctive, and the heritage of the Gypsy community may be used as an additional indicator of origin and membership.

Britain's travellers have not changed dramatically over the last few generations. They have adopted some of the characteristics of the settled population such as styles in dress, and the television habit, and (most important of all) in only the last twenty years they have become motorized and have changed to trailer caravans from the old wagons and tents. It is true that travellers have become more overtly urban—and in the post-war period there has been a gradual decline in seasonal rural occupations in farm labouring and fruit picking—but this is the same movement that has affected the settled population. They appear to have camped closer to settled urban society—and in direct confrontation with it—only because there has been an enormous incursion of new houses into the fringe of rural land surrounding all the major cities of the country. This used to be the 'common' land, which was their traditional haunt. The invasion of inner-city derelict land must be seen in this context: it is available as never before because of the decline of the inner city and rebuilding programmes elsewhere.

The urbanization of Gypsies and other changes in their life style may have been exaggerated by some commentators. Scrap-metal dealing springs naturally from the crafts of the tinker and the coppersmith. The widespread belief that the modern motorized caravan-dwelling traveller is not the direct descendant of the romanticized 'true' Gypsy of the rural camp—the wisp of woodsmoke, the horse and wagons, and the clothes pegs and fortune telling of the past—is a myth. It is one perpetrated by two false premises: firstly, that the Gypsy is by nature rural; and secondly, that in the past he lived in horse-drawn wagons (*vardos*). The wagon, as opposed to the cart (which was not the actual living accommodation of the family but the vehicle which carried their tents and so on), seems to have developed only in the mid-nineteenth century. It was, therefore, a significant form of dwelling for less than a century of the Gypsy's five hundred years in this country. Likewise, there is accumulative evidence, collected partly by the Centre for Environmental Studies, that the greatest agricultural employment of Gypsies started towards the end of the last century after the major initial phase of the Industrial Revolution had deprived the farmer of seasonal harvesters—the Gypsy thus filling the gap left by rural depopulation. His current decline as a harvester has been caused by a new phase in mechanization (especially in the hop-growing and reaping processes and in potato lifting) and by the employment of cheap casual labour of students by the large canning companies which own so many of the fruit farms.

Broadly speaking, then, the origins and history of British travellers may be simplified into the following picture. It is now widely accepted that native nomadic craftsmen and entertainers existed throughout the British Isles long before the arrival of the first Romany tribes, probably already in the process of breaking down into extended family groups, in the late fifteenth and early sixteenth centuries. These indigenous nomads were more numerous in Ireland and Scotland than in England and Wales. On arrival, the Romanies were probably either absorbed into these existing groups in Ireland and Scotland, or, seeing that the areas of their traditional trades and crafts were already adequately catered for, they turned to England and Wales where they tended to absorb the less numerous indigenous nomadic groups. There has also been a continuing flow of settled people into the nomadic community by marriage and a corresponding loss of nomads to the settled community. In spite of all these movements, the over-all picture has probably been essentially stable for centuries: with a gradual dilution of the original Romany stock and yet a dynamic kinship system regulating the structure and patterns of life. The intermittent immigration of more traditional European Romany families, which continues to this day, has tended to invigorate British Gypsies' Euro-Romany heritage and genetic structure.

The origin of the Irish and Scottish Tinkers is more obscure because so little is known about this indigenous Celtic nomad group, which would seem to pre-date the Romany influx. Neither the Irish *Report of the Commission on Itinerancy* nor *Scotland's Travelling People* is very precise on this issue, though the latter recognizes the strong possibility of such a group.[20] Scottish crofters dispersed as a result of Highland clearances, Irish peasants dispossessed during famines and journeying craftsmen and metal workers are generally thought to have fused with this ancient group. The added Romany ingredient makes the position even more clouded. Yet the great interlocking kinship patterns, the survival of secret languages and dialects, even of similar customs amongst Irish and Scottish Tinkers, and the historical interconnexions between Scotland and Ireland known to exist within host community groups supports the idea that the existence of the Tinkers pre-dates the arrival of the Romanies. How far back their real origins go is conjecture: Sampson's study of Shelta led him to propose a twelfth-century genesis in Ireland, and Spence indicates the beginnings of the Scottish Tinker in the thirteenth century.[21]

In this respect both countries resemble Holland, where there are some 3600 traveller families, of whom 2% are classed as Gypsies, 8% as 'ordinary citizens' most of whom have opted for caravan dwelling as a solution to the housing shortage after the Second World War, and 90% as 'nomads'. The latter have roots going back several centuries.[22] The situation in England and Wales more closely resembles that in most other European countries where the percentage of those with obvious Romany heritage tends to be much higher. Some countries, like Sweden, report that three groups can be detected: indigenous Tinker stock, mixed and diluted Gypsy stock, and recent immigrant Romanies from Central Europe and Russia (indeed, Sweden itself operates a Gypsy quota system in its immigration regulations).

The origin of the Romanies is generally thought to be found in an extended exodus of several tribes (possibly two major groups) from northern India over an extended period before and after the turn of the tenth century A.D. There is much debate about the cause of the exodus and whether these tribes were nomadic before their exodus, but this will probably never be solved.[23] However, the exodus was followed by dispersal in most directions but mainly westwards. Circuitous routes were apparently taken, sections of the tribes settling en route in the Near East, in Greece and Turkey and throughout Central and Western Europe. The westward journey continues to this day with migration across the Atlantic to North America. During the last century in Britain, many Romanies were transported to Australia. In the twentieth century the major exodus has been from Western Europe generally during the Nazi era and from Central Europe into Western Europe or America since then.[24] There may even be some truth in the folklore of many Gypsies of an Egyptian or Berber phase of temporary settlement after the Indian exodus and before a second-phase drift to Europe.

It is hardly surprising that during the long trek westwards, supposedly lasting five centuries, many families married outside the tribes in various countries they passed through and there were linguistic accretions to the Romany language from many tongues, including Greek, Turkish, Hungarian, Rumanian, and others. It is certain that the language (or collection of individual tribal languages) was already much changed by the time the first families reached Britain.

What is perhaps even more interesting is that there is growing evidence from many European countries based on genetic studies which seems to confirm a distinctiveness from indigenous society and the theory of a northern Indian origin. Incomplete work undertaken by Sunderland and Clarke[25] at Durham University with only a small number of families considered to have a fairly strong Romany heritage suggests to some extent that the situation here is similar. The over-all picture indicated so far by genetic, anthropological, and philological studies is of two main ethnic groups, resulting perhaps from two distinct origins or a major process of 'genetic drift'. Briefly, studies in Hungary, Romania, Yugoslavia, Uzbekistan and France seem to confirm the northern India hypothesis, but others in Sweden and Slovenia produced partial evidence which pointed to the Indian origin, but with a significant variance from the former countries, which Sunderland and Clarke also discovered in their British studies. The precise nature of this variation has yet to be analysed, but it may support the theory of a temporary settlement by some of the tribes in North Africa, possibly with the Berber community, although this is at present sheer conjecture.[26]

Classification of travellers by extent of nomadism and settlement

Although the preceding consideration of the definitions and origins of the travellers of England and Wales is largely an academic question, it was thought necessary because there is such widespread confusion within the teaching profession, among local authorities and the public about the Gypsies and Tinkers that no clear policy decisions can be made or curriculum development initiated unless the nature and origin of travellers is understood. The explanations offered in this report lead to the conclusion that the travellers, though genetically very mixed, are a separate community, with value systems, membership patterns, and heritages different from those of the host population. They are not drop-outs from society now seeking assimilation but a distinctive and unique minority group. They are extremely secretive about their life and heritage, often very misleading on the question of the 'true Gypsy', and tend to hide their culture because they feel themselves to be a stigmatized group. They fear that they would make themselves vulnerable to compulsory assimilation if they revealed too much and became too friendly with the host community. They live their life by choice and feel that they are part of a very old nomadic tradition—either Romany or Celtic. Those who wish to be assimilated will probably succeed, as those of former generations have. The rest want merely to improve their present conditions, but to continue that traditional style. By no means all are committed to local authority sites, and there is much jealousy between the sections of the travelling community over the selection of tenants. The theory that they are at present facing acute economic crisis must be challenged. Though placing of permanent sites could cause such a crisis, nearly all travellers make an adequate living and do not suffer privations due to poverty, though this is not necessarily true of the position in Scotland and Ireland.

Any categorizations of travellers for the purposes of social policy or educational provision based upon distinctions of race or heritage are highly suspect. Nor are they helpful from a purely practical viewpoint, because the main groups have common life styles and social needs. The most important factor to be taken into account in policy making is the extent of their nomadism or settlement.

The best precedent to date for a categorization of travellers by extent of travelling is that of the report of the committee set up by the Department of Education of Eire to study provision of education for travellers, entitled *Educational Facilities for the Children of Itinerants*, published in 1970. The Committee recommended that there should be three main categories:

(a) families who occupy quasi-permanent sites and for whom houses are being provided, and families who were recently housed and are in the process of being settled;

(b) families, constituting the majority of itinerants, who move in a narrow circuit around the cities and towns and whose itinerancy is generally unvaried;

(c) families who move in a wider circuit embracing many counties and who break the regular route for particular occasions, e.g., Ballinasloe Fair.[27]

For the first category of families, the Department recommended normal schooling when numbers were small, though special schools and special classes might be thought a temporary expedient for children from very large settlements and for older children. The Department had established an experimental school in Dublin with a staff of four and a limit of sixty-six pupils, but does not in general favour the concept of separate small schools. Instead, it suggested that special classes attached to ordinary schools would be a more fruitful approach.

For the second category of children, the Department suggested the concept of a school within the circuit area covered by the travelling patterns to be designated as suitable for itinerant children—a centre to which they would regularly go. The Department admits that if the circuit is a large one, more than one school would have to be designated. Special transport grants might be available in certain circumstances, and local authorities were to be encouraged to set up 'halts' (rather than settlement camps) near to designated schools.

In the view of the Department, the third category of children present such intransigent problems that little can be done other than casual enrolment of the nomadic children in ordinary schools coupled with a programme of persuading families to 'limit their movements at least during the greater part of the school year'.[28] The whole educational programme is based on the clear objective of eventual full integration into the school system, but the Department admits that this may not be feasible until the itinerants have been assimilated into the host community and abandon nomadism.

It was not possible to make any assessment of the effects of the initial phase of the educational programme for travellers in Eire, because it is still in an early and partial phase of implementation. It is dubious whether the Irish solution is entirely relevant to England and Wales. This is partly because the Caravan Sites Act, Part 2, and relevant ministerial circulars never set assimilation as an aim as does the *Report of the Commission on Itinerancy:*

In so far as the itinerants are concerned absorption into the general community can be achieved only by a policy of inducing them to leave the road and to settle down. It is not considered that any worthwhile progress could be made by a policy of compulsory settlement, even if it were legally possible.[29]

A large proportion of travellers in Eire almost certainly face economic crises, unlike their counterparts in England and Wales. There is therefore no such humanitarian need to 'rescue' (a word adopted by the Commission) our travellers from economic distress.

Thus there is no similar pressure on educational administrators here to support such a programme. There are also other (perhaps ethical) considerations: the likelihood that travellers will continue travelling for many years to come, and the question whether a family wants assimilation and integration of its children into school. It was also felt that the threefold classification was simplistic when applied to England and Wales, for there appear to be four clear categories:

(a) *The settled:* these include housed Gypsies and Tinkers, and those travellers living a sedentary life on private all-traveller caravan sites or on mixed residential sites. Those families who remain permanently on the local authority sites set up under the Act are also included. There are other would-be static families who occupy unauthorized encampments but are subject to eviction. They present greater educational problems arising out of their alienated position and the lack of educational experience that most of their children exhibit. Although their ambition is to settle they are unable to do so. At present their 'recognition' by LEAs is hampered because it may be interpreted by councils as condonation of an illegal camp.

(b) *Short-distance travellers:* perhaps the largest single group of travellers in England and Wales, these tend to remain within a restricted, sometimes 'ancestral' area, moving not more than ten to twenty-five miles. It is debatable whether they are the type of family which would want to be permanently settled on a single site, but they would almost certainly tend to make frequent moves between sites in close proximity to one another if ever the choice arose. Designated centres or particular maintained schools, as suggested by the Eire Committee, may be relevant in their case, providing that considerable transport facilities were available.

(c) *Middle-distance travellers:* perhaps almost as large a group as the former, these move in a radius of anything up to fifty or one hundred miles. Sometimes a regular circuit is followed, but most are haphazard. They need to do this for economic reasons, because of their extended kinship patterns, and because nomadism is a strong tradition that they follow by choice. If they were to be catered for educationally under existing methods, they would have to attend a series of centres or schools offering a common teaching programme; it is doubtful whether that would be sufficient in itself, even if it were instituted.

(d) *Long-distance travellers:* among these must be considered the habitual nomad—the type of traveller who makes it a practice never to stay in the same place for more than a few days, those who travel the length and breadth of the country. The English and Welsh habitual nomads may even regularly visit Ireland and Scotland. Many of the Irish and Scottish travellers come into this category, but by no means all of them. Some are clearly recognized groups, like the large group of Irish Tinker furniture dealers who collect their ware from all over the British Isles (one of the main advantages of being nomadic is that they can explore remote areas) and who work a systematic and highly organized business culminating in the export of furniture from the port of Southampton to the United States. Others include those, especially Irish, who return to Ireland annually for short durations. The impression gleaned from discussions with Scottish travellers was that they normally stay in England for, say, two or three years at a time before returning to Scotland. Sometimes they will repeat their stay in England five or ten years later.

Virtually none of the long-distance travellers wants to settle, and few seem to be very happy with permanent local authority sites: they talk about 'transit' sites and pitches or of minimum-facility stopping places where they will be safe from eviction. However, they may become increasingly vociferous about their exclusion from sites and resent the fact that precedence is given to 'indigenous' Gypsy groups.

Long-distance travellers obviously present the most intransigent of educational problems if the aim is to integrate them within or even partially within the normal school system. Although they are among the strongest in resisting attempts to enforce school attendance, it must not be thought that they will not respond to educational opportunities of a relevant kind. Experience from the voluntary sector suggests that there may be a considerable demand for literacy especially from the adolescents. Television and correspondence courses may not be ruled out, but would need thorough preparation.

Some qualifications must be made about these arbitrary but—from an educational viewpoint—useful categories. There may be seasonal fluctuation affecting the patterns of settlement within these groups—including the housed Gypsies' absence from May to October. Families may fluctuate among the categories over periods of several years or generations, as when the children of an apparently settled, assimilated and housed family take to the road. Different branches of the same family may fit into each of these main divisions. A school serving a particular locality *may* have to cope with children from each category, and this will to some extent undermine any specific educational strategy.

There is every indication at present that these four categories may continue to present administrative problems for many decades to come, especially in view of the slow implementation of the Caravan Sites Act and the probability that demand for pitches will continue greatly to exceed supply.

It should also be remembered that to an extent the fairground child falls, at least seasonally, into either the third or fourth category and may benefit from any strategies developed for the Gypsies and Tinkers.

Demography and health

Three points can be made on the question of the total traveller population of England and Wales. Firstly, the 1965 census figure of 'at least' 15 000 individuals from 3400 families (4·5 persons per family) was an underestimate. It should be seen in the light of the two Scottish censuses of March and August 1969, which revealed that over 50% of the August families were not counted in March (the same month as the single English and Welsh census). Even accounting for the fact that more Scottish travellers resort to winter housing, it must surely be accepted that the English and Welsh figure may have been nearer 20 000 than 15 000, but it could easily have been 30 000—there is no way of knowing for certain. Secondly, it has been known for some time that each year there is an influx of families from Eire. There are indications that this may involve fifty to eighty families annually, though it is impossible to substantiate this estimate; nor is there any reliable indication of how long each family stays, nor how many families return each year. Most observers would agree, however, that there is a net influx which does swell the number of travellers in England and Wales. Thirdly, the 1967 report gave a projection of the traveller population (based on fertility and mortality rates) which suggested that the population would increase from 15 000 to 28 000 between 1965 and 1985 providing that there was no substantial movement into houses. So far, there is no evidence that the number of families moving into houses is any different than it has been in the past—for example, there has always been a two-way movement in and out of houses.

In these circumstances, what can be concluded? Firstly, that at the present time we just do not know the total population of travellers but that there are many reasons for thinking it to be substantially higher than 15 000 and likely to continue to grow in numbers. Secondly, that both on a national and local level the targets being set for site provision are well below what will be required; thirdly, that this has a significant implication for schools and educationists because it means that unauthorized camping will continue for many years, and even where there is a site there are likely to be large numbers of surplus families on the road with no stable base from which schooling can be controlled.

There are no data whatsoever on the size of the housed Gypsy and Tinker population. All figures given so far are for caravan dwellers. It is possible that it is a substantial one, larger even than the traveller population on the roadside and on camp sites. As far as schools are concerned this is an important consideration for, educationally, children from these homes present the same problems, though usually less severe.

If it is impossible to assess the true population figures for travellers in England and Wales, at least one can use the figures that do exist in the 1967 report as a sample from which to draw conclusions about family size, proportion of children, longevity and so on. Traveller families are on average much larger than those of the host community—4·5 persons as compared to 3·0 for the rest of society. The proportion of children is extremely high, which means that teachers will be dealing with a group with a larger sibling unit than among others. Longevity is correspondingly poor. This is best illustrated by the table below extracted from the 1967 report.

Table 2 Comparative longevity of Gypsies

Age group	Gypsies	Total population England and Wales
0–4	16·8	8·6
5–15	24·6	15·8
16–34	30·6	25·3
35–44	11·6	13·3
45–64	13·0	24·8
65+	3·4	12·2
	100·0	100·0

Source: *Gypsies and Other Travellers*, p. 9.
(The over-all male/female distribution was 50·9/49·1% for Gypsies, and 48·7/51·3% for the total population.)

The raising of the school-leaving age means that the proportion of school-age travellers is now well above 25%. A close look at ten local authority returns in 1965 reveals an almost complete gap in the five to fifteen age group (see Table 3). This means that the traveller age structure may be even more 'radically different' than was described on page 9 of the 1967 report:

The traveller age structure was also radically different. The high birth rate among travellers is reflected in the proportion of children—twice the national proportion for the 0–4s, and half as many again for the 5–15s. In all, over 40% were less than sixteen years old. On the other hand, the proportion over 65 was less than one-third of the figure for the country as a whole.

The age distribution of the travelling people bears a marked resemblance to the age structure of the total population of the country in 1841, before the advent of widespread industrialization. It is also very similar to that of the Irish tinkers and the travellers of Finland, Sweden and Yugoslavia.

Table 3 Age group distribution of travellers in ten local authorities

Local authority	No. of persons per age-group				No. of families
	0–4	5–15	16+	Total	
Darlington, County Borough	10	2	24	36	9
Yorkshire, East Riding	1	3	24	32 (sic)	6
Bradford, County Borough	10	6	25	45 (sic)	8
Oldham, County Borough	14	nil	19	35	8
Wigan, County Borough	4	nil	12	16	2
Lincoln, Parts of Holland	3	2	22	27	5
Derby, County Borough	5	2	10	17	4
Birmingham, County Borough	nil	nil	17	17	6
Walsall, County Borough	17	2	49	68	23
Soke of Peterborough	3	2	18	23	7
Select local authority totals	67	19	220	314	78
Overall national traveller totals	2302	2384	7376	13 762	3043

Source: *Gypsies and Other Travellers*, pp. 79–80.

Abnormally high infant mortality rates due to poor health and proneness to accidents probably make such a distribution even more remarkable. Though traveller children appear robust, the incidence of motor vehicle and other accidents on muddy sites, combined with the dangerous environment generally, results in a host of minor injuries, a remarkable quantity of scar-tissue from unstitched cuts and burns, and numerous untreated and infected sores that may linger on for months. Many suffer from endemic winter colds and catarrhal infections. The travellers' life is not a soft one, and most parents interviewed took a fatalistic view of accidents.

One child was observed, one icy afternoon, by the project's Consultative Committee, running barefoot over a piece of ground covered with jagged pieces of metal, and it was not easy to distinguish between the broken glass and the cracked ice. The child denied being cold. Later, her mother said: 'If little Rita isn't tough enough to be running about like that, she'd not be alive today. Travellers has to be hardy.' Rita, incidently, received severe burns from an accident some months later.

Life expectancy of travellers must be far below the norms of the settled community—probably close to that of the mid-nineteenth century. One of the major benefits of authorized sites should be ease of access to the National Health Service, and it is to be hoped that this will lead to the reduction of high infant mortality and to increased longevity. There can be weekly site clinics, and if the children go to school they will receive some medical screening. Most travellers have not been immunized against the common illnesses, which in some cases may make school attendance a dangerous proposition, for the child may contract a disease he would otherwise avoid. Dental treatment is another worrying problem. Partly because of a cultural reluctance to go to doctors and dentists, most travellers seek medical treatment only in absolute emergencies—childbirth, chronic illness and bad accidents. They may sometimes be forced to resort to traditional 'Gypsy remedies' because nomadism prevents a traveller being accepted on a doctor's panel; and, sad to report, some doctors are reluctant to make home visits to families on rough camping land.

Though no medical investigation in depth has yet been made into the general health of travellers and the incidence of genetic disorders, a strong and rather disturbing impression was gained during the project about such physical problems as eyesight (long-sightedness and cross-eyedness especially), psoriasis, and other minor ailments which may sometimes be hereditary. Very few travellers indeed were observed to be wearing glasses, although in their occupations there is little need for them. With children in school, however, this has an obvious bearing upon learning potential; and a cultural aversion to glasses is not always easy to overcome. It is not just a question of harsh surroundings, the rigours of the travelling life, and the lack of medical supervision: travellers treat hospitals and doctors with suspicion: 'The discrepancy that exists between the extent of hospitalization and the extent of illness is further exaggerated by the reluctance of travellers to enter hospitals unless absolutely necessary' (*Scotland's Travelling People*, page 66).

There may be other factors involved in traveller health: an over-reliance on 'quick-fries' and nutritional deficiency among the poorer groups. Although no objective studies have been conducted, it was not the impression of the project that the following statement on page 24 of *Gypsies and Other Travellers* tallied with current opinion: 'However, most observers frequently remark on the good health of traveller children. . .' They are robust and resilient, with a remarkably high tolerance to pain—a trait valued within the community—but by no means all are healthy. Those who are healthy are the ones most likely to have already come into contact with teachers, schools and permanent sites.

The corollary to the health of travellers is the problem of whether they themselves constitute a public health hazard to the sedentary society. This was beyond the scope and the capacity of the project's inquiry. In general, travellers have to adopt standards of hygiene higher than those within the host community—because of the absence of the means of refuse disposal, of running water, sanitation, refrigeration and so on. Cases of substantiated health hazards reported by Public Health Inspectors are rare,[30] but more commonly inspectors report industrial pollution affecting Gypsy camp sites or pre-existing hazards such as rats or stagnant water.

The incidence of educational subnormality is another area for inquiry. Certainly, it is not justified to see low IQs and poor results in attainment tests as an indication of innate inferiority among Gypsy children, for results are invalidated by cultural background and lack of regular schooling. Some teachers are certainly concerned that severe abnormality might be proportionately more common in travellers than in the settled community. Evidence from extensive studies conducted by Drs K. Sieteram among Dutch traveller children revealed the predictably low mean scores, but the incidence of acute educational subnormality was found to be no different from that in the total population of Holland.[31] Whereas similar studies here might reveal the same evidence, this might not be entirely valid if infant mortality is as high as is suspected.

Regional and other differences

Many other factors should be taken into account because they have a direct bearing upon possible educational policy and provision with respect to traveller children. These include regional, occupational and social differences that may exist, and differences in the degree of acceptance of travellers by the host society.

In general, travellers in the South East, and particularly around London and the Home Counties, have had greater contact with schools, officials and other members of the gauje community. They seem more articulate, sophisticated and better informed than the more isolated travellers elsewhere. Many are quite used to academic researchers and have become adept at providing the anticipated answers; some will even admit to creating pseudo-Romany words or mythological customs to satisfy the folklorist market. They are also likely to have come into contact with pressure groups and individuals from the host society working for their rights and welfare: Norman Dodds in the fifties,[32] members of the Gypsy Council from the late sixties, the National Gypsy Education Council, the Advisory Committee on the Education of Romanies and other Travellers, and the Romany Guild in the early seventies, and other localized political or welfare organizations.

Urban travellers in the South East and in the large conurbations of the Midlands and the North West tend also be to more affluent, their trailer-caravans more luxurious, and their life style more modern than elsewhere. In parts of the West Country, in North Wales, and in the North East (particularly in the East Riding around Hull) more old-fashioned horse-drawn wagons may still be found than elsewhere, and rural life is in general more primitive. Travellers in these latter areas, as in most rural areas, tend to be found in small, isolated groups: in three or four wagons or trailers rather than the large encampments of the Midlands and Home Counties. They are mainly left alone, and there seems little need for the defensive 'safety in numbers' policy adopted by their urban counterparts.

Information about regional differences in traveller occupations is less reliable. The general impression gained during research for the project was that travellers' occupations depended on whether they lived in rural or urban areas, their involvement in agricultural and horticultural work obviously being proportionately higher in the former, and scrap and general dealing, and tarmac laying being staple urban occupations. However, there is considerable diversification; car breaking amongst rural travellers and seasonal fruit picking by urban groups, expecially in the important picking areas of Herefordshire, Worcester and Evesham, the Wisbech area of Cambridgeshire, and Kent. Potato lifting was once important to the Scottish travellers, but now, because of mechanization and the importation of non-traveller Irish gangs, contributes to their catastrophic economic decline, although the occupation is still prevalent in many areas, especially East Anglia.

Hawking and fortune telling by women is often widespread both in towns and in the country. The traditional side lines—peg making and carving of wooden flowers—which are gradually dying crafts, were seen on various occasions throughout the land. But otherwise, travellers seemed to be involved in very similar occupations—scrap dealing being the largest single source of income.

The most obvious regional difference is in the density of the traveller population, which in general follows distribution levels for that of the settled population; however, most travellers are found on the fringes of industrial areas, where large concentrations of motor vehicles and scrapyards exist. The implementation of the Caravan Sites Act may change this distribution pattern of travellers, and will, to some extent, control the size of encampments and determine which schools will be affected.

The degree to which there may be regional differences in the host community's attitude to travellers is not easy to assess, but there are some general indicators. Much depends upon the history of travellers in the area and the extent to which the local community is stable. Where travellers have had a long history and where their presence in schools may still be remembered by parents, there is far less likelihood of popular antagonism towards them. Where the travellers appear to be intruders—for example, as recent arrivals, or on a new housing estate that constitutes some of the overspill from a large city—they are considered less acceptable socially. In general, stable rural communities have developed a tolerance towards their travellers which is not evidenced elsewhere. Irish travellers are far and away the most likely group to be subject to host community protest and prejudice—not merely because they are frequently the most untidy travellers but because they are Irish.

Conditions of life

This section deals with the conditions and environment of traveller life—the living conditions inside trailers, the immediate environment outside the trailer and on camp sites.

LIVING CONDITIONS INSIDE TRAILERS

The great majority of today's travellers now live in trailer-caravans, which are towed either by scrap lorries or medium-sized vans. It is interesting to remember that the use of trailer-caravans is relatively recent: many families seem to have exchanged their old horse-drawn wagons for them in the late 1950s. Before then, travellers used *vardos* (horse-drawn wagons) and, because of their more confined capacity, resorted also to tents, which were most often used as day-rooms. It would be wrong to think that Gypsies and other travellers have used wagons for living and sleeping in for more than a few generations. In the early nineteenth century most families had tents and flat carts and periodically resorted to houses, especially during the winter.

Probably fewer than 5% of today's travellers retain horse-drawn accommodation. Several of them also possess lorries which are used for scrap. Those families who have resisted modern trends by staying in wagons or in tents, like many of Scotland's indigenous travellers, tend to live a more primitive or traditional life, and because facilities for washing are less adequate than in trailer-caravans, the children may need extra sensitive help in hygiene and dress. Here, however, the concentration is upon life in trailer-caravans because the majority of children live in them.

Trailer-caravans vary enormously in size, luxury and cleanliness, relating obviously to the travellers' income, mode of existence and cultural aspirations. The majority are 22 feet long or slightly shorter (the legal limit for normal towing). They can easily be distinguished from holiday-makers' caravans by the solid fuel fires and the familiar chimneys of the Gypsy trailers. Problem families and those in dire economic straits obviously tend to have small, old, poorly equipped conventional models, but many families buy 'Gypsy caravans' (especially designed and fitted models from well-known suppliers), or secondhand models from other travellers. Many families exchange their trailers frequently, and this is often a good gauge of their current economic circumstances.

Several families possess 'flash' or luxurious trailer-caravans which cost several thousand pounds. Many of these have flower-design cut-glass windows, the exteriors are embellished with quantities of stainless steel and are kept immaculately clean. Richly coloured carpets, cushions, upholstery and curtains, glistening formica and cut-glass mirrors, more stainless steel in the cooking utensils, bowls and kettles, all add to the reflective brightness and kaleidoscope of colour. Most families have collections of ornate and tradition-

ally patterned china, cut-glass bowls, gold, silver and other antiques. These
are investments and become family heirlooms in the absence of job security
and bank accounts. Cooking is done mainly on bottled gas cookers, but a
few families still continue to cook outdoors over an open fire. Trailers are
also lighted by bottled gas, though many trailers are fitted out for electricity
in anticipation of well-supplied permanent caravan sites.

It is interesting to note that this almost oriental quality of interior decor
can be seen in trailers belonging to prosperous Irish and Scottish Tinkers,
probably because of the mingling of Romany ancestry and the cross-fertili-
zation of traditions among the different nomadic groups. It is also universal
among Europe's Gypsy and nomad populations, as among the Dutch non-
Gypsy travellers. Whereas this love of colourful ornament and possession of
valuable objets d'art may be common among all communities which have
been nomadic and used to living in confined quarters (such as the bargees and
the fairground people), there are distinct cultural factors involved. An example
is the Gypsy's traditional dislike of plain white clothing or bedding because
white is considered the colour of death. Economic expedience may reinforce
cultural tradition.

The insides of trailers are thus warm in a physical as well as an emotional
sense. By the standards of house dwellers they might be considered as overcrowded, but it is important to grasp that caravan dwelling is as natural an
extension of traveller life as the tent is to the American Indian or Bedouin,
the igloo is to the Eskimo, and the barge cabin to the canal boaters. The
confined space reinforces the sustaining family unity and may be cause for
concern only when the life style of the family is dramatically changed—for
instance, on compact permanent sites where children have little room for
play, the men are forbidden to sort scrap in the area around the trailer, and
open fires, the traditional family meeting place, are not permitted. This
problem has led some local authorities, such as Hertfordshire, to provide
additional facilities such as day rooms for each pitch on their caravan sites.
It is also quite normal, and often considered essential to its sexual mores,
for a family to acquire a second trailer when children reach puberty and
menarche, so that separate arrangements can be made for sleeping. Several
families whose children have grown up and married retain a second trailer
for daytime living and transform their first into a showpiece reserved only
for entertaining important visitors and for sleeping accommodation. A permanent caravan site for fifteen caravans may therefore contain only eight or
ten families, and even here a close analysis might reveal that extended family
networks exist and that there may be four generations of the same family
inhabiting four or five trailers, further reducing the actual number of families
on the site. In such situations there is great flexibility, and the extended
group may break into distinct nuclear units for travelling purposes.

In a perceptive discussion of European stereotyping of Gypsies, Dr

Donald Kenrick and Grattan Puxon suggest that the travellers' own customs of hygiene are overlooked by their critics. They also explain why travellers' trailers never have indoor lavatories:

Let it be said too that Gypsies often express contempt for the low standards they see kept by householders. Remember that in western Europe at least Gypsies engaged in scavenging occupations come into daily contact with the littered backyards and grubby kitchens of the same Gaje who condemn them for uncleanliness. Gypsies have a healthy abhorrence of city slums, lodging houses and cheap snack bars.

They regard the indoor lavatory with suspicion as a source of infection, and its use by both men and women as most undesirable if not immoral. They will not use the chemical closets provided in their modern caravans for these reasons. The instinctive rejection of communal lavatories provided in blocks on caravan sites has distressed ignorant officials. It is interpreted as more evidence of Gypsy dirtiness. In fact it is their insistence on ritual cleanliness which leads to the misuse of the communal arrangements and sometimes to their deliberate destruction. . . . In brief, hedges are considered far cleaner than block toilets.[33]

There is always this strange paradox in the traveller attitude to tidiness and hygiene as opposed to his external messiness and uncleanliness. It can often be seen in school.

The child in school has to adapt himself to the use of communal toilets. If he has not experienced running tap-water before, this may be an advantage, for the fascination with endless supplies of water mollifies natural aversions to the proximity of toilets to places for washing.

THE IMMEDIATE VICINITY OF THE TRAILER

This is a work area, the children's 'backyard' playground, a storage place for the family's impedimenta and the tools and raw materials of its trade, as well as the area where the family keeps its animals, parks its motor vehicles (at least when this is permitted by authorities) and stakes its claim to possession.

Although Thomas Berger's *Little Big Man* is a work of fiction and one does not know whether an authentic picture of Cheyenne life in former days has been drawn, there are many passages which ring true to Gypsy attitudes today. When Jack Crabb wakes up after his first night with the Indians, he follows the boys to tether the horses on new pasture, participates in some horseplay in a creek, and then, having been given a breechclout and moccasins, distributes his white man's clothing:

Nobody had use for the boots, which were just laid there on the ground and were left behind in the same position when the camp moved away. If an Indian isn't interested in an item he does not so much as see it, will stumble over it repeatedly without ever considering he might kick it aside.[34]

There are many uncanny resemblances between present-day traveller attitudes to the immediate environment of their camp and those described as typical of the Cheyenne Indians.

The most common accusations against travellers concern the neighbourhood of their trailers. In most cases it is not very tidy or safe, though on well-established sites with permanent tenants it may be converted into a smart and ornamental garden with flower beds, gnomes and model wagons, fencing and gates. Generally, however, the unseemly mess and the burning of rubber and plastic on open fires give cause for complaints by local residents. There may be various lean-to and dilapidated structures—hutches, kennels, bird-cages, huts or wind-breaks for sitting outdoors. In stark contrast to the normally neat interiors of trailers, this area is directly symptomatic of the travellers' attitude to the environment, which sets little store by aesthetics or preservation. Several trailers owned by the same extended family group may share the site, and their arrangement may follow kinship or hierarchical patterns. Here, however, the child spends most of his waking hours; indeed, he may be severely restricted in vulnerable encampments, perhaps near the roadside. But it is an interesting and stimulating environment: there may be water churns, prams, scrap, rags, tools, toys and, most important of all, animals.

Travellers have traditionally kept many animals, and this may be considered as a cultural attribute of great importance. Horses were retained by several families even on permanent sites though they were tethered some distance from the site. Some families still breed and deal in horses, but most keep them out of nostalgia and for the children. Travellers have distinct preferences for certain breeds of dogs, especially lurchers (the traditional Romany hound), terriers, and Alsatians, all of which may be found in great numbers. One family has more than twenty dogs as well as the same number of horses, and keeps ferrets, rabbits, bantams, chickens and turkeys. Others kept donkeys, goats, parrots, mynah birds, finches, canaries, ducks, geese and foxes, but rarely were travellers seen to possess cats. The most important animal to most families is the dog, for it gives security against rats and unwelcome strangers. Some families are involved in coursing and, it is sometimes intimated, cock fighting.

In the immediate environment of the trailer therefore, there is much that the children can explore and play with, though little that is useful to them in terms of school skills. They are involved in work from a very young age—helping to sort scrap and rags, fetching water in churns balanced on prams, chopping firewood, minding babies and toddlers, and helping with vehicle maintenance.

A different disciplinary regime applies to the area outside the trailer as opposed to the very strict control evident within the trailer itself. The children often engage in destructive play, imitating their father's breaking of scrap, and little effort may be made to train them to be tidy outside. In the vicinity of the trailer harsh physical punishment is meted out by older children in charge of younger siblings, and the boys are not discouraged from solving their problems by fighting. Play, in general, is imitative of family life and occupations rather than projective or fantasy seeking.

In such rough and dirty surroundings it is extremely hard to keep the children clean, though it is wrong to judge the traveller's sense of hygiene by his outward appearance: traveller jobs are dirty, and they are undertaken at home. On unofficial encampments, parents have to cope with the absence of washing facilities and running water, as well as the condition of the land itself, which may become a great sea of mud, puddles, vehicle tracks and debris. Living in such conditions demands considerable hardiness and powers of endurance. The children seem as oblivious to the damp and cold as they are to the large quantities of broken glass and rusty, jagged scrap-metal objects which are at the root of their accident-proneness. Highly combustible materials are frequently thrown on to open fires, and in general the children have to discover the danger of fire for themselves. Trailers are narrow, and the solid-fuel stoves are not normally guarded: there is little space for such precautions. (The 1967 report, *Gypsies and Other Travellers*, does, in fact, document this lack of facilities, pages 20–4.)

As a training area for future traveller life, the immediate environment of the trailer is, of course, eminently suitable, and the children grow up, if they survive, strong and resilient to pain and hardship. Teachers, however, may have to compensate for the many facilities and activities which most children from houses and literate homes have had since infancy.

CAMP SITES

Camp sites fall into four main categories: official local authority sites, normally for fifteen to twenty trailers; private sites or yards, usually smaller; mixed residential sites with travellers and gaujes, sometimes very large; and unauthorized encampments, which vary greatly in size from isolated groups of two to four trailers, to one-hundred-trailer encampments along roadsides, on waste ground or commons.

Official local authority sites
Much has already been said about local authority sites (see pages 39–41). Though it has been pointed out that there is a uniformity in size and design, there has been a wide range in actual standards—from sites with individual family washrooms, hot and cold water, shower baths, day rooms, community buildings containing wardens' offices and recreational facilities which can also be adapted for educational use, play areas provided with sand-pits and climbing equipment, grazing land and all main services except gas, to sites built on old tips, with poor sewerage and drainage, no mains-supply of electricity (even to toilet blocks at night), minimal water supply,

perhaps only one outside tap, no sinks or basins, communal (sometimes Elsan) toilets, absence of play areas and community rooms. Most sites have individual caravan pitches, tarmac or concrete, and some of them are long enough (40 feet or more) to accommodate two trailers. The area between these pitches is often left without topsoil for cultivation and may be covered with a loose hard-core of red shale or cinders; only the best are turfed or covered with a surface which is both dry and clean. Some sites seem to be little more than a car park, the whole area covered with tarmac and white lines drawn to indicate individual caravan locations. Many of the sites consist of a central access road leading to a car and lorry park cul-de-sac; the caravan pitches are lined up regularly on either side of this road. Occasionally, the placing of pitches is in a herringbone design, which at least prevents windows overlooking each other. A few sites are designed with much thought to traveller family structures; family trailers are grouped around the family wash-house and divided off from the other family clusters by hedges or neat fences, a design based on one of the model site plans in the Report of the Joint Working Party on the Caravan Sites Act agreed by the local authority associations and the Gypsy Council.[35] Very few of the sites have transit pitches for visiting relatives and short-stay families; regulations governing such pitches are difficult both to frame and to implement.

Rents may be as low as £2·00 for one caravan a week, but there are some where £3·50 is paid and, at the time of writing, no electricity, hot water, or sink or bath units have been provided. While the unit cost per pitch has probably risen dramatically since 1968 when the Act was passed, it must have been realized then that there would have to be considerable local authority subsidy.

The appointment of wardens varies: some authorities manage their sites without any resident warden or even part-time non-resident warden or caretaker but rely on officers from housing departments or social services. Some authorities have used travellers as wardens or caretakers, but although it is possible to find examples of this which appear to be working well, it is rarely successful and normally requires other officers to collect rents and act as arbitrators on such issues as tenant selection (traveller wardens may turn away families unrelated to their own). From an educational point of view a good resident warden, able to help families with literacy problems (reading and writing letters, completion of forms and so on), and to act as liaison with EWOs, social services, and local schools, has an obvious value. On some of the sites, pre-school units have been established, sometimes by voluntary organizations, in rare instances with local authority support or by attachment to a local nursery school, as an on-site over-spill classroom still under the aegis of the headteacher.

Probably the most important point to be made about sites is that they are a totally new experience to most travellers who have been used in the past to unauthorized camps. Sites may have an impact on occupations, socialization of the child, family feuding, reliance on the 'welfare', living within the law, coping with bureaucracy, social aspiration, and—perhaps most significant of all—schooling. Access to school is unquestionably one of the major changes that sites bring. Though withdrawal at puberty continues to be a major factor, the attendance of the younger children is made very much safer for the families. Also, for reasons already discussed, they are more accessible to EWOs.

One of the most uniform features of the sites has been their tenant capacity. Partly, one suspects, because of the limit in the obligatory provision of county boroughs, the vast majority of sites have been designed for between fifteen and twenty caravans. To some extent the Gypsy Council and the Joint Working Party are also responsible for this arbitrary size. It is obviously far too soon to assess the success of sites and of their long-term effect upon travellers.

Private sites or yards
It is certain that the number of these was drastically reduced after the Caravan Sites (Control and Development) Act of 1960, which resulted in many sites and yards owned by Gypsies being closed down and dramatically diminished the number of farmers who allowed caravans to stay on their land while the families provided casual labouring. Though no figures are available, it may well be that the visible increase in roadside and wasteland campers has been caused not so much by a population increase supplemented by an Irish influx, but from so many families who used once to be tucked away on private sites, farmland and yards having been forced on to the road.

In the course of the project, it was found that a significant number of children who were in school came from private sites still existing. Some of these were fully licensed and had planning permission; some were 'unauthorized', but were not interfered with because the local authorities had seen that to close the site down would merely increase their own problems with roadside and wasteland families.

These private sites vary greatly in size and general aspect. One remarkable example, now no longer in existence because the land has been compulsorily purchased by the relevant council and developed into a local authority site, consisted of a long row of individually owned yards alongside Harrow Manor Way in the Abbey Wood area in South East London. In all, some fifty families lived there. Each yard accommodated between four and eight caravans, some yards being occupied only by members of the same family, but some consisted of a landlord Gypsy and his caravan and several rent-paying tenants and their caravans. It appeared that these vacant lots had been purchased by the Gypsy families and fairground people some time after the beginning of the twentieth century. Thus this community had been in existence some sixty years and had evolved naturally. A large number of shacks and fences had been erected—not all of them very sightly. It was a relatively stable Gypsy community with many landlords who had inherited their yards from parents who had been original purchasers, but there had been considerable fluctuations in tenancies.

Another private site seen was a much more recent one. A Gypsy and his family had bought a third of an acre of derelict land—actually a traditional stopping place—in one of the semi-rural stretches of land beside the main A34 to the north of Birmingham and south of Cannock. Eventually, after summonses, fines, applications for planning permission and licence, the refusal of each and further summonses and fines, an appeal was made to the Department of the Environment which upheld the Gypsy's case. The site, which had been occupied by the family for nearly two years, became official and fully authorized. A small triangular piece of land, it has four concrete pads and a gravel access road. The family has been joined by three married children and their families. There has been much gardening and, during the summer months, it is a spectacular sight. The young children go to school, although one older girl, aged about fourteen, started but has since stopped attending. She had been almost totally illiterate before the age of twelve, but was given individual tuition before starting school by a volunteer teacher and his wife who visited the site over three months, roughly three evenings a week. During this time, the girl's reading age in the simple Schonell Graded Word Test rose from 5·2 to 11·0. For a short period she went to the junior school nearby, though she was at the time thirteen years old. Transfer to the secondary school unfortunately coincided with the death of her father, but she continued for a while. She is now learning the art of hawking from her mother and assisting in bread-winning. She feels that school has nothing to offer her, especially as she proudly announces: 'I learned to read *before* I went to school.'

Such a site has much to recommend it. The family is near to the local village community, and in fact nearly one hundred local people signed a petition to support the Gypsy's desire to be allowed to stay on his land. Yet the family retains its traditional life style, except that it is now static, though when the children marry they will probably want to travel. However, the older generation will stay at the base. Owning the land on which their trailer stands, the surround and the whole area of the camp site creates a totally different attitude to the environment, and the neatness, hygiene and extravagant decorativeness of the interior of the trailers is extended outside.

Mixed residential sites
An unknown proportion of travellers are tenants on residential caravan sites. One site in particular stood out from the visits made to schools during the project. Just to the south west of Wellington in Somerset, almost on the

Devon border, this site has been operating since the 1920s, initially as a fairground base for winter quarters. For many years it has been tenanted by both Gypsies and gaujes. The division between the two groups is clear-cut and unmistakable, and is also apparent in the children at the local primary school. The Gypsies are very superior about the gaujes, who are mostly the genuine drop-outs from society, with whom travellers are sometimes mistakenly confused. Their problems in school are quite different; the gauje children nearly all come from broken homes and have emotional and maladjustment problems. The Gypsy children, on the other hand, are backward in terms of educational attainment but do not exhibit psychological disturbance.

Although there are many similar examples of such sites, there are not as many as one might expect—mainly because most residential sites provide caravans, very often of the chalet type, and do not allow tenants to bring their own: and also, travellers are frequently excluded on grounds which can only be called prejudice, or because they tend to have large lorries and bring scrap on to the site. The site referred to above is owned by a family that has been in contact with travellers for over a generation and has a special relationship with them.

Unofficial and unauthorized encampments
The great majority of travellers camp on unauthorized land, and the conditions of their sites have already been described.

Encampments may vary in size from two or three isolated trailers to those of forty or sixty which can often be seen in conurbations, where a 'safety in numbers' policy is adopted. One hundred or more caravans are a rarity—only one camp of this size was observed during the project (that is, excluding the vast collections seen at Appleby Fair during the second week of June each year and on Epsom Downs during the races).

They may be set up on open wasteland, tip-banks, and derelict land on the outskirts of towns; or they may be much closer to the centre of towns, on land made available through demolition, even on car parks; some camps are situated on roadside verges, and in rural districts down country lanes. Very often there are subsidiary encampments in close proximity to official sites. The hazards of camping have already been pointed out but in addition there are eviction and what Gypsy supporters call 'harassment' by police and local authority officers. Earthworks and barriers—even 'anti-tinker ditches'—have been erected by local authorities. On the other hand, unauthorized encampments have many advantages for travellers: there is no rent, they come and go as they please. They can break cars, sort scrap, burn off unwanted materials from non-ferrous metals, and live true to their traditional life style—with open fires, free grazing and no limitation on the number of dogs, family grouping of trailers and so on. Many encampments consist of related family groups; sometimes this may be true even of forty-trailer sites. Sometimes they are closely related, though a large travelling family group such as the Irish antique dealers consisting of up to fifty caravans is very rare.

The size of camps varies greatly, and for the purposes of educational action is of crucial importance—for there are difficulties in taking a 'school on wheels', capable of accommodating eighteen children, to a forty-trailer encampment which may easily produce as many as 120 children clamouring to get in. In addition, getting such children to attend maintained schools is difficult if not impossible, because the camp may be closed by eviction at any time. The parents on these transient sites are least disposed to take advantage of short-duration schooling, and few schools could cope with a sudden and temporary influx of such numbers of children with their typical educational problems.

Two further related factors are important to understand about the Gypsy and his sites: firstly, that many of them have been camped on for generations (and this includes some of the local authority sites); secondly, almost always there are housed Gypsy communities nearby which will have kinship links to the families on the sites. If no such community exists near to a local authority site, it will soon be created by the families who want to settle or try to settle, not always very successfully. Gypsies have traditional haunts, and some local authorities have thought it wise to place their sites in these areas because local people are conditioned to the idea of having Gypsies as neighbours and because there is a suspicion that Gypsies will boycott a site outside their normal paths and work centres. The existence of housed Gypsy families near to sites swells the numbers of children that local schools will receive, and it may be predicted that the number of housed Gypsy children will eventually equal that of the site children.

Cultural heritage, customs and language

When discussing the culture of travellers, it is impossible to avoid mention of the outlawed and stigmatized context in which they live. Much of their attitude to life is conditioned by the exigencies of survival and finding camping places, water and work, and avoiding police and local authority attention. Coping with their own image or stereotype and the latent hostility from the host community (the director of this Schools Council project was himself mistaken for a Gypsy and stoned by some thirty pupils of one comprehensive school) is not easy and results in attitudes of aggressive solidarity in the face of any external threat. Centuries of harassment have left their mark. It is, moreover, necessary for teachers to remind themselves that they are dealing with a culture that has developed and evolved in a minority group which is still discriminated against—'No Gypsy travellers' signs in public houses, bye-law prohibition of camping, and even in legislation: 'If without lawful authority or excuse, a hawker or other itinerant or a gipsy . . .

encamps on a highway he shall be guilty of an offence.'[36] All this results in travellers often exhibiting an understandable disrespect for the law and a highly suspicious attitude to officialdom. In comparison with this 'culture of the stigmatized', the vestiges of Romany folklore, the use of Anglo-Romany and Shelta, traditional personal adornment and taste for opulent decoration appear secondary, especially as much of the extant Romany customs and heritage are closely guarded secrets.

Many aspects of traveller life are essentially no different from those common in large lower working class industrial or agricultural families: preferential treatment is accorded to the men and boys at mealtimes, for instance, even though the community has many matriarchal characteristics. General eating times and habits are similar, though travellers do not sit at table. The television has replaced the cinema as a regular source of escapist entertainment, the traveller sets being run mostly from vehicle batteries; the choice of programmes follows the working class pattern. Clothing, especially the wearing of dark suits by the menfolk for menial work such as sorting scrap or laying tarmac, is very much the same, though the travellers retain a distinctive flair for jewellery (rings, ornate watchstraps and belts, ear-rings among girls and women, pendants, bracelets and so on, especially the mounting of gold coins, mainly sovereigns). When travellers dress up for an important occasion, the culturally determined tastes are much more apparent: the dyeing and plaiting of the women's hair in Gypsy styles, the dressing of the boys as adults and the young girls with exotically frilly and colourful dresses, hair-ribbons and additional jewellery. The men often prefer traveller cravats (*diklos*) to ties, and the boys, whatever their ages, will not wear shorts. In comparison to more traditional, often tribal groups of Romany Gypsies in Europe who may still be involved in trades which benefit from traditional customs, travellers in England and Wales at first sight appear to have had several generations of assimilation into settled gauje society. Yet there are telltale clues to their identity which can be distinguished.

Attitudes to childbirth, pregnancy and menstruation similarly appear to be much the same as in lower working class groups—somewhat old-fashioned and ridden with old wives' tales and superstition. But Gypsies' attitudes may be linked with the survival of customs and beliefs which have an Indian origin: *mokkadi*, or ritualistic uncleanness taboos, may involve separate washing of men's and women's clothes, strict rules about the washing of bodies, clothes and crockery (including dish-cloths, which must never be washed with clothing) in quite separate bowls; during menstruation or the immediate post-natal period a girl or woman may be forbidden to cook, wash up, or even touch the food or cooking utensils used by others. This is certainly not always common practice amongst traveller groups who make a practice of moving with the times, but many families have retained this aspect of their traditional past.[37]

Ritual surrounding death is probably the most persistent of all these cultural factors. This may involve the ceremonial burning of the trailer or wagon of the deceased—or a substitute model usually in a dilapidated condition, bought cheaply for the occasion. In cases where the grief is strong because the father of a family has died young, his possessions (crockery and so on) may be smashed and animals disposed of. It is customary to burn the clothing of the deceased, a task often entrusted to the oldest male child still in the household. On a visit to a site during the project, a mother explained that her son, a fourteen-year-old, should not be approached because he had just collected his father's best suit from the cleaners, and was in the process of burning it—the last piece of clothing to be treated this way, and two months after the father's death. It is certainly wise to be extremely careful about mentioning the name of a dead traveller for a year or so after his death. Teachers wishing to pay respects to a traveller need not be too discouraged to do so, and may be advised to visit the site and approach the closest relative (the wife, for instance), expressing sympathy. If—and only if—the teacher does know the family well he may ask whether it will be acceptable for him to attend the funeral. Travellers take death very seriously, for it has long been the most crucial event in the family life: funerals are usually attended by the entire family, cavalcades may include more than a hundred vehicles. The close relatives may mourn a death for at least a year by giving up meat, smoking or alcohol. The widow may wear black for the rest of her life.

One headteacher was puzzled when a traveller child came running to his office bitterly crying out that another traveller had been 'calling over my dad'. He eventually discovered that this meant taking the name of his dead father in vain. No other insult is so severe as this within traveller society, and it may be wise, for once, not to refer back to parents for explanations on this, for fear of creating a feud on a site. Headteachers who wish to understand such behaviour may wish to cultivate a special relationship with an impartial traveller adult for advice.

Practices such as these suggest a stronger cultural tradition than many observers report, though the *Journal of the Gypsy Lore Society* is full of them. It is wise to include under the heading of culture the *way of life* itself: caravan dwelling, nomadism, the family and kinship patterns, traditional and recent forms of self-employment, attitudes to time and the environment, child-rearing practices and inculcation of traveller value systems. The deeper cultural aspects such as language are harder to describe because their secrecy makes documentation so difficult, and gauje novitiates may be asked to respect confidences.

The extent to which the secret languages are spoken within traveller society, especially when strangers are not present, is not known. Indeed, travellers express mixed and contradictory views about this, some denying that the younger generation ever use them, others suggesting that they are widely used by all ages of traveller. The degree to which travellers will reveal

Anglo-Romany or Shelta to teachers and trusted visitors also varies greatly, but one suspects that they are far more extensively used than is usually thought. One informant, a house-dwelling youth who had lived eighteen months with some Irish travellers in England, claimed that the secret languages were used, mixed with English, very regularly indeed when there were no strangers other than himself present or when communication was essential in front of officials without the latter understanding. Outside their own environment, however, travellers are extremely adept at hiding these aspects of their life. Schools certainly reported that there seems to be little cultural exposure by traveller children when mixed in gauje classes.

The language of travellers is distinctive not only because Anglo-Romany and Shelta may be spoken privately or a few words interlarded with normal English sentences, but because travellers have many mannerisms of speech which, taken together, create major educational difficulties. A more detailed discussion of the actual form of Anglo-Romany and Shelta may be found in Appendix A (pages 181–5). Restricted sentence construction, rapidity of delivery, vagueness of pronunciation both of assonants and consonants (particularly the liquids),[38] and reliance on supportive gesture, confuse many teachers when the children first enter school, and may create extreme problems of communication. Travellers frequently become tongue-twisted when attempting long, especially latinate words, which often results in amusing inexactitudes that may be obstinately retained even when the correct version is mastered—for example, 'lectif' for electricity, 'fleeflabs' for pre-fabs, 'all-michaeled out inside' for formica surface interior.[39] Many archaic or quaint usages persist: 'brazen' for naughty, for instance. Travelling results in importation of regional dialects and accents into other parts of the country, and these, like the strong Irish and Scottish accents amongst Tinkers, may linger for several generations.

The heritage of travellers and their value systems are central to the dilemma that their education poses. The educational *system* is to a large extent based upon the ideal that every child has the right to choose his future and that social mobility through school attainment is a fundamental agent in any democratic and fair society. This point explains why so much attention is being given to the culture and ideology of traveller society. If the education of travellers had been thought only to be a question of mechanics, this would have been a very different report.

Providing for the education of migrant children during the regular school year creates many difficult and complex problems which have many social and economic ramifications. The seasonal impact of migratory children on school systems along the routes creates problems of finance, school transfer records, grade replacement of pupils, and provision of teachers and school facilities. There is, in addition, the problem of getting migratory children to enroll and attend school regularly.[40]

A study of American Indians and their education by Miles Zintz includes an interesting juxtaposition of Pueblo Indian children's values and those held by teachers. Although the differences between Pueblo Indians and British Gypsies are only too obvious, the extent to which the value systems of pupils and teachers may conflict is no less severe:

(a) Harmony with nature as juxtaposed with mastery over nature.

(b) Present time orientation rather than future time orientation.

(c) Inclusion of mythology, fear of the supernatural, and sorcery rather than a total commitment to a scientific explanation of all natural phenomena.

(d) A level of aspiration which prefers to follow in the ways of the old people, to co-operate and maintain the status quo rather than develop a keen sense of competition and climb the ladder of success.

(e) Preference for anonymity and submissiveness rather than individuality and aggression.

(f) Working to satisfy present needs and being willing to share rather than always working to 'get ahead' and save for the future.[41]

The Gypsy and traveller community has its own ladder of success, but even within the community not all pay homage to it—not all want 'flash' trailers and the latest models of Range Rovers. Gypsies save for the future—they collect china, glass, silver and gold—not to accumulate wealth but to insure against catastrophe: their basic attitude is to be able to face and overcome the worst rather than to seek the best. To put it in the words of one old travelling man: 'Look at it this way, pal—if an atomic war started and all your houses, shops, power stations, sewers, firemen, public health inspectors, police, politicians, and governments was knocked out, you gaujes would kill yourselves with fire and disease and starve yourselves out. There'd be nought but travellers left 'cause travellers knows how to live. There'll always be travellers.'

This belief in his capacity to survive without school, politics, the law, and all the trappings of gauje society is central to the traveller heritage; it accounts for his tolerance of discomforts and pain, of the sometimes outrageous conditions of unauthorized camping areas, and for his disregard not only for time but for counting. This disregard is captured to perfection by Jack Crabb in *Little Big Man* when he returns to the white man's world:

That's the kind of thing you find out when you get back to civilization: what day it is and time of day, how many miles from Fort Leavenworth and how much the sutlers is getting for tobacco there, how many beers Flanagan drunk and how many times Hoffman did it with a harlot. Numbers numbers, I had forgotten how important they was.[42]

This ability to survive and face the worst and his regard for the family are the most important components of the traveller philosophy and culture. Religion, taxation, the vote, science, the pursuit of what is good—moral and aesthetic—are of minor consequence; they are not traveller but gauje values. The ideals of the traveller may be listed thus:

(a) To survive by one's own wits, out-bargain and be one step ahead of the next man, especially if he is a gauje; to endure the worst and make the best of reality.

(b) To respect the family, honour its elders, never to betray it; to father children who will continue to uphold these traditions and be able to stand up for themselves. To make a living *with* not *for* the family.

(c) To acquire wisdom—that is, not knowledge, not enlightenment, but a deep understanding of human nature and, in the popular sense, a philosophical view of life.

Against these three simple principles, what should be the curriculum, what role should the school play and what should be the teacher strategy?

Profile of the traveller child as a case for education

All children are individuals; and traveller children are no less heterogeneous than other groups of children. But the child-centredness and individualization of learning which leads to the plea 'You are talking about Gypsy children as if they were all the same. No! They are all individuals!' is not necessarily the wisest approach to the traveller. The stress in current educational thought is on the development of each individual's potential within the socialized group (the community). Take, for instance, the Schools Council Working Paper 42, in which appears a digest of teacher working parties' views of the aims and objectives of the middle school:

1. Pupils should be members of a socialized group.
   Pupils should be capable of working harmoniously with others.
   Schools should foster home/school relations.
2. Schools should foster understanding of the interaction of man and his environment.
   Schools should foster understanding of values, relationships, social and moral obligations, manners, and the sense of community.[43]

There are four other stated school objectives which are interesting in themselves but are less relevant to the point being made here. The list of aims for children in the middle years starts with the following three prescriptions:

to be adjusted to community living;
to be aware of problems of living with other people;
to have social awareness.[44]

If indeed these are the aims and objectives (or at least the important social aims) of middle and other schooling, there is a genuine conflict between the ideals of the traveller and those of his teacher over and above those outlined by Miles Zintz and that of education as an agent of social mobility. For the traveller child has more than an individual identity, he has a family identity; and it is this which should probably be the main determinant of teaching approaches and organization. He is not and does not wish to be 'adjusted to community living'—that is to become a socialized member of the gauje world.

Whatever his family's economic status, his ethnic or regional origin, the nomadic habits of his parents, their degree of social acceptance by the host community or the extent of the child's previous educational experience, the traveller exhibits a personality in common with all other traveller children. It is quite different from that of any other children most teachers will meet. Of course he will also exhibit characteristics in school in common with other children and specifically and *apparently* those outlined by Maurice Chazan as the classical 'disadvantage' syndrome:

1. language inadequacies, especially an inability to cope with abstract symbols;
2. perceptual deficiencies, with problems of visual and auditory discrimination;
3. a relative inability to sustain attention, particularly in the face of structured cognitive demands;
4. a short-term view of life which seeks immediate pleasure rather than future advantage;
5. a poor self-image, with feelings of inferiority both as person and learner;
6. a lack of motivation towards school learning and educational achievement;
7. a high incidence of early withdrawal from school;
8. a relatively high incidence of behaviour problems, especially truancy and delinquency.[45]

But these *symptoms* or teacher expectations can be unfair when read into the traveller; for he is an educational virgin when he first comes to school. Johnny Connors, an Irish Tinker, describes the extent of this virginity:

If we teach a settled community child how to spell C–A–T, cat, he can go home from school at the end of the day and he will ask his parents to spell 'dog' for him. Naturally his parents will say D–O–G. But with the travelling child it is the opposite. If he asks his parents to spell dog, it is like asking a deaf and dumb person to say sound.[46]

But where education is voluntary or when it is initially taken to the travelling child, there is more eagerness than is usual, and parents may use the threat of not being allowed to go to school as a disciplinary measure. When the child first comes to school he is reserved, regardless of his age, very much on his guard against the slightest hint of prejudice against him; but he is also uninhibited emotionally, having little experience of meeting adults other than parents and relatives, aliens such as policemen and eviction officers, or potentially gullible gauje customers.

Being inexperienced in pupil–teacher relationships, he is particularly prone to possessive affection (teacher as parent), to studied indifference, even treating them as a skivvy (teacher as Tinker's dosser), or to outright incompatibility (teacher as *divvi*—mad—gauje). The headteacher may be either a 'bad big man' or a family elder to whom one goes for arbitration in disputes. The other children are potential threats, against whom there must be a united front. Literacy is an attribute of the gauje of which he is jealous; it is a skill which, with his superior ability to survive and outwit the gauje, should be able to be mastered as quickly as it takes to learn to sort aluminium from tin. But very quickly it may be seen as magical territory, part of the scorned gauje value system, something to be indignantly suffered, or rejected.

School is alien for many reasons other than the fact that it cannot move and has no wheels. Children in great numbers are divided by age into separate 'gangs', brothers and sisters parted; rules and regulations seem without rhyme or reason. Dinners are good, and traveller children may quickly charm kitchen staff into serving extra portions. The central heating in winter may seem excessive to them for the daytime—though the insides of trailers, in the evenings especially, reach much higher temperatures; but there one is expected to sleep and one can always cool down by rushing outside. Doors, cupboards and rooms kept locked, staircases, corners and corridors are a fascination, not without sinister associations, for the younger children. Taps and abundant, sometimes, hot water may be the first real attraction (the churn upstairs or in the roof never seems to become empty), and the water is sometimes as scalding as that from a kettle.

Sitting down and keeping quiet is punitive and real labour, especially if there is nothing of interest to do. Though wary of gauje children, traveller children may snatch crayons or books from other travellers as if they were scrap metal, and the strongest man takes what he can.

Teachers must be there to teach them—'schools is where you learn your ABCs'—but teachers often seem not to spare enough time, and perhaps they may feel there should be a teacher to each child. They may sulk and walk out of the classroom if they are denied attention, and are very jealous of other travellers who seem to be getting more of the teacher's time.

If divided from siblings, they are under strict instructions from their parents to 'mind' the younger ones and may disobey teachers' direct commands in order to check on a sister in the reception infants' class. All the time they feel cooped up, and once the novelty of being inside the classroom wears off, in perhaps a day or two, they wait for—but do not count the minutes before—breaktime and the freedom of the playground. They are self-conscious about drama, dance, P.E. (especially if this means exposing their bodies, as the boys think shorts unmanly and have a cultural aversion to showing their knees).[47] Painting, art and craft, drama, movement, pre-reading games may be thought silly and irrelevant to ABCs. If the gauje children can produce two paintings in half the afternoon—and they do look rather better than his—the traveller will out-bargain him and produce eight; he is used to working at pressure, dismantling and sorting. Educational equipment like pencil sharpeners and tidy boxes hold a fascination, and he is more interested in the possibility of valuable metals inside. He is by nurture a breaker and a scavenger, not a builder.

But they come in wide-eyed and expectant. Their apprehensions, claustrophobia and their guardedness about information on their families are paradoxically mixed with lack of inhibition, temperamentality and elemental emotional response patterns. Their hyperactivity and spontaneity are frequently mistaken for maladjustment. They are physically robust and can withstand pain, wet and cold, appear accident-prone because the boys (at least) value bravado, strength and fearlessness above gracefulness and co-ordination. Fighting is adult style: hit hard and straight before the opponent can retaliate, and make sure that one punch is enough. It does not have to be elegant. When hurt they may resent mothering, which may be the cause of even greater indignity than the hurt itself. The traveller child recognizes a real danger (though he is a dare-devil), and many teachers report that they rely upon older travellers to tell them when a younger child is really hurt. When beaten in a fight or humbled on the site, the child will often walk a hundred yards away, sulk or cry bitterly; but when he reappears he may show no signs of grudge or embarrassment—in fact, he is admired because he has overcome his problems and faced the worst.

He comes to school with the same spirit as his father when visiting a horse fair or a factory: he is on the look-out for a bargain, seeking something he can make use of. The traveller child obviously enjoys enjoying himself, but he is always more interested in mastering skills that will help him to achieve the three ideals stated on page 85. Marriage amongst travellers, especially Gypsies with strong Romany heritage, is an economic and child-production partnership above all else. Barrenness in women and infertility in men are unquestionable grounds for separation. For the traveller child, school should be similarly functional: parents do not question the grounds for truancy if the child claims that he is not learning anything and was better employed during the period of absence. The traveller child is as curious a creature as the gauje child can be, but unlike the gauje child he will not tolerate and suffer something that does not satisfy his curiosity or his need to master relevant skills.

Traveller children have trained memories, not necessarily sequentially ordered (the time attitude again) nor indiscriminate (he remembers only what is necessary—Jack Crabb's pair of boots again). A non-literate society cannot take notes, keep records, make lists of things to buy or read maps. It must carry its map in its mind; its reference book and memo pad is there too. The traveller child has a highly developed sense of what to *reject*. Given jumble clothing by the do-gooder, the traveller will value it, sell it or discard it as *mokkadi*, but he will rarely wear it himself or give it to his children to wear.[48] The words of the teacher and the knowledge imparted by the school receive the same treatment.

But for all this, the traveller child is consciously submitting himself to schooling for another ulterior purpose: to understand the gauje's ways. Thus, although he might refuse to conform to and socialize and become, in school, like any other child, what he is really doing is training himself to be able to deal better with gauje customers, to exploit their weaknesses and gullibility; to develop ways in which to combat the gauje official. This may account for the traveller children's talent in winning the hearts of their teachers. It may account for their ability to exploit weaknesses in teachers, sometimes to test them out in the most unscrupulous fashion, just to see how far they can go or to deceive an inexperienced or over-maternal teacher. The extent to which a traveller child may intentionally mislead a teacher on such matters as extent of literacy, previous education, 'restricted' language and social competence is very interesting. For instance, besides the quite common factor in travellers as well as non-traveller children of revealing general attainment on entry to a new school which is well below that already achieved in the previous school, traveller children have been known to present themselves as totally illiterate and inarticulate when this is indeed far from the case. In one remarkable instance a teacher in a Bromley school even discovered one of her most regularly attending 'non-readers' fluently reading quite difficult books in the remedial classroom. When challenged the child admitted that although he had hidden the fact completely from her eyes, he had accomplished the task of learning to read in the same teacher's reading lessons. Herbert Kohl describes several similar cases among Negro children in Harlem in *36 Children*.

So far, the emphasis has been placed on the traveller child *in* school. What of the ten-year-old from the unauthorized site, not in school? What of the nomadic child? The Millie Taylors and Amos Prices and Paddy Murphys of the tip-banks and wastelands do not yet really know what they are being asked to buy. To 'educate' them may require great expertise—with the teacher as dealer. It may require listening more than anything else. But it cannot be achieved except on their terms and in the full context of the family. The traveller child is a functioning member of the family, and any teacher who does not work from that initial premise may make little progress.

The heritage of the traveller child, his position outside the host community and his attitudes towards education are interconnected with the style of his life and his familial aspirations. They are all part of his 'culture' in the widest sense. The profile of the travelling child as a case for education which has been portrayed above may be bordering on the extreme; many teachers, especially those whose work is described in the next chapter, may feel that unfair criteria have been raised. They may feel that the attitudes adopted in this report are uncomplimentary and undermine what they feel they are achieving. This is far from the intention of this report and far from the truth;

the insights of the preceding sections, especially this child profile, are very much the composite expression of the most profound teachers who provided the project, like Karshish in Robert Browning's *An Epistle*, with 'learning's crumbs'.

Notes and references

1 For these and all other works mentioned in this survey of previous studies, see Bibliography, pp. 191–3.

2 'Remarks relating to our Gipsies, show, van, and other travelling women and children, by George Smith of Coalville', Appendix 25, Report of the Select Committee on Canals, *Parliamentry Papers* Hansard, 1883 (252) XIII, p. 318.

3 Scottish Development Department, *Scotland's Travelling People* (HMSO, 1971), pp. 19, 21.

4 Ministry of Housing and Local Government, *Gypsies and Other Travellers* (HMSO, 1967), p. 3.

5 Ibid., p. 43.

6 T. A. Acton, 'Changes in ethnic stereotypes of British Gypsies', Proceedings of NGEC Conference, St Peter's College, Oxford, 1971, pp. 58–74. Also CES Gypsy Project Draft Report (1972), chapter on Gypsy identity.

7 B. C. Smart and H. J. Crofton, *The Dialect of the English Gypsies* (Detroit: Gale Research Co., 1968; first published 1875), pp. ix–xiii.

8 Cf. T. A. Acton, 'Who are the true Gypsies ?' in Proceedings of NGEC Conference, 1971, ed. Acton, especially section entitled 'The Didecai as scapegoat', pp. 65–70.

9 CES Gypsy Project Draft Report, chapter on Gypsy identity.

10 *The Book of Boswell*, ed. John Seymour (Gollancz, 1970), pp. 169–74, and inside front and back cover for the tree itself.

11 *A Romany Life* (Methuen, 1935), Chapter XLVII, 'Romany v. Gorgio Eugenics', especially p. 161.

12 *Gypsies and Other Travellers*, p. 1. Members of the Showmen's Guild are specifically excluded from this definition.

13 Viz., the 'Romanestan Institute' and 'Romanestan Publications' (Romanestan = the equivalent of Israel—but see D. Kenrick and Grattan Puxon, *The Destiny of Europe's Gypsies* (Sussex University Press/Chatto-Heinemann, 1972), p. 206). Also the Romany Guild, the Romani Site Owner's Guild, etc.

14 *The Dialect of the English Gypsies* (see n. 7), p. 51.

15 T. A. Acton, 'Changes in ethnic stereotypes of British Gypsies' (see n. 6), pp. 60–1.

16 Ibid., p. 61.

17 *The Dialect of English Gypsies* (see n. 7), p. 80.

18 Significantly this problem is avoided by Charles Duff's 'Supplementary notes on British and American Gypsies' in his translation of Clébert's *The Gypsies* (Penguin, 1967), though Clébert himself deals with the problem, pp. 112–13.

19 *The Book of Boswell*, pp. 164–5.

20 See *Report of the Commission on Itinerancy* (Stationery Office, Dublin, 1963), p. 34; *Scotland's Travelling People* (see n. 3), pp. 9–10.

21 For discussion of J. Sampson, see R. A. Stewart MacAlister, *The Secret Languages of Ireland* (Cambridge University Press, 1937), pp. 130–8; L. Spence, 'The Scottish Tinkler Gypsies', *Scotland's Magazine*, vol. 51, no. 2 (1955), pp. 20–4. There are also numerous articles and notes on the problem in the *Journal of the Gypsy Lore Society*.

22 Information provided by Janssen (see Chapter 3, page 43, n. 5).

23 Bart McDowell, *Gypsies: Wanderers of the World* (National Geographic Society, 1970), Chapter 9, 'The mystery remains intact'.

24 *The Destiny of Europe's Gypsies* (see n. 13), especially chapter 9.

25 A. Clarke, 'The sero-anthropology of human population groups with special

reference to European Gypsies', Proceedings of NGEC Conference, 1971, ed. T. A. Acton, pp. 19–24.

26 See Gipsy Petulengro, *A Romany Life* (Methuen, 1936). Also the maps in Clébert's *The Gypsies* (see n. 18), pp. 52–3 and *Gypsies: Wanderers of the World* (see n. 23), pp. 16–17.

27 *Educational Facilities for the Children of Itinerants* (Stationery Office, Dublin, 1970), pp. 4–6.

28 Ibid., p. 6.

29 'Itinerants to be induced to settle', *Report of the Commission on Itinerancy*, Chapter XVI, p. 106, para. 2.

30 Numerous short references to Gypsies can be found in: A. H. Hays, 'The Gypsy problem—solution ?', *Sanitarian*, vol. 69, no. 10 (1961), pp. 422–3; F. W. Owen, 'The place of the Gypsies and other itinerant families in a changing Britain', *The Royal Society of Health Journal*, vol. 85, no. 1 (1965), pp. 50–3; R. A. R. Wade, 'A conference of public health inspectors on Gypsies', *Journal of the Gypsy Lore Society*, third series, Vol. XLVII, nos 3–4 (1968), pp. 113–16; 'Gypsies and other travellers— a one-day conference on 24 January 1968', *Public Health Inspector*, vol. 76 (March, 1968), pp. 291–324; L. N. Gould, 'Assessment of Gypsy living conditions', *Community Medicine*, vol. 129, no. 7 (December, 1972), pp. 163–4; Arton Wilson, *Caravans as Homes* (HMSO, 1959).

31 Drs K. Sietaram, *Opvoeding van en Onderwijs aan Woonwagenkampkinderen* (Utrecht: University of Utrecht, 1968), pp. 69–70, 167. The only English studies other than those undertaken by some students on a poor sample were those of H. Gordon, *Mental and Scholastic Tests among Retarded Children*, Board of Education Pamphlet No. 44 (HMSO, 1923), p. 49. Gordon tested bargee and Gypsy children, and reported that the only conclusion that could be drawn was that there was a measurable decline in 'mental ability' with advancing age. Not unexpectedly he found a close correlation between test scores and school attendance regularity.

32 Norman Dodds, M.P., *Gypsies, Didikois, and Other Travellers* (Johnson, 1966).

33 *The Destiny of Europe's Gypsies* (see n. 13), pp. 37–8.

34 Thomas Berger, *Little Big Man* (Penguin, 1968), p. 59.

35 *Caravan Sites Act 1968 Part 2*, Report of Joint Working Party of the Local Authority Associations and the Gypsy Council, Appendix 2, Plan III. (Obtainable from the Association of Municipal Corporations, 36 Old Queen Street, London SW1H 9JE.)

36 Section 127, 1959 Highways Act.

37 T. A. Acton, 'The functions of the avoidance of moxadi kovels', *Journal of the Gypsy Lore Society*, third series, Vol. L, nos 3–4 (1971), pp. 108–36.

38 *The Dialect of the English Gypsies* (see n. 7), p. 9—'The English Gypsies are in the frequent habit of confusing the liquids . . .'

39 David Smith ,'Can the Gypsies adjust ?', *New Society*, (26 May, 1966), pp. 9–11.

40 George E. Haney, 'Problems and trends in migrant education', in *Education of the Disadvantaged*, eds A. H. Passow, M. Goldberg, and A. J. Tannenbaum (New York: Holt, Rinehart & Winston, 1967), p. 102.

41 Miles Zintz, 'Problems of classroom adjustment of Indian children in public elementary schools in the South West', in *Education of the Disadvantaged*, paraphrased from p. 91.

42 *Little Big Man* (see n. 34), p. 112.

43 Schools Council Working Paper 42, *Education in the Middle Years* (Evans/ Methuen Educational, 1972), p. 96.

44 Ibid., p. 95.

45 Maurice Chazan. 'Compensatory education: defining the problem', in *Compensatory Education: an Introduction*, Occasional Paper No. 1, Schools Council Project in Compensatory Education (Swansea, 1968).

46 Johnny Pops Connors, 'An essay on the education of travelling children', in *The Shadow on the Cheese*, ed. John Wallbridge (NGEC, 1972), pp. 10–11.

47 *The Shadow on the Cheese*, p. 44.

48 *The Destiny of Europe's Gypsies* (see n. 13), p. 37.

5 Methods of organization and class allocation

Introduction

This review of organization and class allocation is based upon the relatively small sample of forty schools with travellers which were visited during the project, supplemented by very short visits to many other schools of different age ranges, in the vicinity. The sample ensured that a wide range of practice would be seen, that proportionate size of traveller intake, regional distribution, urban/rural setting, age range, and designation of children (Gypsy, bargee, fairground) would vary greatly. The choice of schools seen and those which are used as the basis for the case studies presented here is arbitrary and not based on any objective form of assessment. The purpose has been to outline the main strategies which seem to have been developed to deal with travellers, many of which are expedient and pragmatic responses by schools and teachers rather than subject to a thoroughly worked-out educational theory.

The reason for this is twofold. Firstly, schools are not in the position to determine approaches on much more than the resources available (staffing, accommodation, their existing organization) and the general attitude of the LEA involved. Secondly, it is not possible to make assessment objective, as Townsend and Brittan report in their study, *Organization in Multiracial Schools:*

The question of the most equitable system of organizing class groups in multi-racial schools is still left wide open as far as this report is concerned. There are, however, indications that streaming, unless there is considerable flexibility of promotion and transfers, can cause an early placement in a slower stream, because of language difficulties, to affect an immigrant pupil's career through the school. More detailed research would be required before any more definite statement could be made about the relative merits of streaming and mixed ability groups.[1]

Townsend and Brittan also explain that there are many different forms of organization, often depending upon the age range of the school, and that the terminology for describing them (induction/reception/bridging, class dispersal/grouping/streaming—vertical, horizontal, family, mixed ability—

withdrawal/remedial/special, and so on, integration/assimilation, separatism/ segregation) is confused and sometimes coded.[2]

There is a further important consideration which must eventually be faced concerning travellers, and that is the relative importance to be attached to preserving identity and to achieving academic progress when these two may be mutually exclusive. It may be that no definite policy line could be adopted anyway because of the heterogeneity of the groups and their varying needs. Certainly many teachers are already well aware of the central dilemma which is posed by the traveller; it is the same that perplexes educationists involved with different minority groups with cultural traditions outside the mainstream of settled majority society:

Studies demonstrate that the [American] Indian child achieves more in an integrated school than under segregation [that of the old separate educational provision made by the US Bureau of Indian Affairs], however his exposure to children from other cultural backgrounds tends to have an eroding effect upon his cultural identity. The moral question arises as to whether it is right for the school to attempt making over the Indian traditions which have a long, rich history, even though these traditions present a handicap to material success and enlightenment in twentieth century America. . . . The traditional American dilemma over whether to preserve cultural pluralism or to make our society one of the world's great melting pots.[3]

The whole problem is far more complex. It may be possible to develop 'culture fair' tests which even out the discrepancies between minority groups' scores on IQ and educational potential (though the work of Jensen may be thought to some extent to undermine this).[4] If so, then the liberal conscience is salvaged by establishing that abilities are not innately affected by race, ethnic or cultural background. But as yet no tests have been developed which can measure cultural erosion. Most of the assessment programmes that have been developed in England and Wales with respect to immigrants, for instance, are limited, as Judith Haynes admits in her *Educational Assessment of Immigrant Pupils*:

Although attendance at school clearly helps mental development in general, there is very little evidence for or against any particular kind of schooling in favouring educational progress, particularly of the kind of progress which is being assessed in this study which is a rather restricted type of assessment and does not include any assessment of general knowledge and other skills which the children may have been developing.[5]

How, it must be asked, can what is learnt at school be distinguished from what is learnt at home, especially in view of the comparatively short time a child is actually in school and in learning situations there?

If we can become more adept at devising 'culture fair' tests, there is no doubt that some could be developed which would indicate that school attendance itself could be eliminated as a causal factor in developing general mental ability with Gypsies—tests which, for instance, could measure a child's skill in sorting and assessing the value of metals, in dealing with eviction officers, in sizing up what sort of sales talk is relevant to what kind of gauje customer. It might even be shown that the views of some Gypsies are justified: that school may hinder the development of abilities needed by their children.

Ingrid and Arne Trankell have studied the education of housed Gypsies in Sweden, and made an assessment of an educational programme devised in Stockholm. In their report of the initial phase of this programme they suggest that attendance at school is not all and that progress in school may be related to many other factors:

The programme was set in action in a pilot study in which twelve of thirty six gypsy families with children of school age were given combined socio-curative and therapeutic treatment during the first year of action (1965–6). The analysis of the resulting increase in school attendance supported the view that a considerable amount of school days could be saved by the treatment; it was assumed that around 33 school days had been gained per child in the families treated. . . .

The observations during the first year also revealed, however, that the rise in attendance did not in itself lead to any clear gains in knowledge or increased ability of the gypsy children to avail themselves of the instructions provided by the school.[6]

Although *diagnostic* tests of learning disabilities or high potential have an invaluable part to play in any teaching, this is too complex an area for a project such as this to explore.

The criteria used in the selection of case studies for this chapter and the compendium of teaching approaches in Chapter 6 were developed and refined during the research and inquiry stage of the project and during the report-writing stage. The major criterion has been to present a wide range of current practice; whereas there has obviously been some selection in stressing certain approaches, what is presented is by no means intended as a prescription.

At first, emphasis was laid upon the initiation and maintenance of regular attendance at maintained schools, the effectiveness and amiability of the adaptation and socialization of the traveller child in the school and classroom, progress in the basic skills (particularly in literacy, as this was believed to be the area of the curriculum most desired by traveller parents), and a rather vague field usually called 'school–home' contact. There was a general feeling on the part of those concerned with the project that actual teaching approaches most likely to be successful would be those which took account of the background and culture of the children.

Increasingly, it was realized that more account had to be taken of the heterogeneity of the educational needs and problems involved with the different types of children (see the section on categorization of travellers by extent of nomadism and settlement, pages 61–5) and the length of previous educational experience and the general 'social acceptability' of the traveller family involved. No one set of criteria would be valid for all situations.

Some of the initial criteria were refined: regular attendance at maintained schools had to be widened to general education—that is, to include teaching units outside school. Although the stress on literacy was still thought to be critical, more attention was given to the depth and quality of the wider impact that education was having upon the children *and their families*. Because so many of the children were entering school late, were subject to frequent casual absences, seasonal patterns in attendance and premature drop-out, there was an obvious justification for believing in the importance of teaching which was designed to make the traveller pupil self-reliant as a learner. This would enable him to continue his education in school subjects while away from school—by homework, vacation work, taking advantage of potential 'teachers' of literacy such as the family scribe, milkmen, shopkeepers, casual site visitors, and the inanimate teachers—literacy on TV, bill-boards, road signs, and so on. The methods of teaching, not dissimilar to those employed in the early board schools, which involved developing teaching ability in the pupils themselves, were also seen to be crucial, for several cases were discovered of children teaching reading and writing to younger *and* older siblings and parents. On the wider impact of schooling and education, it was clear that the family's over-all attitude to teachers and education was important. What parental attitudes would contemporary pupils exhibit in years to come?

However, to use regular attendance as a criterion or indicator of 'good practice' was unfair to schools, for the extent of travelling could hardly be within their control. Likewise, the raising of literacy and other educational standards could hardly be expected to be achieved when attendances were only of very short duration.

It was also realized that 'good practice' was not limited to the maintained schools. There were many interesting developments in the voluntary sector and in liaison between the maintained and voluntary sectors, some of which were initiated after the research and inquiry stage of the project had been completed. Although some of them have hardly had time to take shape and some have not even started, examples have been included in this chapter, e.g. mobile schools, peripatetic staff, on-site classrooms, appointment of joint local education authority supervisors.

One further criterion was necessary: however imaginative and ambitious a programme is, however much it reflects traveller heritage, it is essential that it be feasible and practicable. Resources of manpower, materials and accommodation, finance and the presence of the co-operation of LEAs, school staffs and other official personnel such as wardens and site managers are all required. Some methods which seemed theoretically admirable were not working successfully because they were too easily suspended, casualties of insufficient staffing and facilities. Withdrawal classes and certain voluntary programmes especially were among these.

Actual citations of individual schools have mostly been avoided for two reasons: firstly, that many schools had developed almost identical strategies, and to select one rather than another would have implied a value judgement; and secondly, that teachers in some schools which have already been well known for what they are doing with travellers have been deluged with inquiries and visitors, and feel that the children have prior claims to their attention. Although well-organized and co-ordinated action–research work undertaken, for instance, by students at colleges of education can be very fruitful, especially in the areas of contemporary language studies, the under-supervised term paper or minor thesis is an encumbrance to teachers and often an impertinence to travellers.

Primary level

For the purpose of this report the advent of middle schools has been ignored. The age range dealt with here covers both the five- to seven-year-olds (infants) and the seven- to eleven-year-olds (junior). The range of educational organization for travellers during this primary period is dependent upon the main methods employed in the school itself, and there is a very great variety in that. However, it is possible to outline the main ways in which travellers were placed by schools visited during the project:

(a) The children were allocated to classes in just the same way as everyone else.

(b) As above, but with substantial withdrawal or remedial group work either in traveller only or mixed traveller–gauje classes.

(c) As above at infant level, but with special methods and exclusive traveller classes at junior level, by which time differences in attainment were so great that assimilation seemed to be unwise, or the number of travellers without infant experience so high that they needed separate inductive education before being dispersed.

(d) An initial infant-level induction class for travellers, into which some of the junior-aged travellers coming to school for the first time were also placed temporarily, and normal dispersal at junior level, with withdrawal/remedial attention when necessary.

(e) Parallel traveller infant classes and gauje infant classes, followed by integrated junior classes (there was sometimes a year's delay before the travellers were integrated into the junior level).

(f) A totally separate system of classes at infant and junior levels.

(g) An all-age traveller class throughout the primary level, with transfer into the normal classes of the school only when appropriate and only for a few children. Sometimes this class was housed in the infant, sometimes in the junior department; in some cases it was housed in a mobile classroom or caravan parked in the school grounds.

Which of these systems was used often depended upon the general opinions of the headteachers and LEAs, and upon accommodation available, more than upon the background of the traveller children—except that the more educationally raw the children, the more likely that withdrawal would be considered necessary. Withdrawal was also most frequently adopted when it was known that there was only likely to be a very short stay at the school—during summer fruit picking or, incidentally, with fairground children during the show season. In general, there had been a movement away from special classes towards assimilative dispersal in schools which had been serving sites for a number of years prior to the project. Since the project began many more pilot projects have been established and children previously unschooled have started to receive education. Both factors have tended to tip the balance back towards special, sometimes separate provision.

CASE STUDIES

Assimilative dispersal: junior and infant
One such infant school has had between twelve and twenty-five traveller children from a Hertfordshire permanent Gypsy caravan site since 1966. In that year, the LEA brought thirteen previously unschooled travellers, ranging in age from nine to thirteen, to the school unexpectedly one morning shortly after Christmas. In the early weeks they were taught by the headteacher in a converted staffroom. There was then a period of roughly four years during which a special teacher operated a Gypsy class in the school as the children from the twenty-six-family site were gradually dispersed in small groups to several other schools in the area. Now the separate class has been abandoned, and the school takes all the five- to nine-year-olds from the site. At the junior level they are also dispersed into normal classes.

The special teacher has been replaced by a special and additional ancillary helper. The school itself is relatively new, run on progressive patterns with integrated day form of organization. The atmosphere is refreshingly friendly, and the headteacher and her staff now know the families well and are experienced in dealing with the children. Progress in the basic skills appeared at least as satisfactory if not better than elsewhere, though because the school is in a basically middle-class commuter catchment area the travellers inevitably lag behind the other children. The headteacher hopes to meet this problem by developing a special language development and literacy work unit to which all the children in the school will have access, but which will be especially useful for groups of Gypsy children.

E.T.C.—4*

One of the main aims in the school is to socialize the Gypsy children so that they can take fuller advantage of the educational system and eventually enable them to choose whether to follow the old way of life or to adopt a new one. Certainly the children seemed to fit into the school easily and to be extremely happy there. Attendance irregularity and tenancy turn-over continues to be a problem, and the school relies heavily upon the special ancillary helper, whose job includes visiting the site regularly, chasing up non-attenders and dealing with welfare problems. In fact, she is involved in many activities that one might associate with an 'educational visitor'. She provides liaison with the site warden, the pre-school play-group leader, and assists the coach driver in delivering and collecting the children to and from school. She works with the parents and encourages them to play an active role in the school. For these duties she has a special car allowance paid by the LEA, which also provides the transport for the children—an example of positive discrimination, for the site is within the three-mile limit.

The school believes that it is important that the travellers are assimilated into normal classes for many reasons: the old separate system had tended to reinforce their social isolation. They were now getting five-year-olds from the start, and very few were joining the school late at seven or eight. Attendance, which varied among families, had generally become a habit with the children, though this was far from true by the time secondary education age had been reached. Benefits were accruing from the integrated situation in the classroom: travellers were learning from non-travellers. A policy of separatism seemed no longer defensible on social grounds.

What was most impressive about the school was the genuine interest and sympathy shown by the staff to the children, and their 'unsentimental tolerance' (the headteacher's own words) of the travellers' behaviour in school. Though the assimilative policy had been operating some time, it was still seen as an experiment subject to periodic review, and account was constantly taken of the cultural difference between the travellers and the other children.[7]

A second example of primary-level assimilative dispersal is a large junior mixed and infant school in the south-east area of the Inner London Education Authority. Its catchment area contains multiple deprivation communities as well as an unusually large Gypsy site—fifty families—capable of adding up to eighty primary-age children to the roll. Unlike the previous school, this one has had wide experience with the teaching of settled children who find it difficult to learn the basic subjects and have educationally unconducive home backgrounds. The school has a nursery unit, though at the time of the visit no Gypsy children were in attendance. The school has been the base for summer projects for several years, and in these some of the Gypsies had participated. Having both infant and junior departments in the same building complex and under the same head gives advantages in terms of common methods of instruction and liaison among teachers. The site has been in existence for several generations, and, although there is a degree of tenant turn-over, the situation is much more stable than usual. A very energetic EWO, who has long experience of working at the site, plays an important role in ensuring good attendance. In general he is firm, and though there is considerable casual absenteeism, he is affectionately known on the site as 'old School Board'.

The staff of the school adopt a positive and strongly held policy of integration by dispersal into normal classes. They feel that any separate treatment is unjustifiable in the circumstances. Because the site is very close indeed, attendance well established and progress, though comparatively poor, not too far behind the norms of the school, separatism might be viewed as discrimination by both traveller parents and gauje parents, and, most important of all, there are positive advantages for all children to be mixed together. The staff are caring towards the travellers but feel that they are part of the total intake of the school, warranting as much help and attention as other children. They believe that the integrated approach works and is ethically less suspect than a separatist system, which would be extremely difficult to institute anyway.

The visit confirmed the staff's impression, and though many of the travellers were making slow progress there seemed to be no viable alternative. Attendance at the secondary level was somewhat difficult to determine, but it was generally admitted that this was far less satisfactory and that it was there that the real problems had still to be solved.

A third case study in assimilative dispersal at primary level is in the school already referred to (see page 16) in Devon where the Small and allied families have been attending since the beginning of the century. A fairly small Church of England primary school has been dispersing its Gypsy children for some years now. Most of the children come from families settled in or near the village, and are the third or fourth generation attending school. The number of children involved is very low—six to nine at any one time, spread throughout the school from reception infant class to top juniors. Seasonal absence has long since ceased to be a factor, and attendance and progress in the basic subjects is satisfactory though in general well below what is normal for settled children. The extra attention the Gypsies need is easily given without additional special staff and without special withdrawal groups. Were they to be introduced, it is hard to imagine what reaction would come from the Gypsy parents, for they have long accepted the fact that their children are treated with the same fairness and understanding as any other children. The present system works well.

Dispersal into normal classes at infant level and dispersal with withdrawal for special attention at junior level

The first example is a county primary school that serves a varied catchment area containing a suburban over-spill estate with many social and educational problems, a middle-class housing area, an old-established farm labouring community, and a ten-year-old local authority Gypsy site with poor facilities and an undistinguished aspect: it is built on an old corporation refuse tip. There tend to be intermittent unauthorized encampments in the vicinity of the site, which sometimes swells the number of travellers to above thirty. The site is within easy walking distance of the school, which has to be passed in fact by any traffic between the main road and the caravan site, which is at the end of a dead-end track. Attendance is still affected by seasonal absences, though less so than a few years ago; nevertheless it obviously makes assimilative dispersal difficult, and class teachers start the year in September with classes sometimes only three-quarters of their eventual size.

The infant department is situated in a Georgian mansion with extensive and pleasant grounds, at one corner of which is the fairly recent junior school. The school has gradually developed its spacious acreage into an adventure playground. The infant department had plentiful accommodation, and at the time of the first visit to the school a daily pre-school play group run by local volunteers was operating in one of the rooms in the building, and catered for several Gypsy children as well as a few gaujes. An old caravan donated to the school through the efforts of local Community Service Volunteers is parked in the school grounds and will shortly be reconditioned and converted into a playroom or 'home from home' for the Gypsy children and a meeting point for Gypsy parents.

In the infant department the travellers are dispersed normally into ordinary classes, though the free atmosphere allows siblings to be kept together if necessary, and several children are transferred to the junior department at a later age than is normal. Special attention is given to the travellers but in the normal classroom situation, usually not more than two or three to a class.

At the junior level where mixed-ability classes are run, the travellers are dispersed, but a system of withdrawal for intensive literacy and numeracy work operates for them. Unfortunately, the school does not have additional staffing for this, and it is only accomplished because of the devotion and enthusiasm of an experienced staff. These withdrawal classes are thought necessary because not all the junior children have had full infant schooling (there are often complete newcomers who suddenly appear), and because of almost universally low levels of attainment by the travellers, which cannot adequately be remedied in the normal classroom. The staff recognize that they are facing a very long-term educational problem and have established a close relationship with their traveller families. Part of the problem, they realize, is connected with the conditions on the site and the low morale of some of the families. The headteacher hopes to be able to create within his school an environment for the traveller children and their parents which will go some way in compensating for the site—the playroom caravan, the community atmosphere he is trying to develop. To an extent, the travellers represent an extreme but numerically small section of the school, which has also to cope with other groups of children who need extra attention and nurture. The over-all aim is to create within the school an atmosphere which will attract the travellers to participate in after-school activities and gain a sense of belonging to a wider community. During the second visit to the school there was much evidence of this: parents with prams, toddler children using the adventure playground and several traveller children at the school staying on to play football and climb on the playground equipment.

The main problems of the withdrawal group system are staffing and accommodation. During the winter, when staff illness becomes a very important factor in a school with large classes, the withdrawal group has to be suspended or taken by a sequence of different teachers. The headteacher is very aware of the problems created, realizing that withdrawal classes need to be held almost daily if they are to be effective.

What was most impressive about this school was the thoughtfulness and energy of the staff and the obviously successful attempt to create something for the travellers in addition to school 'learning'—a place which not only cared for them and welcomed them but valued their contribution to the community.

The school certainly benefits from the activities of a local Gypsy support group, which not only runs the pre-school play group but also undertakes educational welfare on the site—encouraging attendance, providing transport for families camped illegally some distance away from the site, helping with preparing the children for school (washing, clothing and so on) and attempting to set up educational projects with adults.

Infant inductive classes followed by dispersal at junior level
This is an interesting case because it points to the problems of a large site established in a remote rural area which has small village schools. The site caters for at least fifty families and has been officially open over ten years, though it was an unofficial camp as far back as 1947, for it is mentioned in one of the local school registers. The primary-age children are dispersed to several local schools, which creates a complicated transport problem.

The local school in question is a small county primary village school. It regularly receives between twenty and thirty travellers, proportionately over 40% of the total roll. The Surrey County Education Authority provides a coach to fetch and return the children from the site, which is two miles away. Even though there is a professionally run pre-school play group on the site, financed by one of the larger children's charities, the travellers come to school at age five at least a year behind the other children in terms of general intellectual and physical development. The school also receives four fairground children from a privately owned winter-quarter site, which means that roughly half the children in the school are traditional caravan dwellers.

Before 1964 a strictly segregated regime had been in operation, but the new headteacher at the time mixed the traveller and village children throughout the three age-group classes in the school (infant, infant and junior, junior). This was the situation in January 1970, when the present headmaster took over; but in September 1971, after consultations with his staff, an experimental revision of the distribution of the children throughout the school was tried because real difficulties were envisaged in view of the fortuitous preponderance of infant-age travellers. This would have produced an infant class consisting of six village children, three fairground and ten travellers, manifestly an unfortunate proposition, which was likely to cause gauje parental objection, possibly withdrawal of some to private schools, for it is a wealthy area. The new system was also thought necessary because of the difficulties of teaching mixed classes in which such a wide difference in ability and background existed.

The new system consists of a mixed traveller and village junior class (roughly twenty children aged between eight and eleven) and two parallel infant classes: a village and fairground class of twenty five- to eight-year-olds, and a traveller infant class with a slightly wider age range, some of the nine-year-old travellers being subject to delayed transfer into the junior class. (Incidentally, this was one of several cases where fairground children were socially accepted and educationally adequate in comparison with travellers.) In fact, the pattern is flexible in that transfer to the junior class may be delayed or brought forward as the case demands, and the two infant classes can be mixed for P.E., games, television, and so on, and team teaching.

It is perhaps too early to analyse whether the new system has brought all the benefits that were expected. The school has been visited twice during the project but was not seen when the former system was in operation. However, there seemed to be a very pleasant atmosphere in all the classes, and there certainly was a need for special methods and progress rates in the traveller infant class. The headteacher sent the project the following notes:

1. For the Gypsies we find that they are beginning to enjoy having a classroom of their own in a gauje world. It is their own room and everything in it is theirs. Whatever they touch they will not be distressing a sensitive gauje child who probably cares more than they do about personal possessions. The displayed material relates more to them and their way of life. The Wendy house is a 'trailer'. We find that the children are becoming increasingly aware of all this and are keeping their own room in the way they like it.
2. Their work can be more geared to their speed of learning and their much lower ability and because of this they are gaining in confidence in their work.

If one of them learns to write his name all his friends can applaud and appreciate because they all have the same problems. A similar situation in a mixed class would have inevitably produced a gauje who said: 'Cor! I could do that when I was four', which would have resulted in shattered confidence and withdrawal.
3. Very much the same can be said for the village class—work is geared to their faster speed, taking much more initial learning for granted, and a room of their own with displays suited to their way of life and needs. The bulk of water and sand play apparatus is based in the Gypsy classroom because they need it far more than the village group.
4. An advantage of this system which must be admitted to, with a little shame, is the response from village parents. In the past we admitted infants from the village aged 5 only to have them sent away a few terms later to other schools because of the Gypsies in the class causing so much disturbance to the education of the villagers. There are already signs of this stopping. Parents sending their children here now show every sign of keeping them here until middle school (1974/5) age is reached and, as the word spreads round, the village atmosphere seems to be improving.
5. Our duties are to do the best we can for all sides of the field. We are sure that everyone here is gaining more now than they did in the past. The Gypsies are getting a carefully guided education suited to their abilities. The village children are getting an education comparable to any in the county and the staff are enabled to work more efficiently than in the past. The village children in the past were really handicapped by the high proportion of Gypsies—this is a simple statement of fact—and it hardly seems fair that the village group should be asked to lose so much for the sake of questionable integration. I consider that the relationship between the two groups is happier now that they only meet at playtimes instead of all the time. I'm sure the friction is less and that, surely, is closer to integration than anything we had in the past.[8]

Separate system of classes for travellers at infant and junior levels: caravan classrooms and unattached teachers
The first example of a caravan classroom for travellers parked in a primary school is that in a Bedfordshire voluntary controlled primary school, which is thought so successful that it has been duplicated in another school in the same county. The first caravan, provided by the Gypsy Council, a 'Romano Drom' (Romany road) trailer classroom, had been used on a voluntary basis for teaching travellers when it was formerly parked in the back garden of a local traveller supporter. The LEA and the headteacher agreed to having the caravan classroom moved on to the school grounds, and it has now been equipped with electric lighting and heating at the expense of the authority. The experienced ESN teacher who had been teaching in it without pay for several months was appointed full-time to operate the project under the aegis of the headteacher, who was strongly in favour of the experiment. The National Gypsy Education Council had also been involved in the initial negotiations with the LEA, which provided special transport for the traveller

children who came from unauthorized roadside encampments in the neighbourhood of the school. The families had little previous educational experience and were thought not to be ready for integration into the normal classes in the school.

The unit caters for between twelve and sixteen children at any one time, but there have been considerable fluctuations in the roll reflecting nomadic patterns. The age range of the children varies from week to week, but the majority of the children are between seven and twelve, though five-year-olds and sixteen-year-olds have attended. In the early stages some of the children attended for only half the day, for it was confirmed that they needed carefully planned induction into regular schooling. Access to facilities in the main school, which cannot, of course, be provided in a small caravan, is free, and several of the 'regulars' have begun transfer to ordinary classes at their own request. The teacher and headmaster believe that with such children (from the roadside and not from an old-established camp site) they have developed an ideal temporary solution at a mere fraction of the cost of a conventional 'mobile classroom'. The caravan can be moved at very short notice to another school in the county if there is a major move by the traveller families. Furthermore it provides an environment which prevents claustrophobia and social trauma. The response from the parents has been encouraging, for some families continue to bring their children to the unit even though they have moved several miles away. The teacher has established a close relationship with parents and has a special travelling and time-tabling allowance to enable her to carry out the vitally necessary home visiting.

Visits to the unit during the project revealed not only warm and stimulating personal relationships in the caravan but also significantly more culturally based materials and activities than were seen elsewhere. The co-operation between the voluntary and statutory bodies concerned was perhaps the most impressive aspect.

The experiment obviously had the advantages of the services of a skilful and trained ESN teacher with a thorough grounding in early literacy work. By having the classroom in the grounds of a school, both the teacher and her travellers felt part of the school community and did not seem in any way alienated or socially divided from the gauje classes. The families felt that they were welcome in school: indeed, they had been invited to attend in the first place.

A similar unit was visited during the project in north-western Somerset. In this case two schools were involved, and the solution was the pragmatic reponse of the LEA to an urgent call from the respective headteachers who were trying to cope with a sudden influx of roadside travellers in the middle of a school year, the influx being proportionately large because the two schools were small and had small staffs.

The county already had a team of experienced peripatetic remedial teachers and a pool of caravan classrooms. A peripatetic teacher was allocated to spend half his time in each school, and the caravan was parked in one of the two schools. The schools serve rural communities in which there are families with children who require almost as much special attention as the travellers. The remedial teacher takes mixed traveller and gauje withdrawal groups for intensive literacy work. There seemed to be little attempt in comparison with the Bedfordshire experiment to incorporate traveller heritage and culture into the teaching, but it seemed not to have a deleterious effect upon their progress: many were learning to read quickly and were obviously very happy to be in school.

Another example of a separate all-age traveller unit at primary level but in a normal classroom rather than in a caravan was seen during a visit to Wigan. A temporary site—built on the foundations of a former slaughter-house, surrounded by tips and deep sunken areas full of stagnant water and rotting car hulks, rat-infested and swarming with blue-bottles in summer—had been opened by the council the previous year. The area is a fast declining city centre, and the local primary schools were in the process of being run down and were shortly to be replaced by a new open-plan school. Because there were staffing difficulties at the infant school, all the traveller children went to the junior school. After a short period of attempted assimilation into normal classes, the LEA appointed a special teacher and an assistant to operate an all-age traveller class divided into two groups (five- to eight-year-olds, nine- to seventeen-year-olds) taken in two interconnecting classrooms which were no longer needed by the junior school because of its rapidly decreasing roll.

With approximately twenty children in all, the teachers have their work cut out and are frequently helped by the headteacher. The class was also assisted in the term before the visit by a college of education student on teaching practice. The staff and the LEA are experienced at dealing with children exhibiting Plowden priority needs, but realize that their travellers presented problems which could not be met in the normal ways. In this situation it is possible to retain sibling and kinship relationships and integrate an educational programme for all the travellers to prepare them for school attendance in a conventional manner when the new building is open. Though the LEA views this experiment as a temporary inductive measure, it is recognized that this might be a multi-generation problem.

On-site extension classrooms
Several examples were found of teachers within a school undertaking teaching of travellers on caravan sites where there was a community building. One such example was seen at a Hertfordshire site, which has recently been opened and where a pre-school play group shared one of the community rooms with

a teacher from a nearby primary school who held preparatory classes for the school-age children. The reason for the adoption of this system was expediency rather than specific educational innovation: the families were not prepared to send their children down a country lane to the school, because the lane carried a rush-hour traffic of such proportions that it was obvious that the children were in danger. Plans to divert the traffic and make the lane part of a one-way system were being made, but as a temporary measure the teachers were released from normal duties at school on a rota basis to hold afternoon classes on the site. This obviously gave the teachers, who would eventually receive the children in school, time to prepare the children for this and also to understand their social and family backgrounds.

SUMMARY OF METHODS OF ORGANIZATION AT PRIMARY LEVEL

It is apparent from these case studies that the longer a site has been open and the greater the educational experience of the children, the easier it is to facilitate dispersal into normal classes at the primary levels. Nearly every headteacher, however, stressed that without extra staffing and accommodation little could be successfully achieved without serious loss of attention to the non-traveller children in the school and the likelihood of putting too great a strain on existing staff. There was universal agreement that the attendance of travellers, especially from newly opened sites or from the roadside, created enormous pressures for the school. Few teachers were absolutely satisfied with the methods they were operating, and there was a general impression that most schools were perpetually reviewing their organization of classes, regardless of whether there were travellers in attendance or not. In this healthy but slightly unstable situation, the arrival of travellers sometimes worked to the advantage of a school, for LEAs which had delayed expenditure on additional facilities for the school frequently showed a readiness to respond quickly to the call for immediate help when the travellers arrived. Sometimes facilities provided initially for the travellers became available for other children in the school.

It must be emphasized that this collection of case studies gives an unbalanced view of present educational provision for travellers at primary level: the great majority of schools deal with their influx by normal dispersal to classes throughout the school. Yet it must be understood also that most of the schools selected for visits had had several years of experience with traveller children, had passed beyond the phase of separate inductive education and were dealing with children from atypically sedentary and socially accepted families. In general, withdrawal groups and separate classes were most common at junior age levels.

Secondary level

It must first be admitted that more traveller children of secondary age were seen in primary schools than in secondary schools during visits undertaken during the project and that the great majority of travellers who were attending secondary schools were from well-settled, often housed Gypsy families and tended to have had primary education beforehand. It was so common to find that secondary attendance fell short of expectations—even of primary head-teachers who had sent many children on to the secondary school—that the total LEA survey figure of 622 secondary-age travellers attending, or at least appearing on the rolls of secondary schools (see pages 24–5), began to be questioned seriously.

Lack of motivation to attend at secondary level and (in gauje terms) pre-mature involvement in the family economy is partly the explanation, but blame must also be attached to, and is often admitted by, the secondary school itself. It is, after all, a more depersonalized institution compared with the family atmosphere of the primary school—and when it comes to school attendance for travellers, nothing is more important than personal relationships and a welcoming atmosphere. In several schools visited, indi-vidual members of staff—the remedial teacher, for instance—were directly responsible for attendance regularity. When that member of staff was ill or otherwise absent from school the travellers tended to absent themselves too. It is far more difficult for a secondary teacher to establish a close personal relationship with individual children, because he sees a succession of different classes, unlike the primary teacher, who tends to have the same class all day and every day. The size of secondary schools and the complexity of their buildings are further factors which may keep travellers away; their play-grounds are also rougher places, and gauje children more likely to be actively anti-Gypsy than at primary level, where hardened social attitudes are rare. But perhaps the most important factor is one of curriculum: most travellers would consider that the secondary school offers little of relevance to their older children. And in spite of what one headmaster described as the school's 'strong and steady unrelenting policy on attendance', traveller parents' traditional attitudes are most likely to prevail.

Yet in certain cases secondary schools have been able to achieve attendance rates in the upper 90% level and have even managed to attract some of the travellers over the school-leaving age. The factors which seem to be present in all these cases are important to distinguish: the children either come from well-to-do housed families or from permanent sites, where paradoxically there may be widespread traveller unemployment; there is an exceptional headteacher or remedial teacher who is a frequent site visitor; and within the school there is a genuine effort to give special consideration and, if necessary, make special provision for the travellers, which includes an emphasis on pastoral care.

There is generally a narrow range of organization at secondary as compared to primary level. The main methods include:

(a) Normal class dispersal.
(b) Dispersal with substantial remedial withdrawal group lessons.
(c) Attachment of all traveller children to one teacher—normally the remedial English expert ('I always have the two travellers sitting with me at the table in front of the class').
(d) The creation of a special traveller/remedial unit within the school.
(e) Withdrawal with extra assistance from the Schools Psychological Service or a peripatetic expert.

Rather more children were discovered to have been placed in special schools than was indicated by the LEA survey. There were mixed feelings about this amongst parents of such children; however it was an aspect of traveller education that was to a large extent neglected during the project.

CASE STUDIES

Normal class allocation at secondary level
The school in question receives around thirty-six traveller children (10% of its total roll), most of whom are housed or have been housed by the local authority. Only one family involved lives in a caravan, on a temporary (probably unauthorized) site. The rest are strictly Gypsies rather than travellers; most have had full primary education though a few were still 'totally illiterate'; attendance averages 70%.

The headmaster has de-streamed the school, though the children are divided into sets for 40% of the day, with the result that the Gypsies almost invariably find their way to the lowest sets. Some of them are 'retarded' educationally and receive special attention from remedial teachers, but most participate in ordinary classes and subjects. The headteacher occasionally allows the Gypsies to devote extra time to practical projects—building spectator seats overlooking the sports field, for instance. He also finds that the boys are particularly adept at motor mechanics and that several members of his staff have been given free diagnostic inspections—'Your tappets are over tightened up, Miss'. In general the children seemed happy in the school on the evidence of a short visit and a discussion with a vociferous group of them in the headmaster's study. They were certainly prepared to voice and discuss opinions about the Caravan Sites Act and whether they wanted to travel when they got married (most did).

For all their apparent assimilation into the school, the headteacher was well aware that they created special curriculum problems in his school. He wrote in a letter to the project:

My previous experience with Indians, Maoris and Backwoodsmen in New Zealand has helped me to tune in sympathetically to the gypsies.

It seems to me that if schools are not very careful they either harden or create something similar to the adversary sub-culture that Hargreaves writes about in *Social Relations in a Secondary School.*

I am aware of different value standards sincerely held and a rather touching willingness with some of these gypsy children to confide once their suspicions have been lulled. They speak of being disliked. They also talk of much violence in their own upbringing.

Sensing that the traveller children have a need to confide and discuss their own place in society and their heritage, the headmaster makes time to see them often, without gauje children present. He believes that these sessions have a value over and above their shortness of duration, for few traveller children will use education as a stepping-stone to trades and careers other than those followed by their parents.

Substantial periods of remedial class withdrawal
The second secondary case study is of a school quite near to the previous one but serving a well-established local authority caravan site. Several of the families are housed nearby, and in all there are between twelve and fifteen travellers and Gypsies in the school (a little over 2% of the roll). The children fall into two groups: those who are in the lower streams but not in desperate need of remedial attention, and those who clearly are in need. The latter group spend the majority of their time with two remedial teachers (a married couple) in a terrapin mobile classroom unit which is well equipped especially with teacher-prepared remedial English and number games. There are many other children in the school doing remedial work, who join what amounts to a special Gypsy class intermittently throughout the day. The Gypsy boys also go to metal-craft and woodwork classes, and they participate in games, swimming and P.E. The girls go to needlework classes, not always enjoyed, and to some other classes but are not especially keen on games and P.E. The remedial teachers remarked upon a tendency, not reported elsewhere, for attendance to decline sharply amongst the girls after thirteen years of age, and thought that this was sometimes because they were sent to live with grandparents or uncles and aunts in other districts. Both teachers have established close relationships with the families on the site and invite the children to their own homes.

Perhaps the most successful innovation found in this school was the involvement of the Gypsy secondary pupils in a project to set up a play group in the remedial classroom for their younger siblings and cousins between 3:00 and 4:00 P.M. Fortuitously, the infant school serving the site is situated on the same campus as the secondary school, and the Gypsy infants are released a little early so that they can join the remedial class before being escorted home to the site. The older children prepare word games and stories for reading and telling in the early part of the afternoon. This creates the family learning situations with which the children are most familiar, and establishes the concept of education independent from school and teachers—something which was of great interest to the project.

It is hoped that this will eventually be integrated with a child-care course run within the school and that the Gypsy girls will actively participate in a pre-school play group in the village, perhaps bringing the under-fives from the site.

An ESN-traveller unit with a specially trained teacher in a comprehensive school
This school receives around fifteen traveller children from a local authority site that has been open seven years. The school also serves a large London over-spill housing estate, deep into Kent. There is an abnormally high incidence of educational subnormality amongst the gauje children in the school and insufficient special school places locally to cater for all of them. After considerable difficulties both with these children and the Gypsies, the LEA set up a special ESN/traveller unit within the school under an ESN trained teacher with an extensive knowledge of travellers—in fact coming from Gypsy stock himself.

Most of the Gypsies had had full primary experience, but with a few exceptions remained illiterate or severely sub-literate. The unit had been in operation nearly three years when it was visited. By this time several of the Gypsies had been integrated back into normal classrooms, and one would have been head boy had he stayed on after the age of sixteen. The rest, however, were still in the ESN unit with six to eight gauje children with different but equally severe learning problems. The teacher devoted considerable time to site visits, frequently with his class in school time. He had established close relations with parents and reported regularly to them on their children's progress; this enabled him to investigate absenteeism and to distinguish between absence with parental approval and truancy.

Outdoor activities played a major part in a carefully planned and structured programme—though a casual observer would not necessarily have gained much sense of this unless experienced in unconventional approaches to re-medial and ESN teaching.

Although there were the usual interdepartmental jealousies and suspicions towards a unit with such freedom, the benefits to the whole school were by no means limited to taking apparently maladjusted and retarded Gypsy and gauje children off the hands of class and subject teachers. The impact was deeper than that: every child in the school received diagnostic testing for learning difficulties; sociometric studies had become routine, and in general remedial methods in the teaching of English throughout the school were professional. If there was a criticism—and it was one of which the teacher was aware—it was that some of the Gypsy children did not want to leave the special unit and would stop making progress if it was believed that transfer into normal classes was imminent. However, it was noticeable that the families on the site, an unprepossessing one at the time, were to some extent problem families with a low general morale—their children exhibiting symptoms of actual maladjustment as well as those directly linked to the trauma of site-settlement and transition from roadside economies.

Though the original ESN teacher has now left, the unit was still functioning along the same lines on the last inquiry to the school.

One of the annual problems that the previous teacher had tried to solve was the seasonal absence of several of the families who still participate in fruit picking, especially in May and June. He had attempted to continue contact with the children by visiting them on the farms and giving them work to do. Unfortunately, different families went to different farms, and there was considerable movement from farm to farm; besides, the children were picking fruit and tended to consider it as a break from the dull routine of site life and regular school attendance. The teacher could maintain contact with most of his pupils only intermittently and only by accumulating a very considerable mileage in his car. It is not known whether this practice has been continued by his successor.

SUMMARY OF METHODS OF ORGANIZATION
AT SECONDARY LEVEL

There is a striking correlation between attendance at secondary level and the degree of permanent settlement and housing. Methods of organization at secondary level are more limited than at primary level, and most travellers who have either been late starters or made little progress during their primary years end up in the remedial streams. Their general lack of educational motivation at secondary level can to some extent be offset by special remedial class treatment under a sympathetic and skilful teacher—but only partly so.

Whereas at primary level all kinds of methods can be devised to ease the introduction of the traveller child into the maintained system, at the other end of the period of schooling virtually no thought has been given to devising ways of easing the traveller out of the system. In other words, bridges can be provided to get the child into the primary school, but by the time the child has become an adolescent he has become a reluctant passenger in the secondary school and tends to find his own solution by escaping suddenly back into the life he is accustomed to and has wanted to return to all along. The expenditure of effort to socialize the child into school has largely been wasted. If it is thought that the traveller child should be schooled, then it is felt that the most important area of all for development and innovation is at the 13+ age level. This is the perennial problem of the secondary level of education and, of course, is applicable to a good many gauje children—the 'secondary failures'. But in the case of the traveller one is seeing the problem in an extreme form. It can occur even at the top of the junior school, as one head-teacher from a Teesside primary school reported:

One interesting fact that has come to light 2 or 3 times is when a boy has reached the age of 11, he is then a 'man' and therefore leaves school the day before the end of the summer term. This last happened 2 years ago. The boy had been with us for 2 or 3 years for 5 or 6 months a year. He was popular and fond of school. He informed the class teacher he was leaving, thanked her and gave her a present and bid farewell to the class. From then on (he is 13 now and I still see him regularly) he has helped his father in the business (scrap and ponies).

What should I have done with this child/man? Should I have chased him up to come back to school? (His brother and sisters were still with me.)

I didn't—in their life he was a man. I respect their life.

If I had chased the boy—the family would just have moved on and I would have lost the lot—or rather they would have lost their schooling.

He could neither read nor write but he is a grand lad, far older than his years.

One factor which proved constant in determining the success of whatever form of organization was adopted was a teacher attitude which was sympathetic and friendly. Travellers who know that their children will be welcomed in school and that there is someone there whom they can trust, *in loco parentis*—that, in fact, the teachers have their children's best interests at heart—will approve of any method of organization.

Special measures in the maintained sector

One of the most important conclusions that can be drawn from the head-teachers' questionnaire and the project's visits to schools is that—as with immigrants but with travellers perhaps more so—traveller attendance puts additional stress upon the resources of a school. This stress is disproportionate to the numerical strength of the traveller intake. It is felt at every level in the school: staffing, administration, accommodation, capitation allowance, welfare and health, catering and playground supervision, EWO and other allied services, and, not least, by the other children in the school.[9]

Nearly all headteachers in schools with a significant traveller intake would agree on the need for the following special measures and allowances:

(a) *Staffing and ancillary help:* there was a general consensus that at least one teacher and perhaps one ancillary helper in addition was needed for every fifteen traveller children.

(b) *Accommodation:* the need for additional classroom or remedial withdrawal group accommodation is universal even in schools aiming at assimilation. (Seasonal attendance patterns were confirmed still to exist by 65% of the questionnaire returns and this necessitates careful planning in advance; few headteachers can predict accurately in September the numbers of traveller children likely to arrive in late October.)

(c) *Administration:* the problems caused by irregular or seasonal attendance patterns, social problems and the need for liaison with welfare and social service officers put a considerable additional burden on the school administration.

(d) *Capitation allowance:* it was widely believed that travellers' demands upon raw materials (paper, paints, writing implements and so on) and upon pre-reading equipment, which a junior or secondary school might not possess at all, virtually doubled *per capita* consumption of stock. Absence of suitable reading matter necessitates the production of teacher-prepared materials which are also costly.

(e) *Transport:* paradoxically perhaps, travellers need positive discrimination with transport. Car allowances for teachers who undertake regular site visits may also be necessary.

(f) *Welfare and health:* this depends upon the families, but in general travellers make considerable demands upon the school in terms of free meals, clothing grants, medical inspection, routine hygiene, sometimes (especially in cases of poor sites or unauthorized encampments) washing facilities. Some LEAs arranged weekly medical clinics in the school.

(g) *Liaison:* under this broad sub-heading there is a wide range of needs. Liaison is needed among schools of different age levels receiving siblings and cousins, for the transfer of records and to establish continuity of methods with the seasonal attender. It is also required among schools affected by multiple attendance by the same children (sometimes in different LEAs), and there must be liaison with EWOs, social services, site wardens and managers and with voluntary bodies working with travellers. These extra liaison needs create further administrative burdens which, in a small school, have to be time-tabled.

On many of these points LEAs had shown generosity, but there were several schools which had to improvise short-cuts and devise measures for sharing the additional work amongst staff and ancillary helpers. During the course of the programme of visits to schools, an admiration was felt for the ingenuity with which the teaching profession was endowed in being able to convert broom-cupboards into language laboratories and train caretakers and coach drivers into teachers' helpers. There was a sense of urgency and enthusiasm in many schools which might, in fact, not have existed had purpose-built accommodation been miraculously provided overnight. However, no staff can sustain such a sense of urgency and enthusiasm without something giving —usually the health of the teachers.

Special measures to compensate the school as well as the traveller pupils are obviously a priority, and this is true whether 'segregation' or 'integration' is the dominant policy.

Recent and planned innovations

During the latter stages of the project several experiments were being introduced or in the early planning stages. Though it would be unwise to attempt any actual assessment, some are obviously important and of value, as they might well multiply as pilot ventures.

AN ALL-AGE SEPARATE SCHOOL FOR TRAVELLER CHILDREN

A pioneer project for a group of very traditional Gypsies camped by the roadside in the Woodmansey area of the East Riding of Yorkshire has been established by the LEA. It is accommodated in a large hut rented from a local youth club. The hut is set in an open field, which affords considerable use of the outdoors. Three full-time teachers, an ancillary helper and a peripatetic headteacher have been appointed. This staff is supplemented by teachers in local schools released by rota. Voluntary helpers are also involved and are drawn in from a locally based Gypsy support group, which was instrumental in making the first social and educational contact with the travellers during a successful summer school programme in 1971.[10] In fact the leading teacher on the staff of the school was involved in this before she was appointed officially to that of the new experimental unit.

It caters for anything up to thirty travellers aged from five to thirteen. Over half of the families concerned still live in horse-drawn wagons, and in the past have led a very sheltered and 'old-style' life with little or no contact with gauje society other than in their economic capacity as general dealers, mostly in scrap metal. They are fairly nomadic, wintering around Hull and during the summer months gradually moving southwards eventually, some as far as the Wisbech area of Cambridgeshire. It is hoped that the staff can follow the families when they start their southerly migration: there is a caravan–classroom available, and the LEA hopes to provide a towing vehicle. With five or six staff at any one time the unit has a very favourable staffing ratio (one to five), but this is needed, for the children display patterns of behaviour and learning difficulties as extreme as any travellers seen elsewhere. Though similarly traditional families may be found in many other parts of the country—even in the Black Country where 'flash' trailer-caravans have become almost the norm—this particular group is well known as one that has altered very little in this century.

The LEA's aim is to provide a viable inductive or preparatory education before normal school attendance and class assimilation is introduced—thought to be at least five years into the future. Though this is the LEA view, some of the teachers expressed their doubts about the advisability of normal assimilation even if they could succeed in socializing the children and bringing up their standards of attainment in the basic skills to a sufficiently high level to warrant class dispersal. However they were hoping that relationships with local schools could be developed further, which would mean access to better facilities and a feeling of being part of the mainstream of the educational system.

The school began operating on a full-day basis, but this was soon curtailed to a morning session only, the LEA coach picking the children up from their roadside camps at 10:15, school dinners being provided at 12:30 and the coach returning the children home at 1:15. The afternoon is not wasted, for home visits are made and materials prepared for the next day. Recently the session has been extended into the afternoon.

The school—'special class', rather—is a pioneer venture that could never have been contemplated but for the activities of the support group, which broke down the barriers of suspicion and fear that education would be used as a means of moving the families on or exposing the children to gaujes and the gauje world in an attempt to make them change their ways. The response from the travellers has been very encouraging, and regularity of attendance is better than in many schools visited during the project.

The high staffing ratio makes the unit a costly one but there has been minimal capital expenditure: the premises are rented. This enables the project to be very flexible, and if the families move to a new location twenty miles away the LEA can rent alternative accommodation nearby.

USING SECTIONS 39·3 AND 56 OF THE 1944 EDUCATION ACT

The 1944 Education Act makes it the duty of a parent of every child of compulsory school age to 'cause him to receive efficient full-time education suitable to his age, ability and aptitude, either by regular attendance at school or otherwise' (section 36). There is a similar responsibility upon LEAs to provide facilities for such suitable education and to bring proceedings under clause 39 against parents not fulfilling their duties. However, sub-section 3 provides a loophole for itinerant parents and LEAs. It is worth quoting the relevant passage, though for the purposes of clarity the complexities involving children of 'no fixed abode' and the walking distance from school, paragraph (c), have been removed:

39·3. Where in any proceedings for an offence against this section . . . the parent proves that he is engaged in any trade or business of such a nature as to require him to travel from place to place and that the child has attended at a school at which he was a registered pupil as regularly as the nature of the trade or business of the parent permits, the parent shall be acquitted . . . providing that, in the case of a child who has attained the age of six years, the parent shall not be entitled to be acquitted under this subsection unless he proves that the child has made at least two hundred attendances during the period of twelve months ending with the date on which the proceedings were instituted.[11]

This clause, which extended the implications of section 50 of the 1921 Education Act to nomadic children other than bargees (the group for which it was originally intended to apply), has rarely been invoked in recent proceedings, though several LEA officers met during the project said that the clause had been taken into account in deciding on a policy of not enforcing section 39. This clause, however, is obviously applicable to families who continue to resort to a series of unauthorized encampments or who are moving from one permanent site to another frequently during any year. The 'no fixed abode' exemption is difficult to define anyway but is not an essential part of the substance of the 'two hundred attendances' specification for itinerants.

The application of this clause seems to have had virtually no effect in the past and is largely ignored now in England and Wales. In Scotland, where it is invoked much more frequently, it may account for the fact that 42% of the children recorded in the March census in Scotland in 1969 were claimed to be attending school—though it is not clear who 'claimed' this and whether attendance was regular; and, of course, a large number of families recorded in the second census in August were absent from the March data on which the 42% attendance is based.[12]

Clause 39·3 is a negative rather than a positive justification for a special policy: it defines the legal minimum sessions for attendance (half that imposed for the host community's children). Besides, the real aim should not be strict application of educational statutes, but the best and most efficient education provision that can be made. Nevertheless, it may prove a very useful legal basis from which to operate.

The relevance of section 56 is perhaps a more profitable one, for it enables an LEA to make provision other than in school and also for less than the normal academic year:

56. *Power to provide primary and secondary education otherwise than at school.* If a local authority are satisfied that by reason of any extraordinary circumstances a child or young person is unable to attend a suitable school for the purpose of receiving primary or secondary education, they shall have power [with the approval of the Secretary of State] to make special arrangements for him to receive education otherwise than at school, being primary or secondary education, as the case may require, or, if the authority are satisfied that it is impracticable for him to receive full-time education [and the Secretary of State approves], education similar in other respects but less than full-time.

The importance of this clause is partly the concept of *suitable* education, which cannot be provided within normal schools, being made available in the form of special arrangements. According to Taylor and Saunders' footnote (c), the *Manual of Guidance, Special Services No. 1* recommends that 'the amount of individual tuition given should not normally exceed five sessions per week' (page 172 of *The New Education Act*, 1971 edition).

It is therefore possible for a local authority to formulate an educational policy for primary- or secondary-aged travellers based upon the principles outlined in clause 56. In fact such provision is not much different from that system applied for immigrant induction centres or physically handicapped children who attend normal school but are released part-time to attend specialist therapeutic centres.

Briefly, the clause could enable a secondary- or primary-aged traveller boy, for instance, to be released from school attendance on several days each week (or on a block, say on a two- to three-week basis) to receive industrial training in the company of a parent or uncle, by actual participation in scrap dealing or car breaking. Though this may give rise to administrative difficulties within a school unaccustomed to such innovation, the children would need intensive literacy work and could be attached to the remedial English teacher whenever in school.

This programme would create an important precedent which involves the admission that an area of vocational training cannot be supplied by the LEA within its schools—there is no one capable of teaching it—and would be expedient because this is what happens anyway when the economic needs of the family clash with attendance. Several LEAs already encourage work experience projects and need not look further for a justification for extending it to travellers.

A PLAN FOR AN EXTENSION CLASSROOM ON A SITE

Though not yet put into practice, similar solution was proposed for one of Cheshire's first Gypsy sites. Long before the site was built, the County Education Committee called a joint meeting in a local primary school of its staff and governors, representatives of other council departments and LEA officers. The purpose of the meeting was to decide how to cope with an expected influx of twenty travellers into a new but already crowded building.

The village is situated on one of the major traveller migration routes followed by many of the Irish families bound for the Midlands. There is also an indigenous Gypsy traveller population of rather traditional life style. A previous experience of having two Gypsy children at the school had persuaded the headteacher that special measures and facilities would be needed.

Various solutions to the problems were debated, but the most favoured one (which was later adopted at a governors' meeting) involved the building of an additional classroom and 'quiet' dual-purpose corridor area in the school itself, and the development on the site of an extension classroom unit. This on-site unit was to be serviced by a specially appointed teacher and an ancillary helper but with a flexible brief to hold tuition groups both in the school and the site classroom and to establish on the site a parent counselling system. These plans are most interesting as well as realistic, and represent a pioneer plan in educational provision for transit families.

PLAN FOR A JOINT LEA SUPERVISOR FOR FIVE AUTHORITIES, TO BE RESPONSIBLE FOR TRAVELLER EDUCATION

Recently an application has been made by one LEA for Urban Aid on behalf of itself and four others in the West Midlands area, and the Home Office has agreed to the grant for a five-year period. The five county boroughs involved have a 'floating' traveller population of around 300 families (obviously likely to be drastically reduced if each provides a site and is granted designation under the 1968 Caravan Sites Act); thus they have the highest density of travellers per square mile anywhere in the country. In the past the authorities have operated an 'open-door' school policy for travellers but have not made many attempts to encourage unofficially encamped families to attend. This policy has palpably failed to attract school attenders, and it is hoped that the creation of the new post of supervisor will have a dramatic effect. Each LEA reserves the right to make its own policy decisions about traveller education and is responsible for providing accommodation and staff; but the supervisor will help to co-ordinate the whole operation, especially in cases where the families concerned move regularly among the boroughs and can therefore be designated as 'pool' families.

The officer appointed (September 1973) has suggested an over-all plan which includes a systematic record-keeping centre based in the Wolverhampton Education Offices, the acquisition of some fifteen to twenty specially designed mobile classroom units, the appointment of about thirty teachers, and a policy of providing for traveller children in local schools. The mobile units, each served by two of the teachers, will be based at chosen schools and will accommodate both the travellers and a proportion of the remedial gauje children already in the school, thus ensuring mixing of travellers and gaujes at the earliest opportunity and benefiting the school generally. Further details of the record-keeping centre are given in Appendix B, see pages 186–90.

The role of the independent schools

The contribution of the independent sector in the education of traveller children has been a major factor over the last five years. Their importance has been not only in focusing attention on to the problems and helping to initiate attendance in maintained schools, but they have also succeeded in actual provision of education and innovatory practice which may be capable of multiplication in maintained schools. Their contributions may be summarized in these areas of education: on-site pre-schooling (sometimes for children of *all* ages); summer school programmes; mobile educational units ('schools on wheels'); educational visiting; adult education and community development projects; and national and regional co-ordination.

ON-SITE PRE-SCHOOLING

There are now more than a dozen voluntarily run play groups and pre-school education units established on permanent caravan sites throughout the country. It would therefore be unfair to single out any particular one for description. To call many of them play groups at all is somewhat less than fair, because in many cases they operate almost full-time (as nursery schools), have qualified teachers, are run with considerable professionalism, and do far more than play. Various charitable organizations have provided the finances: the Church of England Children's Society, the Save the Children Fund, and Rowntree. Certain individuals have played important roles: Yul Brynner, Barbara Cartland. One unit in particular has been based on Montessori methods, which have an obvious application to travellers especially in the early perceptual training stages. Many of them have been generously supported by LEAs and local schools and in several cases operate in buildings provided by the local authority.

What is interesting is that the same problems tend to be experienced as in maintained schools—irregular attendance, family orientation, initial apprehension and so on. Nevertheless, they have established the importance of the early years in the socialization and preparation of young children for later schooling.

The main contribution of these units has been in discovering that travellers do respond well to educational opportunities that are relevant and protective. The fact that many of the teaching sessions have to be extended after 4:00 P.M., because the school-aged attenders return from school still demanding more and with plenty of energy in reserve to take advantage of it, is symptomatic of a genuine motivation. A further factor which has been discovered is that there is a similar need amongst adults and teenagers—one which cannot be met at this stage by school attendance or night schools in further education establishments. It can be met only by very sensitive and individualized home tuition.

SUMMER SCHOOL PROGRAMMES

The last few years have seen the development of summer projects for many groups of children. For travellers, who may enter school late, be casually and seasonally absent and withdraw prematurely, they have an urgent relevance —as has been shown by American programmes in education for migrant Mexican agricultural labourers' children.

Especially in the case of the unauthorized camper and the traveller who misses substantial periods of schooling because of nomadism, summer schools may not need to have the recreational element that characterizes those for gauje children. There are signs that travellers expect intensive literacy teaching and more formal approaches; for them it might well be a fourth term in the year rather than a holiday adventure scheme.

In 1971, the summer schools co-ordinated by the National Gypsy Education Council reached well over 600 traveller children—a considerable achievement for the first year of such programmes.[13] Though limited mostly to a duration of two weeks, these summer projects had a significantly beneficial effect upon school attendance subsequently. They were instrumental in several areas in persuading LEAs that active intervention in encouraging travellers to go to maintained schools was rewarding if done with understanding and compassion. Subsequent summer schools have continued to have these beneficial effects.

MOBILE EDUCATIONAL UNITS

The concept of the 'school on wheels' that can be driven on to sites and to traveller halts, where normal school attendance is impracticable or undesirable for a variety of reasons, is by no means unique, but it does have a logical relevance. The floating barge school, the Dutch fairground mobile school (double-decker bus towing double-decker trailer), various 'play-mobiles' in Harlem and Liverpool, for instance, provide precedents. There are now several such units operating in England and Wales, though the major example is West Midlands Travellers School financed by the Bernard van Leer Foundation.[14]

Unfortunately, there are problems which make such mobile units of questionable value if they are regarded as substitutes for full-time education by attendance at school. Firstly, they tend to be small for the job (a floor space of 16 feet by 7 feet) and may necessitate the adoption of rigid disciplinary control, which is as much in conflict with traveller heritage as normal school regimes (sometimes more so). Secondly, when operating on large sites, teachers in such units may have to adopt strategies that cut across family and kinship patterns. Thirdly, the aim of providing continuity by following individual families from one unauthorized encampment to another can easily break down if too many families are involved. Teachers can become over-stretched and over-worked when operating nomadically, and, of course, the school on wheels cannot be on more than one encampment at any one time.

However, schools on wheels have an enormous potential in initiating traveller education for families who are migrant over a limited distance. They are also potentially valuable as an agent of educational propaganda—just as a touring theatre company promotes an interest in drama.

EDUCATIONAL VISITORS

This propagandist role can also be fulfilled by a highly mobile teacher or educational visitor—part EWO, part peripatetic teacher with access to classrooms in the maintained sector, part home tutor for families rather than individuals, and mobilizer of statutory and voluntary resources. Such a role has been developed by the Church of Scotland Socio-Educational project in Perthshire (again financed by the van Leer Foundation).[15] Although the main virtue of such a person would be to work from within the family context, he can also help to bring about a much-needed liaison between schools affected by multiple attendance, and between local schools catering for children from the same family, and can aid in the transfer of children from primary to secondary level.

To some extent, the Advisory Committee on the Education of Romanies and other Travellers has developed such a propagandist in its field officer, but here the role includes that of instigator and adviser to LEAs on a national level.

ADULT EDUCATION AND COMMUNITY DEVELOPMENT PROJECTS

One of the major discoveries of the independent sector has been the demand for literacy amongst adolescent and adult travellers. On some of the better managed local authority sites wardens respond to this themselves or make private arrangements for volunteers to offer home tuition. Some local authorities have toyed with the idea of appointing a 'tutor warden' rather than a 'social worker warden'—in other words, someone who becomes more involved in teaching and explaining rather than casework itself.

To date, only one summer school programme has been specifically designed for adults—the project (with an Urban Aid grant) at West Bromwich in 1972 which also involved the appointment of a part-time WEA tutor.[16] The project was observed to be working reasonably well, but more contact was made with women than with men (though this might be explained by the personnel of the project and their approach rather than any theory about traveller women wanting literacy more than the menfolk). Work undertaken in Kent by support group volunteers would suggest that it *is* the men rather than the women who want literacy, for only the men took part in an unprecedented evening class at a local further education establishment, which ran for several weeks.

Working with adults is not easy and can be undertaken only on the students' own terms, for it is, of course, voluntary. An attempt by some community service volunteers to develop traditional Gypsy crafts as a communal economic activity amongst travellers near Orpington foundered because no account was taken of family patterns of economic competition. It is unwise to try to foster community development in the wider sense too quickly; this can only grow out of a sustained social contact with individual families.

NATIONAL AND REGIONAL CO-ORDINATION

One of the needs expressed by many headteachers in maintained schools was that of creating communication channels between teachers in different

E.T.C.—5

schools and between different LEAs catering for the same children but at varying times of the year. The West Midlands Gypsy Education Supervisor whose purpose is to co-ordinate and initiate on a regional level could obviously be duplicated elsewhere. If this was accomplished then there would be a network of regional supervisors which might make the creation of a central advisory or planning body unnecessary. However unprecedented such a central body might be—the only comparable body would be that operating in the Department of Defence for service children being educated abroad— there might still be a justification for it. Especially in terms of evaluation of good practice and in the unification of systems of record keeping a central national body would ultimately pay dividends.

At present the voluntary bodies exercise a certain amount of national co-ordination but, while their value should not be under-estimated, internal conflicts[17] and the non-statutory influence any voluntary body can wield, which is necessarily of a very limited kind, prevent them being an adequate substitute for an official body. Both the National Gypsy Education Council and the Advisory Committee on the Education of Romanies and other Travellers organize summer school programmes, and training conferences, and issue publications of value to teachers. But the major role has been the appointment of a national field development officer, initially by the former organization and at present by the latter, who has been able to instigate LEA action and influence the type of programmes the LEAs devise.

The establishment of regional and central co-ordinating bodies might be viewed as a priority, not least because travellers constitute only a regionally significant group of LEA pool children and because their numbers in each locality are so small as to make responsibility for them a very minor and peripheral job of existing LEA officers and advisers. Teachers cannot be expected to assume co-ordinating roles and are in great need of the support and information that would result from personnel with a full-time regional responsibility for Gypsy children.

One lesson that can be drawn from the voluntary national bodies' work in the field is the need to involve travellers themselves. This could be achieved either by appointing travellers as welfare assistants attached to officials or by paying expenses to travellers who become involved in work on behalf of LEAs.

The concept of a national body or system of regional co-ordinating bodies responsible for supervising the education of travellers is to some extent one that may strike educational administrators as alien to our system, yet the precedent has been set by the West Midlands conurbation LEAs (see above). The only other model which can be cited is that which operates for children of the armed forces serving abroad. The NGEC, however, has shown that there is a need for such an agency, and perhaps a feasible system could be established.

Notes and references

1 H. E. R. Townsend and E. M. Brittan, *Organization in Multiracial Schools* (Slough: National Foundation for Educational Research, 1972), p. 137.

2 Ibid., p. 39.

3 A. Harry Passow, Miriam Goldberg, Abraham J. Tannenbaum, eds, *Education of the Disadvantaged* (New York: Holt, Rinehart & Winston, 1967), p. 88.

4 Arthur R. Jensen, *Genetics and Education* (Methuen, 1972).

5 Judith Haynes, *Educational Assessment of Immigrant Pupils* (Slough: NFER, 1971), p. 77.

6 Ingrid and Arne Trankell, 'Problems of the Swedish Gypsies', *Scandinavian Journal of Educational Research—Pedagogisk Forskning*, Universitetsforlaget (1968), p. 142.

7 Peggy Blakeley in *The Shadow on the Cheese*, ed. J. Wallbridge (NGEC, 1972), pp. 40–3.

8 By kind permission of the headmaster; report to the project.

9 The same problems are covered in *Organization in Multiracial Schools* (see n. 1), Chapter 9.

10 Megan Edwards in *The Shadow on the Cheese*, pp. 36–8.

11 The footnotes in the 1961 edition of M. M. Wells and P. S. Taylor's *The New Law of Education* (Butterworth) are more detailed than those in the 1971 edition, ed. George Taylor and John B. Saunders.

12 See Scottish Development Department, *Scotland's Travelling People* (HMSO, 1971), pp. 62–6.

13 Arthur Ivatts, *Report on NGEC Summer Schools* (1971), p. 23.

14 Ian Jones and Dick Worrall, various reports on the West Midland Travellers School van Leer project, obtainable from the Hon. Secretary, WMTS, 204B Lichfield Street, Walsall, Staffs.

15 Ibid.

16 Maree Welch, Report on Adult Education and Community Development Project at West Bromwich, 1972 (unpublished).

17 Since this was first drafted, there have been dramatic changes in the personnel of the NGEC. A considerable majority of the travellers and former Executive Committee of the NGEC have resigned and a new body called the Advisory Committee on the Education of Romanies and other Travellers (ACERT) has been formed under Lady Plowden's chairmanship. This occurred shortly after there had been a similar withdrawal of travellers from the Gypsy Council, and the formation of the traveller-only Romany Guild.

6 Teaching approaches, activities, materials and curriculum

This chapter is intended as a review of the most successful teaching studied during the project amplified by observations of a more subjective nature. Much thought has been given to the objectives of teaching travellers and to the provision of a compendium of classroom activities from which teachers may select to supplement their own schemes of work.

Introduction

Three themes ran through replies in the headteachers' questionnaire and in conversations with teachers held during school visits: there is no substitute for a reassuring and friendly approach; it is essential to know the whole family by paying regular visits to the site or camp; and there was an absence of commercially produced materials and reading schemes which were particularly effective with travellers. Indeed, concerning the latter theme several teachers went further, and suggested that the real need was for an almost completely individual approach based upon a variety of materials they had themselves designed.

This chapter is unlike the previous one in that its main readership will be the practising teacher rather than the administrator. Also, because little attention has been devoted to distinguishing between the needs of children of different ages, it will be necessary for a teacher to make considerable adjustments depending upon the age level being taught.

What is said and suggested, it is hoped, is relevant to the five-year-old and to the adult. Stress is given to bridging the gap between home and school, preparing for education, training in the essential prerequisite skills and in the initial stages of literacy. Teachers may find that there is only little on the later stages of education, but this is partly due to the lack of experience of traveller education at the post-literate stage and partly because it is felt important to inculcate an attitude in the teacher which is responsive rather than passive, which follows from the wishes of travellers rather than pushing on to the traveller a curriculum without incentive. The best curriculum is always self-selective.

One major reservation must be made about the emphasis upon literacy skills: education is much more than skills or cognition. It is about human responsibility and growth and about the ways in which we learn to live with and beside one another. To emphasize literacy at this point of time is itself open to considerable doubt. To begin with, there is likely to be continued widespread traveller failure in reading and writing; and secondly, neither we nor they really know whether such priority should be given to these skills. One is dealing with a minority group which has suffered prolonged discrimination and has been 'outside' for too long. No teachers need ever feel dispirited if their literacy teaching is unsuccessful in the early stages, providing that they are meeting travellers on a friendly and mutually respecting basis. It may be that this is what travellers most desire and what is real educational success.

Objectives and principles

The following list of objectives and principles which may be relevant to teachers of traveller children incorporates some of the points made at the beginning of the previous chapter but is more specifically oriented to the practical teaching situation:

(a) the initiation and maintenance of regular attendance or other educational contact, continuity of teachers;

(b) providing 'bridges' into the educational system, socialization within it, and filters back into traveller life;

(c) the involvement of parents by means of extensive home visiting by teachers, and the concentration on the impact of education upon the whole family unit;

(d) the account that should be taken of heritage and life style, and the very tense social predicament of the traveller;

(e) the priority that should be attached to progress in literacy;

(f) ensuring that the traveller child becomes self-reliant as a learner and is equipped to learn the 'living' literacy around him;

(g) exploiting the traveller's capacity to select only what is relevant and immediately rewarding, his trained but discriminating memory, his highly developed reading of human nature, and his training at home to face up to and overcome emergencies;

(h) respecting and utilizing the stress that travellers place on family, respect of elders, loyalty and responsibility towards one another, especially younger siblings;

(i) satisfying the traveller's uninhibited curiosity by a special curriculum developed after discussions with parents;

(j) making time for plentiful conversation and oral interaction between traveller pupils and teachers—sometimes in a very confidential, even confessional, context;

(*k*) creating within a school an active role and viable identity for travellers, situations in which they can reveal adequacy and in which they are not exposed to anti-traveller feeling nor in which their true identity is denied.

Obviously there are many other aims and underlying principles of teaching, but the above have been isolated for their particularly traveller flavour.

It certainly appeared that progress was related to the individual charisma and skill of the teacher rather than to the methods employed. Consequently it is inconsistent to recommend specific schemes in this report. Teachers are limited very often to what is available in a school, and an eclectic approach based upon materials and apparatus familiar to the teacher and personally liked by her is probably the most reliable one. Several unconventional approaches were seen: initially teaching only capital letters; a combination of Dr Seuss and chalks and slates rescued from an old school's dusty attic; a programme based upon visits to local shops and places of interest coupled with an infinite capacity to respond to the red herring (which were at least as successful as, if not more successful than, those employing *Breakthrough to Literacy*, Language Masters, *Racing to Read*, SRA, Stott's Programmed Reading Kit, the Ladybird reading scheme and so on). There was also an impression that traveller children were as likely as not to be more confused when using 'approved' apparatus because teachers tended to underestimate the children's difficulty in understanding their operation and function and because the teachers tended to believe that such apparatus had been so carefully designed that it needed little explanation and could achieve its objectives merely by the child's exposure to it.

Part of the problem is the myth that a better or more culturally suitable reading scheme can on its own provide the answer, or that there is some piece of educational apparatus that one could expose the child to and he would catch reading and writing like some contagious disease. Everything points against such haphazard approaches, especially with the traveller child who is a late starter in school.

David Mackay and Brian Thompson in their *Initial Teaching of Reading and Writing* (Schools Council Programme in Linguistics and English Teaching, Paper 3),[1] which was published before the *Breakthrough to Literacy* materials, point to two very significant factors which are relevant here:

Perhaps the greatest need in the field of literacy teaching and learning is to develop a theory that will account for all that happens to a person in the process of his becoming literate. At present we know something of what the teacher does in her classroom, but we know all too little about how the pupil is reacting, interpreting and understanding her procedures.[2]

... Michelangelo pointed out the absurdity of attempting to represent the natural world by painting on a flat surface, of attempting to depict what the eye sees 'realistically' in three dimensions by arranging selected blobs, lines and patches of colour on a two-dimensional surface. Equally we could say that it is absurd to attempt to render the complex patterns of noise, gesture and face-pulling that constitutes spoken language merely by making marks on a surface; reducing the dynamism of speech to a spatial system of scratches. Children learning to read find the concept of a writing system puzzling and magical. To the four year old one of the inexplicable wonders of the adult world must be the intricate horizontal rows of black swirls, spots, lines and curves that his mother looks at when reading him his bedtime story.[3]

When traveller children are left to their own devices without regular and persistent teacher intervention, their enthusiasm may drive them to develop and condition themselves into reproducing every known symptom of writing malfunction. Their patterns of attendance seldom leave sufficient time for these faults to be corrected, or, in the normal mixed classroom situation, for them ever to receive sufficient teacher explanation of the basic principles underlying the often illogical sound–symbol coding systems of written English or instruction in the directional and positional orientation of letters. On too many occasions during visits to schools, traveller children were observed who had made slow but definite progress through the first two or three graded readers in a series and were still unable to distinguish between a word and a letter. Many were unable to name the letters of the alphabet. They may have missed the reception infants' class pre-reading and reading readiness programmes under teachers trained and experienced in this vital groundwork. Their propensity to drop out of secondary school education may further reduce the possibility of their ever meeting a trained remedial English specialist who would instinctively give them the basic principles of literacy which they had somehow missed in the past.

Though writing of the current confusions over 'dyslexia' and 'developmental dyslexia', Paul Widlake makes a point that has relevance here:

Very often, the only 'expert' this child is going to meet is his class teacher; and if the teacher is convinced that there is an incurable condition with a Greek name, the child may never receive any organised help. I have already met this term in infant schools; 'she's word blind, you know'. Implication: everything possible has been done, but the whole thing's settled in the genes. Poor child; poor secondary school.[4]

Certainly, there were many times during the project when a similarly despairing attitude was met in teachers of travellers: he'll never learn to read and write, he's a traveller, with a social background inimical to attaining literacy. To some extent there is truth in this: it is a background which gives little or no help to the traveller child struggling to learn reading and writing —as Johnny Connors suggests, for the traveller child to ask his parents to spell a word or write a letter *is* frequently like asking a deaf-mute to say sound. The child may, after all, be content with a superficial level of literacy, perhaps a reading age of seven or eight because within his own community that may make him a 'scholar'.

BACKGROUND READING

Teachers may feel ill equipped to deal with such problems and with children with so inimical a background. This may be especially true with junior and secondary teachers with neither experience nor training in infant or remedial methodology. However, knowledge of the background of the children such as has been presented in this report and supplemented by personal observation is at least as important as, if not more important than, methodology. Also, successful teaching of travellers depends upon an attitude of mind— an essential receptivity to the needs of the children—and it is perhaps more important that the teacher read the works of Maria Montessori, Sylvia Ashton-Warner's *Teacher*, Herbert Kohl's *36 Children*, Erik Erikson's particularly relevant chapter in his *Childhood and Society* ('Hunters Across the Prairie'), and Rachel Scott's *A Wedding Man Is Nicer than Cats, Miss*,[5] than that a major study of the literature of literacy teaching and remedial English be undertaken.

Those who wish to gain greater insight into the theoretical basis of literacy teaching and the diagnosis of the causes of literacy failure may wish to consult standard texts by such authors as Moyle, Webster, Schonell, Tansley, Vernon, Daniels and Diack (also helpful with diagnostic tests) and so on. *Reading: Problems and Practices* is a very useful anthology of important articles edited by Jessie Reid; and Alec Williams' *Basic Subjects for the Slow Learner* is a 'student's nutshell' distillation of most of the major writers in addition to containing many practical hints. *Remedial Education* is a very useful magazine and a source of ideas for many activities. Paul Widlake's twenty-four-page pamphlet *Literacy in the Secondary School* contains a review of suitable apparatus and reading matter for older children. But perhaps the most useful of all to recommend is the Teacher's Manual to *Breakthrough to Literacy*, which contains a lucid consideration of the theoretical basis of the early stages of literacy acquisition.[6]

Any programme of teaching ought to be based on solid principles and on an understanding of the learning processes and likely causes of failure. An overview of the basic formation of reading and writing proficiency needs to be gained.

THE FIVE STAGES OF LITERACY

It is not the purpose of this report to offer a treatise on the acquisition of literacy, nor can it be said that we know exactly how any child learns to read and write. However, just as the successful child has to construct a mental model of how spoken language relates to printed matter, the teacher needs a working model on which to base any teaching programme. It must be emphasized that the arbitrary divisions that are made in the following five stages of literacy acquisition overlap and interact, and the amount of overlap and interaction will vary from one child to another:

Stage 1. Prerequisite skills (pre-reading and reading readiness)

(a) *The development of visual, auditory, and kinesthetic perceptual skills.* Before a child can learn to read he must be able to recognize and remember letters, recognize and remember sounds and have developed some ability to 'learn through his fingers'.

The traveller may have highly developed perceptual skills but they are concrete perceptions. Thus he is in special need of a carefully programmed course in developing abstract ones—i.e., not that this is copper worth so much, but that it is bent in such a shape, so many inches long and, if you turn it round, you have produced a different shape pointing in a different direction (its mirror image).

(b) *Understanding and recognition of auditory and visual symbols.* Before moving to sounds and letters it is necessary to have a long period of practice in naming and recognizing sounds and in naming and recognizing symbolic shapes. At this stage useful teaching may be devoted to enabling the children to distinguish the symbol from its reality, starting with pictures and going on to more abstract representations such as squares, triangles, circles and so on. The capital and lower-case alphabet can follow.

(c) *Developing manipulative skills.* Generally speaking, the average five-year-old's perceptual skills are relatively more advanced than his manual dexterity. In other words, he can proceed to reading earlier than he can produce writing. The traveller child coming to school older than usual may be in the reverse situation—being more capable and desirous of productive writing than receptive reading. Obviously, however, manipulative skills, hand-to-eye coordination and complex visual copying are essential.

(d) *Articulacy.* Vocabulary, pronunciation, syntactical variation and power of communication need to be sufficiently developed in advance of tackling literacy.

(e) *Socialization for learning.* This factor is a continuous one that stretches through to proficient literacy. It involves motivation, concentration/absorption, purposefulness and morale. Also important are *rapport* with the teacher, gratification and the necessity for a secure atmosphere conducive to learning.

Stage 2. Initial literacy (an expanding sight-and-write vocabulary)
This includes the recognition of the common grammatical words (namely,

the first hundred or so Ladybird Key Words) and various nouns, verbs and adjectives from the child's *own vocabulary*, and the ability to write and use them in composing sentences. Because graded readers dominate the methods of many schools, most children tend to learn the vocabulary of their reader rather than the one which is more familiar to them. This becomes less and less justifiable in direct relation to the degree to which the children's own language and environment is alien to that of the reader. This stage is a mechanical one—barking at print—and the older child at this stage should understand that it is only a transition phase. For travellers, the vocabulary can include their own names, place names, words like 'trailer', 'dog', 'TV', 'motor', 'scrap', 'slush' and so on.

Teaching methods can be directed towards two main activities: games that reinforce word recognition, and functional use of known words to produce sentences of the child's own making—*Breakthrough to Literacy* can be very helpful in doing this. Reading and writing should be simultaneous and complementary. It is an acquisitive process—letter formation, not handwriting. This continues until between two and four hundred words have been learnt, and time should be taken to make clear to children what they are doing so that they can use the same techniques for learning to recognize recurring syllables (or phonemes) in the later stages. When this stage is well under way there begins the parallel stage 3.

Stage 3. De-coding
This requires understanding of the relationship between visual and auditory symbols. In English this is a complex relationship, and care should be taken to avoid attempting to oversimplify it, thus creating errors which hold up children later. For instance, individual letters have names—'A', 'B', 'C' and so on—and many nearly always make the same sounds, but not always. They are also affected by the other letters around them in a word; and many of them are frequently put together or 'blended' to make a single sound— 'ch', for example. Above all, the use of pseudo-phonics of the kind that states that 'a' stands for 'apple' and 'b' for 'bat' should be avoided. Rather, they should be introduced to the common vowel, vowel-consonant and consonant blends as whole units, as in *cr–a–sh* or *sp–oo–n*.

The successful analysis and synthesis of words is the state at which so many children balk all too often simply because they do not understand what is expected of them. Teachers need to take great care in giving their children full explanations to make sure that they are not adding more mystification. Spelling systems, rudimentary etymology, and punctuation must be systematically taught, for travellers will not generally catch them by mere exposure.

Examples on which to base the idea of de-coding and phonics can be drawn from the children's sight vocabulary as much as possible rather than from arbitrarily chosen word families, though unfortunately it is the most common grammatical words which are the most irregular. It must be remembered, however, that de-coding itself is not 'reading' and children at this stage need plentiful reading matter that can be enjoyed and whets their appetite for more.

Stage 4. Development of speed, comprehension and expression
Continued instruction (as opposed to exercising) in these skills is all too rare once the child has achieved the launching pad of understanding the rudiments of de-coding. Children should be taught to read aloud, developing rhythm, pitch and expression. As they do so it will soon become clear whether they are comprehending and communicating their understanding. At the same time it will be remembered that reading aloud and reading silently are now becoming very different skills.

The technical skills of this stage include learning to recognize syllables and to scan phrases when reading silently. Fast reading depends upon being able to spot unfamiliar words which need to be analysed syllabically or step by step, anticipating the movement of a sentence or phrase from contextual clues. Extremely fast eye movements are necessary and powers of absorption must be extensive. Comprehension can lag behind actual mechanical reading ability, so teachers should take great care to stress its importance.

Handwriting has grown out of the learner's early printing and is developing style and rapidity. Communication of complex descriptions and ideas is now possible, and the correction of spelling and other mechanical errors that the child develops should not just be a formality (or even an overlooked formality) but an opportunity for the teacher to gain an insight into a child's faulty de-coding system and provide specific prognosis.

Stage 5. Proficiency
This is all too rarely achieved even among quite able children, and most of us who are reasonably proficient are often unaware of the effective skills and techniques we employ. These may include selective scanning for important material in long passages, the ability to read slowly and intensively to gain maximum information from complex or badly presented literature and to make value judgements about what we read. In writing, style has been developed, a wide variety of styles and forms can be employed, and scholarly texts can be prepared, revised and edited.[7]

Throughout these stages it is vital to maintain an interest and incentive and to avoid rote and drill learning, and dull routine—which, incidentally, can arise in so-called creative writing just as it can in the project or topic work. Generally, stages 4 and 5 are not 'taught' at all, which is a mistake; they are left to develop haphazardly as the child moves forward chronologically and through the different age levels of the system. Notwithstanding the concepts of reading age and the models (such as this) which we impose on the way in which children become literate, there is reason to believe that there comes a point when the whole thing goes 'click' and somehow the child then really comes to understand what it is all about even though he may have many skills yet to develop. (Those who have learnt to drive a car will remember the moment when they stopped being all arms and legs and when they began to 'feel' the car.) This point may come at a mechanical reading age of 6·5 or even at 8·5, and in some children it may never have taken place even though tests which are not truly diagnostic may reveal a reading age of ten. Obviously, too, the first major 'click' is followed by a series of reverberating minor 'clicks'. They may be defined as a sudden insight into the theoretical basis of the extremely complex operations of literacy. Children accustomed to abstract thought and what Piaget described as 'formal operations' discover these insights often with little help from parents and companions, and sometimes with less help from teachers. The traveller, dominated by 'concrete operations' and bereft of help from parents and companions, needs to be led very carefully through each perception and insight.

With travellers, most early teaching is not concerned with the final three stages of literacy outlined above. There must be a concentration upon the prerequisite skills and the initiation of mechanical reading and writing. Even before one can start on these, educational and social contact must be established and trust built up. The remainder of this chapter is devoted to practical suggestions on providing the bridging operation into school, on developing an integrated course in the basic skills, and on considerations of the wider curriculum and related problems.

The bridge into school and socializing into the classroom

PRE-ATTENDANCE CONTACT

For many years to come teachers will be involved in meeting the needs of travellers of all ages coming to school for the first time or with such negligible previous education that it can be discounted for practical purposes. There will almost certainly be a further development of school induction classes and on-site preparatory education designed to facilitate the bridge into school from family-oriented travelling life.

The development of trust is the first priority, as Fred Wood, a leading Gypsy, has reiterated:

When a Gypsy child first comes to school the place seems very strange to him after life on a caravan site and on the road. School is entirely new to him.

What many teachers do not understand is that coming into a school for the first time is for each child rather like putting a wild bird in a cage. Before a teacher can think of teaching such a child he or she must gain his confidence.[8]

The ways in which trust can be built up obviously include meeting the child in his own environment, the site and his family's trailer. It may be necessary also to allow the opportunity of the child seeing the teacher in *his* home environment—meeting his family, wife and children—and experiencing the school buildings and grounds before attendance starts. This latter point is important not only because of claustrophobia, but also because there are many things in the school which the child may need to be allowed to explore before mixing with other children, who may find his response to familiar apparatus bizarre. An anecdote illustrates this: A voluntary teacher took a party of some dozen traveller children to an exhibition of their own drawings and paintings in a municipal art gallery. None of the children had been to school and many had never been inside so large a building. Their reaction was as spontaneous as it was unpredictable: they totally ignored their own work, and threw themselves on their backs and propelled themselves backwards up and down the large polished floor surface to the amazement of bystanders and the consternation of the librarian and curator. The display continued without let-up for over ten minutes; an attempt to bring it to a premature close resulted in a series of expletives from the oldest boy and the complaint, 'We's not broke nothing yet, has we?' Their response, incidentally, had been identical to that of the volunteer's three-year-old the day before while the exhibition was being set up. The travellers ranged from three to seventeen, but the majority were between eight and thirteen.

SITE VISITING

Visiting a site, especially when it is unofficial and there are many dogs around, can be a daunting prospect. As many travellers will explain, their dogs are travellers not gaujes, and they know a gauje when they see one. Those tied up near kennels are the only really dangerous ones; the others respect a person who walks past them without deviation in direction or speed, or any apparent recognition of their existence (Jack Crabb's boots yet again).

Any visitor to a site is bound to be seen as an intruder—an official, perhaps, or a journalist. A direct approach is best, with a statement about who and what one is and why one has come. But there should not be very many questions about who *they* are, how many children there are, where they have come from and when and where they are going.

EARLY INTRODUCTION OF ACTIVITIES

Pre-attendance or early contact between teachers and traveller children can be oriented towards equipping the children with elementary skills to practise on their own, or experience at activities which they may be in a position to put into effect in school at times when a teacher must concentrate upon the other children in the class, who will be working at a different level. It is partly an attitude of mind: 'If you've got nothing to do, then practise copying letter shapes, tracing words, learning from each other the words that are known', and so on. Many activities can be introduced to the children that they can practise on their own before they come into school: 'brass-rubbing' vehicle registration number plates, copying street signs and so on, playing Kim's game, finding and exploiting literate site visitors (wardens, milkmen, casual passers-by) as teachers ('Show me how to write two words every day you see me and I'll give you ——— in return.') Traveller children are scavengers and very acquisitive. They are used to finding out things for themselves and their parents expect them to be able to make their own ways.

One Scottish traveller child aged about eight spent most of a summer school approaching each volunteer teacher in turn—'Hey, Mister! Will you teach me to read?' After all but one member of the team had tried and failed: 'Och now. I'm wasting your time!' Willie discovered that teachers were not magicians. He had also learnt that literacy was tough work, and so eventually he settled on the only volunteer who had had the insight to refuse adamantly to even try to teach him to read, and said, 'If you won't teach me to read, fair enough. But will you tell me what this word is? Give ye' a poler?'

Pre-attendance contact also serves to prepare teachers, provide them with essential social background information and enable them to conduct a diagnosis of the children's developmental stage and previous educational experience.

PREPARING A DIAGNOSTIC PROFILE

At the earliest opportunity (preferably before regular educational contact begins), it is necessary to assess and diagnose the particular educational needs of traveller children. Only when a detailed profile of the children is developed can the most appropriate methods of organization and teaching be decided. The following arbitrarily ordered questions may be born in mind.

Can they hold pencils, draw pictures and letter shapes (from memory or by copying); when copying abstract shapes (see, for example, Daniel and Diack's visual copying test)[9] do they reverse positions, directions, etc.?

Can they write their own names? Capital letters only? Can they name letters?

Can they recognize any other words: 'POLICE', 'AMBULANCE' and so on, or the first twelve most common words in the Ladybird Key Word list?

Can they name shapes? Classify according to size, colour, texture, distance, weight, direction (left to right, top to bottom, north and south, back to front, upside down, etc.)? Or do they have a different classification system? Strange vocabulary?

Do they understand the meanings of such words as 'letter', 'word', 'page', 'crayon', 'sentence', 'mirror image'?

Are there recognizable perceptual defects—in hearing, eyesight? Can they
    rhyme?
What of their general physical co-ordination? Balance? Strength?
How clear is their speech? Do they have difficulty in pronouncing long words?
How fast is their speech? What sort of syntax? Dialect? Do they reveal any
    Anglo-Romany or Shelta words?
Can they re-tell stories in sequential order? How do they describe pictures?
To what extent does their school speech or the language they use with you
    differ from what they use at home or with their own companions?
Can they handle money? Count and recognize digits? Compute? Tell time,
    day of the week and so on?
Can they play card games, dominoes, do jigsaws?
Do they know (or are they prepared to reveal) their ages? Do they know the
    town in which they are camped?
Can they name birds, trees, zoo animals, metals, makes of motor vehicles?
What are their favourite songs, television programmes?
Can they use a telephone?
Have they been to school before? Where? What were their teachers' names?

Some of the answers can arise from initial conversation growing out of the
first session, during which pencils and paper are handed round. Many
answers will have to develop from close observation and responsive listening,
for if the children feel that they are being pressured for answers or if they are
unsure whether to trust the questioner, they will either avoid giving answers
or intentionally mislead.

   Such a list of questions should not in any way be used (at least overtly)
on a printed pro-forma taken to the site. Rather, it is intended to stimulate
the teacher to build up a picture of the needs which must be met in the later
teaching situations. Parents can help in building up a portrait of the children
and, as it is hoped that they may be enlisted to supervise and even to learn
from homework activities and generally participate in their children's
educational welfare, the earlier they are consulted the more profitable
the eventual relationship.

THE 'CASE DEI BAMBINI' AND MURPHY'S COALPIT—
PARALLELS IN SPONTANEITY

Between 1907 and 1911 in the tenement apartments of some of the worst
districts of Rome, Maria Montessori made some startling discoveries about
the motivation of Italian slum children who did not attend school.[10] One of
her most remarkable experiences was of a spontaneous and initially uncon-
trollable outburst of *imitation* handwriting. Anyone familiar with children
in literate households between the ages of two and a half and five will appreciate what is meant. One informant's first experience of teaching traveller

children on the roadside has left an indelible impression, but such experiences may be re-created on numerous unauthorized encampments throughout the country, wherever there are large groups of unschooled traveller children.

The camp was in the heart of the Black Country and took several hours to locate, mainly because we had been told that the families were on a well-known but improbably named stretch of land—Murphy's Coalpit. In indescribable conditions, about six trailers were eventually found. The teaching session that ensued took place out of doors in and around our Morris 1000 Traveller—which at one time proved capable of accommodating eleven of the twenty children. Each child was given a small packet of crayons but before there was even time to issue the small exercise books, *it* happened. On tree trunks, scrap metal, bricks, all over the coachwork and windows of the car. A flurry of snow did not interrupt it. Some of the older children (there were several teenagers) found the car log-book, left in view on the parcel shelf, and began copying. Gradually the exercise books were passed around. Predictably and logically, the results were a complete jumble of mirror and correct image letters (about 50–50), no gaps between words, upside-downness, reversal, left-to-right and right-to-left in almost equal quantities, transpositions, omissions, perseverations, insertions, substitutions and so on.

After about an hour the children tired, and most disappeared into trailers with crayons and an exercise book each. They left behind them scattered around the car, trampled into the mud, blown into hedgerows the priceless artifacts of their first hectic hour of 'school'. One ruled 32-page exercise book was 'completed' with squiggles imitation writing between every line on every page, not one blank page, and not one single decipherable letter anywhere. Another similar book with two words of self-assertion printed in rudimentary capital letters, not always the same letters and in the same order, on every page—'JIMMY PURCELL'. Two or three of the children had a degree of literacy, limited to capital letters and in one case unmistakably acquired graffiti. Significantly there was not one single picture or drawing, only a touchingly spectacular revelation of jealousy towards other children who could write, and the policeman with his note-pad, the local authority officer with his questionnaire.

These were Irish Tinkers and they had never seen the inside of a school, but experiences of roadside teaching and even an examination of school exercise books in classes in the many schools visited during this project confirmed that this was no unique phenomenon. Teachers also confirmed that traveller children in school were prone to attempt similarly uncomprehending copying from books—one teacher resorted to this as a regular activity just to keep her children occupied.

The traveller does not make the same distinction between work and play as the gauje does. Holidays usually consist of horse fairs where there is, if anything, more dealing, bargaining, trading of trailers and business between travellers than in the normal week. Weekdays and weekends are not so rigidly divided for them, nor do they work specific hours. The child does not make the same distinction between work and play as gaujes do, and a teacher may capitalize on this and be wary of making the division so clear. Significantly, on a recent newsreel report on television, a traveller child brushed aside an interviewer's question on whether the child preferred playing or reading, with the over-the-shoulder and somewhat aggravated reply: 'Oh! We . . . we play reading all the time.'

INVITING ATTENDANCE

Surprisingly, there are many traveller families whose children do not attend school simply because they have never received a friendly invitation to do so. In 1969, the headmistress of a Hertfordshire Roman Catholic primary school discovered this after she had driven several miles across town to a newly opened temporary caravan site tenanted by some notorious Irish Tinker families. The sister was greeted with the usual apprehension, slightly molli- fied because she was dressed in her habit and because the families were Catholic. She wasted no time in coming to the point, explained that she was head of a school the other side of town and that she'd come to see if any of the children would be allowed to come back with her with a view to attending regularly. Three years later, though the site has been closed, the school still takes several children from these families, who have moved into houses nearer to the school; the sister's sudden appearance on the site has become a legend. The initiation of attendance, its maintenance and preparation of traveller children for school can be achieved by an action as simple as hers.

It is not impracticably idealistic to suggest that George Smith of Coalville's notion almost a hundred years ago holds the secret to a massive increase in traveller school attendance:

Upwards of £3,000,000 is spent every year, out of the taxes of this country, for the children of other working classes, one penny of which does not go to the poor boat-children living in the cabins. If education does not go to the children, then the children, 'by hook or by crook', must go to education. If Mahomet cannot bring his mountain of education to the boat and gipsy children, then Mahomet must take his canal, gipsy and show children to the mountain of education.[11]

Most teachers of travellers do not believe that an indiscriminate use of com- pulsory attendance orders will achieve greater and more successful attendance rates. Rather, they feel—and many EWOs would agree with them—that what is needed is salesmanship and customer satisfaction.

SOCIALIZATION IN SCHOOL

Introducing the child into the classroom once his parents have been persuaded to send him (whether to a maintained school or special unit) is a further task—not always as easy as it may appear at first sight. Indeed most schools stress the need for an extended period of social adjustment as the first stage in successful teaching of traveller children. This consists of not just 'knocking the rough edges off', as one headteacher put it, but allowing them the time and opportunity to work out their feelings of strangeness, alienation and a hyper-excitement in the novelty of everything they see and do. For the teacher it may be a period when 'unsentimental tolerance' can become overstrained, as these two headteachers' reports indicate:

It is with some deliberation that I place the social needs ahead of the learning situation. . . . The first to arrive was Ted—a rough diamond if ever I saw one (five years old), possessing a face like a harvest moon and dressed overall in the fashion of the day with every item of clothing newly purchased. How he enjoyed his midday meal but with such disregard of formality. Triumph came to us, however, when the second boy came a few weeks later, and was told by Ted, that when the grub is finished 'he puts his knife and fork at half past six' (on his plate!!) Once settled, the friendliness and warmth shown us by these children makes us forget the early days and their many difficulties. . . . The language the children used was meaningful to them, and of use, we felt therefore that it was not our place to condemn it, but rather extend it by giving them a vocabulary which would gradually enable them to link themselves to the society of school. . . . We discovered that some of the children had a limited span of concentration, and this might have stemmed from their inability to extract the maximum from a situation, or that as young children suspect that tomorrow never comes, they were compelled to have 'a go' at everything.
We must look upon the early days of this experiment in education as an investment in the future and we must not show disappointment if, after two years in the infant school, the child leaves as a non-reader. . . . In their early days the teacher needs to accept the coarseness of their language and habits, a tendency to acquire bits and pieces, tearful tantrums and running off the premises. (*Berkshire infants headteacher*)

Travellers come here for a year or more then disappear only to enroll 2 or 3 years later and have not been near a school. The dull children of illiterate parents are hopeless. Others learn to read and write and take normal lessons, but never reach more than 50% marks. [The main difficulties the travellers have experienced:] Using toilets properly. Using handkerchiefs. General hygiene. Changing clothes frequently. [They have] pilfered other children's lunches, toys, pencils, etc.
Travellers always keep together as a community but if rival outfits arrive then the teacher has a nightmare on his or her hands. They have to obey and be polite to staff always & bad language is not tolerated. On Mondays when they are clean and tidy [they mix with other children in the classroom] very well but this wears thin as the week goes by. . . .
The travellers are fetched by their parents and taken home so they see very little of non-travellers. . . . If rival factions meet outside the school it is a police matter, not the teachers'. . . . Parents will complain to the LEA or

police for minor accidents such as a grazed knee. They will cooperate but one must be careful as their children will bring all sorts of things which you suspect are stolen. E.g. Don't ask for holly at Xmas—you might get a tree—probably from some-one's front lawn.

Here the headmaster must watch that clean delicate [non-traveller] children do not sit near to travellers. Travellers are usually strong, tough & seldom ill, but they can pass on all sorts of undesirable visitors, and they always find the 'posh' only child. The traveller parents will then abuse the posh parents for accusing them. Fun and games thereafter for the headmaster. They need a breaking-in period. A classteacher cannot spare enough time for teaching a non-reader over the age of 7. (*Worcestershire first school headmaster*)

These two complementary experiences and contrasting teacher attitudes may help to define some of the problems involved. Many schools have found it necessary to introduce a structured orientation programme for their traveller children.

ORIENTATION INTO SCHOOL AND CLASSROOM

When attendance starts it is wise to place the travellers under the wing of one member of staff or an ancillary helper whose task is to introduce them to the school buildings, the grounds and the classroom apparatus they will eventually use. Such a person also helps to explain to the children the disciplinary regime of the school—what will be required of them. The familiar facilities for washing, dining, playing and classroom routines may need to be introduced in a sensible manner, for they may be alien to the traveller. This orientation period also introduces to the child the vocabulary of school life, and this is a time when apprehensions are removed and confidence built. Particular attention may be paid to ensuring close contact between traveller siblings—making sure, for instance, that the older brother or sister, who will eventually be placed in the junior department, accompanies an infant sibling to its classroom, meets the infant teacher and spends a little time in that classroom. Schools may find it useful to take advantage of the responsibility for the minding of younger children that a traveller will almost certainly have been given. Some behavioural problems may in fact be referred back to the older child—though it may be necessary for the member of staff concerned to explain to the older child that it is not expected that disciplinary action in terms of a cuff on the ear will be allowed. Such action is not only wise but expedient, for the traveller honours parental sanction and instructions more than any given by teachers.

The advantage of having a staff member without a particular class to look after is important because of minor emergencies that will crop up and because many of the travellers may find the experience of being inside a building for an extended period overwhelming in the early stages. A constructive use of the outdoors relieves the tensions and can be structured in such a way as to

introduce the traveller to the immediate environment outside the school—
shops and the price tags on goods, street signs, the name of the school on the
outside plaque and so on—all the living literacy around which has previously
been an arcane and bewildering world to the non-literate child who has no
literate companions. The acquisitive language and sign activities are important
to establish and may be supplemented by the collection of tangible objects for
labelling and as a source for oral work. It may also be possible to entrust
traveller children with responsible tasks outdoors, which will reinforce the
sense of adequacy and utility so easily destroyed by a premature exposure to
classroom activities.

ORIENTATION OUTSIDE SCHOOL

Many teachers have extended the orientation of travellers to incorporate
educational and recreational facilities outside the school itself. Travellers
may be unfamiliar with community facilities that other children enjoy. They
seldom take advantage of these partly because, belonging to a fringe minority
group, they fear that they will be excluded or meet gauje opposition, such
experiences being a regular daily occurrence. These fears are not without
grounds for, during the project, many substantiated cases of excluding
travellers from public places, public houses, swimming baths, playgrounds,
youth clubs and libraries were found. Teachers need to be aware of this and,
if necessary, accompany travellers to such places until they have won, or
been granted, full access. It is not often fully appreciated how many times
each day a traveller has living proof of discrimination, and much of his
behaviour in school, or as a parent of a child in school, needs to be seen in
this light.

SOCIAL PROBLEMS OF UNAUTHORIZED ENCAMPMENTS

If more travellers from unauthorized encampments begin school attendance,
teachers may have to face up to the realities of the social and political predicament of the traveller over the next decades. Traveller children may
actually be in school while a local authority is in the process of evicting their
parents' trailer-caravans.

Teaching the basic skills—an integrated programme in oracy, literacy and numeracy

What practical suggestions can be made for the practising teacher of traveller
children? If this report does not include recommended reading schemes and
apparatus, and yet makes a strong case for a systematic and structured
literacy programme for travellers, how can the teacher start?

These questions were debated at length in many staffrooms and with many
educationists and reading experts; what follows are some guidelines and
practical hints—though it is hoped that teachers already operating them will

not be offended if they discover what they already know. They amount to an integrated programme of preparatory education in the basic subjects.

According to information received and observations made during the project, the traveller enters school in very special need of attention. Though one must be careful not to insult a child by under-estimating his capabilities, a teacher needs to take *nothing* for granted: a fourteen-year-old may not be able to fit together the simplest wooden Galt jigsaw because he has never met the problem before, though he may be more than able in stripping down, sorting the different metals in, and valuing an assortment of scrap including vacuum cleaners, boilers, heavy goods vehicle diesel engines and 3 cwt of discarded electrical wire and cable from a television manufacturer.

ORACY—THE BASIS OF THE SCHEME

These children present several tricky problems for the teacher: their vocabulary may be extensive, but it includes words which a teacher may not understand and which they are on strict parental instruction not to reveal— Anglo-Romany, Shelta or cant. Travellers also have a form of non-verbal communication which may baffle a teacher, for one child may report the unspoken comment of another. In another sense the traveller has a limited vocabulary—one that is lacking in many of the specifically needed words that are used in school and to describe the literacy and numeracy processes. Even when the teacher has tuned in to the accent and dialect of the travellers, and they into hers, there is still a wide gulf which they must cross before they can take full advantage of instruction.

This oral development is a prerequisite of progress. The school induction and socialization periods can be used to develop a functional vocabulary for learning, though care should be taken to avoid frustrating traveller children in their main desire, which is to write and read (probably in that order of priority).

LEARNING THE ALPHABET THROUGH THE FINGERS

In the early days of school the traveller can be given a whole range of manipulative skills to practise: using pens, pencils, rulers, templates, tracing. There is no harm in a concentration upon drawing and painting letter shapes, in bright colours and with decorative borders and patterns. There should be large display letters and numbers in the classroom and these can become centres of oral work. A teacher might prepare in advance spirit-duplicated, dotted-line outlines of letters for joining up and colouring in. Montessori-style letter cards (sandpaper letters stuck on to a smooth card or tile—possibly arranged in a bright colour system for clockwise or anti-clockwise or straight-line letter orientation), and any other tough, brightly coloured apparatus for letter shape work is useful. Old typewriters can be very effective in the classroom—for left-to-right orientation, making fair copies and so on. A machine with an exceptionally large type face is best. An alphabet scrapbook can be an early project for the travellers: cutting out different typographical styles for letters (perhaps two books—one for lower-case letters, one for capitals); the use of scissors and glue are further exercises in manual and digital dexterity. Throughout such activities there is constant discussion of the essence of letter shape—just a morning may be spent on mirror image, the differences between 'b', 'd', 'p', 'q', '6', '9', upside down, back to front, top to bottom, left to right, straight or curved, and so on—and of the diversity of handwritten, printed and illustrated forms of letters. Styles of letters seen out of doors may be turned into project work—street signs, shop names and labels, and a visit may be made to a printer to get type-face catalogues.

A follow-up project can be the publication of a 'travellers' alphabet book', drawn and illustrated by the children on to spirit duplicator masters and run off and stapled by them.

At this stage the media of art and craft can be oriented towards letter shape —wooden letter shapes pressed into soft clay painted, or even glazed and fired. The aim is to create within a controlled and corrective situation the spontaneous letter writing of the *Case dei Bambini* and Murphy's Coalpit. There is at this stage no need to enter the world of phonics—it can be just a naming of letters, insight into their shape and variety. The activities involve the children in using all sorts of classroom equipment and writing and drawing implements, and also enable them to do homework. But most important of all is the oracy of the situation, the language used by the teacher to distinguish a 'W' from an '8'.

FUNCTIONAL LITERACY

The closer the teacher can approach the practical and functional situation the better. Written language is basically a sign coding system, and initially letters may be given a sign value similar to an arrow. Children can be allotted a letter each, the chairs or desks can be labelled with letters, tidy boxes can be catalogued. Traveller children can be given specific errands: going to the library and finding the book with a certain reference or catalogue number (such a book may also be one that the teacher happens to think might appeal —one on horses, for instance).

However, throughout this reading readiness programme the emphasis is upon language development and an acquisition of a school learning vocabulary, one which pays particular attention to the vocabulary of early reading and writing. It is a time when the child's curiosity needs to be continually stimulated and satisfied not 'on a plate' donated by the teacher but through active exploration and effort on the child's part.

EDUCATIONAL HARDWARE

If a teacher is in a position to acquire educational hardware, a strong and simple camera might well be put on top of the list. It has enormous potential in a classroom with travellers, and there is no better visual stimulus for oral development than pictures taken of relatives, the site, new traveller babies, the children's animals and travellers from other areas. An exchange of photographs between two schools with related travellers accompanied by letters and class scrapbooks is only one of the many possibilities. A camera which the children can easily use themselves can be a very valuable piece of educational equipment, as has been shown by Parfitt, who has used cameras successfully with ESN children.[12] Photographs have a special relevance to travellers because they are one of the few printed possessions which they keep and treasure.

The use of similar educational hardware—such as tape-recorders and junction boxes, cameras, typewriters or duplicators—helps to provide practical manipulative experience as well as offering the teacher a centre of attraction for oracy. The aim is always to unify the approach so that the child sees the relevance of each component, each specific activity and piece of gadgetry.

GAMES RESOURCE CENTRE

An essential task for the teacher of travellers is the accumulation of an educational games resources centre in the classroom. Equipment may include the items below, though the list is by no means exhaustive:

chess (for the older children)
dominoes
dice
roulette
Monopoly
word bingo or Lotto
Snakes and Ladders (left to right
  orientation version)
Lexicon
Scrabble
card games: Snap, games with
  letters and words, Happy
  Families, rummy and so on, but
  with letters and words

crosswords
word jigsaws
word games (commercial sets and
  also home-made sets—48 cards, 4
  sets of 12 key words)
Morris cards, Portholes and so on
Pelmanism, Kim's Game
'Battleships'
farm and zoo model animals
puppets

Breakthrough to Literacy and other early literacy apparatus can be included, with amended vocabulary—what one school termed a 'key site vocabulary'. The educative value of the above games should not need stressing, for they are essential to children from educationally advantaged backgrounds. Many of these games are made of easily soiled and fragile card, and it may be necessary to cover them with transparent self-sealing PVC sheeting, slightly diluted PVA glue, or ordinary PVC sheeting bonded on one of the patent bonding machines. These soon prove their worth, considering the high price of the self-sealing material.

Travellers certainly respond well to situations of challenge, and some teachers have used puzzles (matchstick teasers, getting the Indians across the river, conjuring tricks, and trick question mental arithmetic problems), and these have stimulated a daily session which can be prolonged for months. The children respond to the whole idea of such pastimes because it is part of their background, because of the cut and thrust of the game and the final out-witting of the problem. They are not by nature fiercely competitive among themselves in learning situations. Comparative marks mean little to them, but they enjoy the battle against the odds in a practical situation.

WORKBOOKS

There may also be a need for the teacher to develop workbooks and work cards, handwriting 'copybooks', collections of picture completion exercises, mazes and so on. Such workbooks can be run off cheaply on a spirit duplicator.

They may include shape colouring and copying, left to right series completion underlining odd men out, missing object puzzles, picture and word matching exercises, missing letters in words, anagrams and self-teaching word and picture lists (shopping lists, household or caravan objects). Such workbooks should be abundant and should be left available for any child to 'chor' (that is, steal—if that is an appropriate word when the motive is educational) for they can be used at home and when travelling.

NUMBER

Another aspect of this stage is the 'literacy' of number work and the 'numeracy' of literacy work. For example, how many letters are there in the alphabet? How many are written clockwise? How many capital letters are just bigger versions of lower-case ones? Letters and numbers may be set, sorted and classified. The language of number is exemplified by adding, sub-tracting and taking away, by analysing the configuration of words, how many letters there are in a word, how many words in sentences, how many with tails, how many with long necks. Pages may be numbered in books—an exercise in front-to-back orientation. Further examples are measuring, weighing, taking tyre pressures, examining scrap-metal price lists, telling time, plotting the days of the week and what the children did on what days, who did not attend when, and what percentage of attendance has been achieved.

One of the most perceptive remarks about teaching travellers arithmetic was made by a teacher who claimed to have made a breakthrough when she started adding a £ sign to all the sums she set her travelling pupils. She pointed out that it was not merely a question of abstraction but of social and vocational context. Teachers wishing for some practical suggestions for social arithmetic may wish to consult a symposium on the subject in *Remedial Education* (vol. 3, no. 1 (1968) pp. 11–31).

CONSTRUCTION

There are numerous constructional toys and educational apparatus which provide relief and enjoyment. There are interlocking bricks, construction kits, jigsaws, Tinkertoy, Fixit bits, and so on. Other activities are paper folding, paper flower making (not just the teacher's own styles but examples brought in from the traveller family), the drawing of complex and colourful geometrical shapes and 3–D models, all forms of craft work, including box construction, carpentry and metalwork, clay, papier mâché and collage work. Group work and participation are among the social aims behind this programme. Sharing, lending, possession, neatness, finishing a task, achievement-motivation (goal-seeking) and self-reliance are also stressed.

AUDITORY DISCRIMINATION

There is also a whole range of auditory discrimination activities which can be integrated into this scheme: rhyme lists, I-spy initial sounds, setting of objects from a junk box by initial sounds, action (touching something or doing something) related to initial word sound. Homework tasks can include scavenging for objects which start with the same letter. In many of these oral activities a portable tape-recorder is essential; the child needs to compare how he says a word with how you say it, how the caretaker says it, what it sounds like when whispered, shouted or muffled. Activities such as the use of telephones, party game message relaying, memorizing of precise messages to be delivered to the headteacher, finding out the menu of the day from kitchen staff, interviewing other teachers, the caretaker or visitors, give a functional context. There are in addition many practical follow-up literacy and numeracy activities—among them, plotting menus (predicting what will be the dinner on Tuesday next week) and so on.

TOPICS

A wide range of additional activities common to any classroom can easily be related to this core work: music, nature study (seed sowing is very effective, as, of course, is keeping a classroom animal), P.E. (measuring swings or jumps) and games. But it is the telling and discussing that really matters; and here the traveller's ability as a raconteur can be exploited.

STORIES AND SONGS

Strangely enough, not all teachers claimed success in the reading and telling of stories to travellers. The explanation may lie in the choice of tale and the manner of delivery; it might lie in the fact that travellers do not usually respond well when gathered together in a large group around a teacher. In this respect they are more amenable to smaller group work.

The accent during story-reading and -telling sessions should be on stimulating the child to produce as well as to receive passively. Stories can be started and then finished by the children. Deliberate mistakes can be made to ensure concentration and to capitalize on the travellers' 'kidding' sense of humour. The choice of stories need not be too different from those used with gauje children: folk tales, myths and legends, tales of the lives of children from other lands—Eskimos, Red Indians (a favourite subject usually), 'biter bit' plots, stories of any group pitting their wits against nature or an enemy, traditional nursery tales (even with older children), tales of wild fantasy, superstition and witch-doctoring. They will sometimes ask for the same story time and time again and will often be able to pick up the dramatic intonations that the teacher should use during the telling. Even five-year-old travellers may be able to tell well-known stories to younger siblings, and their telling styles still reveal that the oral tradition amongst Gypsy families is not a thing of the past.

Stories written by travellers or about them are beginning to appear on the market (see the Bibliography), and these may be included. The traveller child prefers either subjects which are fancifully imaginative or those which are closest to reality as he knows it—horses, travelling, his own family. Too many of the existing children's books about Gypsies are over-romanticized, and many teachers have found that one of the most popular of all books with traveller children is the Ministry of Housing and Local Government report *Gypsies and Other Travellers*, because in it are a fine selection of photographs, some being of other travellers they may in fact know. The Scottish Development Department's report, *Scotland's Travelling People*, also contains good photographs, though there is nothing to match *Gypsies: Wanderers of the World* with its beautiful colour reproductions of photographs of Gypsies and nomads from all over Europe, the Near East and in India (see Bibliography).

In a similar way to the appeal of photographs, teachers will quickly discover that almost without exception traveller children love sentimental ballads and often retain pop hits from several years back: 'You've got Kisses Sweeter than Wine', 'I Beg your Pardon, I Never promised You a Rosegarden', 'My Boy Lollipop' may be heard today on many sites. What is one of the most interesting phenomena is the utilization of pop songs, ballads, and *risqué* ditties as lullabies, and their transformation into cradle-songs with the addition of 'hush-a-by' refrains.

Teachers revealed mixed opinions about the capacity of travellers in singing and revealing 'Gypsy' songs, but there is increasing evidence that they have a richer and more extensive repertoire than has been generally accredited them in the past. Ewan McColl, Charles Parker and Peggy Seeger's record *The Travelling People*[13] contains some very stimulating catches of conversation from travellers, provocative and sometimes alarming statements by members of the public and by politicians and officials; but it also contains many gauje folk-singers' songs about travellers, which appeal to the children.

Traveller folk-tales may be found in back issues of the *Journal of the Gypsy Lore Society*,[14] and some can be taped from parents keen to participate in their children's education, though it may be discovered that these are likely to be variants of traditional stories like 'Jack and the Beanstalk'.

The role of jingles, tongue-twisters, nursery rhymes and Dr Seuss in helping auditory discrimination and articulacy can be very important. They are a prelude to blending, and can be used with older children who will not be embarrassed by the babyishness of it all because they are skilled child rearers and minders and can use what they learn in school on their younger siblings. I. E. and P. Opie's *The Lore and Language of School Children* (Oxford University Press, 1959) is a treasure trove of chants, skipping songs, folklore and jingles. The children are themselves an excellent source of ballads, for instance the following which includes some Romany words substituted by the child heard singing it on one site:

As I was slowly passing an orphans' home one day,
I stopped there for a moment just to watch the chavvis (children) play.
A lonely mush (boy) was standing there, and when I asked him why
He turned with yoks (eyes) the tears ran down, and he began to cry:

> I'm nobody's chavvi (child),
> I'm nobody's chavvi child).
> Just like a flower, I'm growing wild,
> No Mama's kisses, no Papa's smiles,
> I'm nobody's chavvi (child)
> Nobody wants me.[15]

The uncanny popularity of this well-known song amongst Gypsies—it can be heard on sites all over the country—is interesting, especially because it illustrates the travellers' attitude to children (no wonder travellers have been thought to be baby-snatchers and receivers of illegitimate unwanted babies) and gives an insight into the sort of story that traveller children will respond to—tear-jerking tales of lost and found children. Noel Streatfeild's *Thursday's Child*, with its setting, horses, bargees and orphanages, should be a hit.

Once the teacher has been initiated into some of the Gypsy ways, he or she may be allowed to hear the children sing some of their own songs (Irish Tinkers are more likely to produce Republican hymns and ballads) and such stand-bys as 'I'm the Romani rai' and 'Can you rokker Romani?' However, teachers should not in general solicit such songs.

DILEMMAS OF ASSIMILATION AND HERITAGE

The degree to which cultural manifestations take place varies widely depending upon the attitude of the family concerned and upon the privacy of the classroom situation itself. But there is reason to suspect the motives of a teacher who overstresses the Gypsy heritage. The real concentration is upon the training of the child in the skills that he needs, not to force him to expose in the classroom what he normally keeps for the site.

Travellers often need to be treated differently from gauje children for purely educational considerations, but two reservations must be borne in mind. Firstly, many traveller children will have been assimilated into gauje classes, will want to be treated as children (not as traveller children); and approaches which expose them to ridicule from other children (remarking on their lack of skill in tasks which gauje children mastered even before coming to school), or to premature exposure of distinctive heritage (bringing the 'Gypsy' out of them) may be resisted by the children and may cause parental objections. The traveller is extremely sensitive to overt and covert discrimination. The second reservation is that different activities may be impracticable in such mixed classes because there is a need for the teacher to involve all the children in a common scheme of work; traveller participation obviously depends upon their proficiency in literacy and other basic skills.

As has been already suggested, the 'bridging' operation into the primary level of the educational system is in many respects the easiest part of traveller education. A harder task is to satisfy the desire of the traveller to acquire skills of literacy and numeracy in view of the educationally inimical social background. Harder still is to be able to respond to the educational needs of the travellers when they have attained partial literacy—a mechanical reading age of nine or ten—when, as one teacher put it, 'Some are keen enough until they can read and compute a bit; until they can at least give the impression that they are "scholars" within their own community, but then work intervenes and they are men. Men don't go to school for that is child's play.' It may be that ultimately the solution to these problems lies in using the travellers' cultural heritage, but while stigma and prejudice remain most travellers prefer teachers to leave culture alone.

The wider curriculum

How can teachers develop travellers' literacy further than the initial stages without schemes and reader sets ? The answer to this must be to some extent hypothetical, for very few classrooms were visited where the travellers had progressed to competent de-coding. Most were still struggling to achieve a sufficiently extensive sight vocabulary to be able to use their skills as tools in achieving other goals—writing letters, reading for pleasure and information.

It must also be said that, although there is an abundance of literature on the initial teaching of reading and upon remedial methods and theory, there is a dearth of material covering the acquisition and teaching of efficient and proficient literacy.

Travellers need to be persuaded that they can become proficient and that it will be a worth-while effort. To succeed, therefore, the teacher must do two things: devise a curriculum which will provide the incentive and driving force to literacy progress; and encourage the traveller to seek proficiency. Some of the arguments that can be presented to him and can be used to explore the sort of curriculum which will appeal can be found by an analysis, brutal perhaps, but telling, of what he *cannot* do if he lacks literacy:

He cannot read a chemist's prescription instructions.

He finds great difficulties in form completion (part of the wider skills of proficient literacy).

He cannot read social legislation or detailed reports of parliamentary debates which vitally affect his livelihood—the Caravan Sites Act, for example.

He cannot communicate in writing with other travellers and gauje supporters.

He is at the mercy of red tape, the policeman's note pad, the local authority officer's questionnaire, whenever petty or important regulations are read to him. He does not even know where to find them to check on whether they actually exist and are relevant.

He cannot mobilize political union amongst the travelling community through broadsheets and newspapers.

He cannot read the highway code, Heavy Goods Vehicle regulation pamphlets, or the multi-page application form for the test—hence his frequent infringement of the new laws.

He cannot read communications from headteachers which affect the educational welfare of his children.

He cannot teach his children to read and write and cannot help them with the problems they have in reading and writing.

His wife cannot risk buying many packaged and frozen foods because she cannot read the cooking instructions.

Unless he finds a literate gauje to transcribe a tape-recorded statement or autobiography, he cannot use the power of the pen.

He cannot read books about him and his people—*The Book of Boswell*, the government reports, *The Destiny of Europe's Gypsies*, *Gypsies: Wanderers of the World*, or even this Schools Council report.

He cannot read a site warden's notices.

He cannot enjoy literature unless it is read aloud to him.

He cannot read a map and plan a route, nor can he read warning notices on motorways.

He cannot keep business accounts.

It must be admitted that there are many Gypsies who want to stay as they are, indeed take a pride in overcoming all these problems:

The Gypsy ways are the best ways. I always say I am a Gypsy. I say to my children. 'Never disown yourself.' If people say, 'What are you?' say, 'Well, I'm a Gypsy.'

My children never had education. I reckon education destroys a lot, I do. That's my belief. Neither one of my kids can read nor write, but I can send them anywhere, trust them anywhere. ... I seen a lot of travelling children being educated, I've seen a lot of it. But I reckon they should be left alone. I reckon if a Gypsy wants to be a Gypsy, if he's going to be a Traveller, let him be. [*Tommy Lee.*][16]

Tom Lee, whose words these are, is a Gypsy who has in fact worked hard to advance the education of travelling children. This impassioned statement therefore represents only half of his opinion on schooling, perhaps more specifically on that type of schooling that takes away from people instead of adding to what they already have.

The wider curriculum that exists which can build upon the traveller's heritage, widen his horizons and still avoid the dangers Tom Lee outlines, might include the following:

(*a*) A social studies course that will explore the history of the travellers, their demography throughout the world, their local, national and international position in society. Why there is prejudice against them; what is the nature of their stigma.

(*b*) This self and group consciousness can lead outwards to study of other minority groups throughout the world, and thence to majority groups —history, politics, sociology, religion, anthropology and natural sciences, astronomy and so on can all follow as curiosity dictates.

(*c*) A course on education itself, its history, philosophy and objectives (how these may conflict with his own value systems, his ability to change them so they do not).

Such a curriculum is organizationally difficult within a maintained school because the emphasis is always on the traveller looking outwards and then internalizing his response; if this is to be effective it must be out in the open —freely discussed between teachers and travellers. This is difficult in mixed classes, especially when the travellers are a tense minority group of three children in a class of thirty. It is possible that this can be overcome by a pastoral or tutorial withdrawal follow-up session for travellers after mixed lessons. Other measures might include summer school programmes for travellers only, which would put the year's conventional schooling into this context.

Even within mixed-class situations there are many occasions on which the travellers can operate as a group, participating in the over-all class project but also specifically working in a traveller-oriented facet of it: for instance, at one school visited during the project a class was doing a local environment study—the history of the town, its industrial development and changing social nature, its rivers, topography and so on. The travellers were exploring their own place in the town's history and their present social acceptance in the community. Their active roles included making a newspaper scrapbook of reports and editorials concerned with travellers from the local press. They tape-recorded talks with their older relatives and other old people in the neighbourhood to discover whether their present local authority camp site had been a former Gypsy haunt and, if so, for how long. They plotted on maps where all the other stopping places were, and compared a present-day map with a pre-war map, which revealed how the spread of housing estates had eaten away their old camping lands. In much of this they were helped by some very able gauje top junior class children, whose special topic within the overall project was to trace the changes between the pre-war town and its present sprawl. The travellers participated with a group in surveying selected areas, and they made a survey of the site and a scale model. The project was sustained for a complete academic year, and involved photography and 'artists' impressions' of the old town and the old Gypsy encampment of horse-drawn wagons. The whole class debated the attitude of the townspeople to the Gypsies and made a study of the false impressions that were given in the press: the present travellers were not Tinkers who had come to the town, but descendants of old Gypsies. Their gravestones were photographed and genealogies worked out showing how the children in the class were related to them. The project resulted in much greater understanding on the part of the gauje children, some of whom were invited into one of the trailers, and boasted of having had tea out of Crown Derby. According to the class teacher, not everything went as smoothly as it sounded: there were moments such as when the survey party was attacked by dogs, and a punch-up on the site which momentarily split the travellers. Most important of all, however, was the fact that the travellers who had almost non-existent reading ages at the beginning had made dramatic strides in literacy, though they had needed a great deal of help, especially in the hunt for newspaper clippings. When open day was held, at the end of the year, one or two of the traveller parents offered to bring in old photographs of their grandparents' wagons, wooden flowers, model wagons and clothes pegs.

Projects as successful as this were not common in the schools visited during the inquiry into classroom practice with travellers. Some teachers had felt them inadvisable in view of the risks involved in exposing the travellers to prejudice from other children. In some cases an attempt to emulate a project such as the one described above had led to traveller parents complaining that their heritage was their business, not the school's. But mostly, approaches like this were avoided because they interfered with the teacher's predetermined classroom syllabus. It must also be reflected that the achievement of such an enormous amount of work must have almost completely dominated every class contact hour in that junior school.

Several familiar problems are met in schools concerning specific subjects in the wider curriculum. In art and craft, for instance, many traveller parents feel that the concentration on 'creativity' and non-representative art is misguided. Their own tastes in decoration are 'old-fashioned': china with a floral design, traditional folk-art painting on the sides of wagons and scrap lorries, horses' heads, Victorian trinkets and china figurines, ornate scrollwork and filigree have high value. This may conflict with some teachers' artistic tastes and the whole movement in art and craftwork in schools. Teachers expecting their children to be talented sign painters and decorators may be very disappointed in their travellers' initial awkwardness, though their love of bright colours and vibrant designs frequently results in the development of bold and noticeably folk-art style which can easily be encouraged.

Craft and practical wood- and metal-work activities are popular amongst the boys and can become a regular and enjoyable part of their curriculum. For the girls cookery and needlework are similarly popular: some of the Irish children may in fact be able to do weaving and crochet work of a very high standard. Fairground children may be spectacularly talented in painting, for they are involved in renovating the side-shows and in decorating new ones. They are also very dextrous and may be good carpenters, model makers and adept at maintaining intricate mechanical gadgets.

It has already been remarked that travellers rarely possess a 'knowledge' of the hedgerows and natural history; but many live closer to it than the gauje and may have a totally different manner of classifying it. Just as the bargee child and the ex-bargee are in fact very frightened of water and resist swimming lessons strongly, the traveller is often too close to nature to have an academic or sentimental interest in it. However, he may be knowledgeable about things in the natural environment which are useful—the best wood to burn or to carve for flowers or pegs, how to catch, shave and cook a hedgehog, what can be eaten and what cannot. In fact his whole attitude to the environment and to animal life is utilitarian: he may know where, when and how to pick strawberries and how much one can earn doing it, but he probably knows very little about plant growth. The only members of the animal kingdom to which he has a sentimental attachment are his pets: dogs, horses, rabbits, caged birds and fowl. Some of the children may be knowledgeable about horse breaking, and many teachers have found this knowledge easy to incorporate into their topic work. The keeping of animals in the classroom can also be a rewarding activity.

It has been suggested in the profile of the traveller child and in the interpretation of traveller values that they do not have a particular interest in the scientific explanation of natural phenomena. Though this is true there are many areas of science which may have a relevance to a traveller child. Electricity, for instance, is often regarded as a mystery, and site wardens sometimes have to intervene to prevent continual fusing of lights because the travellers do not understand the difference between plugging something into a light-bulb socket and using a power point. They may be familiar with stripping down vacuum cleaners and extracting the wiring from electric cookers, but their knowledge of wiring circuits is probably limited to car batteries and motor vehicle electrical systems—and then only on a very practical level. Electricity may provide a science project which will appeal and may be developed into other areas (magnetism, for instance).

Projects based upon metals have an obvious relevance because in this area the traveller is without question knowledgeable, but his knowledge is often limited to where to come by metals that make the best scrap market proposition, and which dealer gives the best price for what. On their properties and production, and on their uses, he may be less informed.

Perhaps the most difficult area of science is biology and, in particular, human biology and sex education. Here the travellers' modesty must be taken into account. Many examples have been encountered of children being withdrawn from school because of the introduction of teaching about reproduction. Johnny Connors suggests that:

Under no circumstances must a travelling child be taught the facts of life. When I say this I mean sex, contraceptives, etc., how he or she was born. They know about sex, it's a natural thing. But the parents don't know that the children know this. It's a kind of religious saga between parents and children. It acts like a close kept secret.[17]

One or two headteachers at secondary level mentioned that though they understood the parental attitude, some of their travellers were prurient on such matters and that as headteachers they had had to talk to some of the traveller girls, in particular, about brazenness. This is interesting and not unexpected, though it is mostly for show and not in any way a genuine promiscuity. A teacher from Sweden who is very experienced with teen-age Gypsy girls from some very traditional families informed the project that some of the girls experience hang-ups because extreme sexual modesty in the home conflicts with the seeming licence in school. Most of the girls, she said, arrived in school each morning with ankle-length traditional dresses but after ten minutes could be seen in mini-skirts. In fact it may be that English and Welsh Gypsy and Irish Tinker men are more modest in this than the women. Certainly all the teachers agreed that extreme caution was required when sex education was attempted in school. On childbirth and birth amongst animals travellers are experienced and matter of fact. A Senior Medical Officer of Health reported that he had once delivered a baby some years ago in a wagon during a particularly hot summer spell. He was helped by what he supposed were sisters of the mother. Because of the heat the wagon door and curtains were left open. During the latter stages of the delivery he discovered that there were at least ten children peering in on the proceedings. Being rather busy at the time, he did nothing about it but remembers that he thought that it was not very advisable. However, some ten minutes later his doubts were removed, when he heard the oldest girl remark that everything was okay with their 'Mam' now its 'dear little head' could be seen. When he next turned round they had all disappeared.

Traveller attitudes towards sex and exposure of the body can be seen in the problems of dress for P.E., which drew comments from many schools. All traveller children tended to be very shy of changing in front of other children and were very reluctant initially to take showers. That boys had refused to wear shorts for games was another familiar complaint or point made in questionnaire answers. In fact, this refusal is not just a question of the traveller boys' view of wearing shorts as unmanly; there may also be a strong cultural reluctance to show knees in public. At Appleby Fair, for example, spectators will frequently see the young men and older boys taking the horses down to the riverside and riding them into the river. Though they strip to their waists, they continue to wear their trousers and braces. At school it was felt that it was wise to be tolerant of this, and some teachers reported that when any of the boys were good at games and played football for school teams the initial reluctance to wear shorts soon disappeared.

Generally speaking, travellers enjoy P.E. and games at the primary levels. Their robustness and the absence of physical fear may make them formidable tacklers in football, and at P.E. they tend to be more enthusiastic than graceful. As the traveller gets older his interest in sport declines, especially amongst the girls. Unable to practise skills, the traveller may lose his former pre-eminence in team sports.

Amongst the girls there is a tendency for premature feelings of womanhood and they may become very shy even by the top junior level. This is not unconnected with sexual modesty; during the course of the project one mother of a secondary-age girl in school was read part of the list of school objectives from the Schools Council Working Paper 42, *Education in the Middle Years*. There was a dramatic reaction to the idea that 'Schools should develop individuals physically so that they may be perceptive of themselves and of the body's potential.'[18] The mother turned to her husband and said good-humouredly, 'My Dear Lord, our Rosalie's not going to school no more.' It would be wrong to over-estimate such cultural factors as these, but because they are related also to social apprehension on the part of the traveller parents that their children are not being looked after, account must be taken of them. Usually, however, a straightforward chat with parents on the site can clear up any difficult matters, for most parental objections arise from anxiety. Teachers usually managed to find a similar way around related problems, such as reluctance to go on school trips and visits.

Cultural clashes are unlikely to arise in religious education for, with the exception of the Irish Tinkers, who tend to be Roman Catholic, most travellers do not have strong denominational preferences. Except for the importance of baptism and burial, religion tends to be peripheral to traveller life—though the adage 'know the family' holds here too. However, travellers are unlikely to relish religious education unless attempts are made to engage their interest through relevant topics which touch upon their own experiences.

CONCLUSIONS

Most aspects of the wider curriculum can be subsumed under the broad heading, 'social studies'. What most concerns the traveller is always the most profitable to explore. The objective is to help the traveller to understand his relationship to society and society's attitudes to him, as well as to give him geater insight into the nature of educational provision and the opportunities available to him. These objectives must always be linked to the development of skills in literacy in order that the traveller shall be able to make a choice whether to change his life style, to remain as he is or to partake of both worlds. Curriculum is to a large extent self-selective, and it is felt that teachers should be encouraged to find out from the traveller children and their parents which areas of teaching should be stressed. The major problems facing such measures are organizational: the extent to which special curriculum emphasis *can* be given in mixed classes, and whether the teaching profession itself approves of special emphasis being given to so proportionately small a number of children.

Utilizing cultural background

It has been indicated that approaches which ignore the travellers' distinctive life style and value systems are likely to fail—indeed, there are one hundred years to substantiate that; and present attendance rates for the school-age traveller population indicate that a major change of professional attitude is needed. Many ways have already been indicated which show how schools can capitalize upon the background of travellers. In this section, however, the focus is upon what can be called the 'deeper' cultural heritage—and whether it *can* be exploited by a teacher and whether it *should* be. The 'deeper' elements include the secret languages (which are not after all very secret because there are word lists and dictionaries). Such matters as *mokkadi* are also involved, but the sort of taboos that some Gypsiologists warn one against seem somewhat superfluous and to infringe them unknowingly is not a catastrophe: walking between a Gypsy and fire, casting a shadow on food, breaking a cup if it touches the ground and so on. Certainly in matters involving toilets there is need for more attention to be given to travellers' feelings about communal facilities and the mixing of sexes. Menstruation in young girls does tend to preclude school attendance, and if when visiting a site one is told that a girl is 'off-colour today', it may be best not to interfere. Broadly speaking, the most sensible attitude is showing respect for different customs and being sensitive to infringing the code. It is certainly unwise to anticipate taboos and customs when they do not exist or when a family does not expect one to know about them anyway.

The use of Anglo-Romany and Shelta is similar, for many travellers feel that it is one of their last refuges against the power of the social worker: they can still talk together without being understood. On any one site the likelihood is that some parents will encourage a teacher to use a *few* Anglo-Romany words but that others will disapprove strongly. In the classroom it will be the children initially who determine whether to respond to any careful probing on the question whether they want to know how to spell any secret words. During a visit to one all-traveller classroom, a very significant reaction was seen to an attempt to test out whether the children were 'itinerant scrap dealers' or Gypsies (there had been disagreement about this during coffee break in the staff room). The oldest boy in the group (about seventeen) was discreetly approached, and several Anglo-Romany words were written down on cards. He was asked to read them. Unfortunately, though the oldest boy, he was by no means the most proficient reader. Several other boys and girls gathered round the table and tried to read them. One, a twelve-year-old boy, shouted 'jukel' and picked up the relevant card. There was a momentary hush, then a lot of pushing and shoving. Eventually the oldest boy and the twelve-year-old had cleared all the other travellers from the scene, and for the next ten minutes none was allowed to approach. Some thirty Anglo-Romany words were written, and as each card was picked up if the younger boy could read it he passed it to the older and whispered it into the ear of the older boy who then gave the English translation. When the younger boy could not read a word he was told what it was. Several of the words needed correction because, though used elsewhere in the country, there were regional variations. Only after school on the site did the older boy actually say an Anglo-Romany word aloud and the others used them freely in front of the visitor. Parents on the site overhearing the exchange expressed mixed feelings about whether it should be allowed in the classroom at school: some suggesting that it would help if they could write Romany letters to one another, others saying that it was not a 'writing language'. Incidentally the oldest boy could still 'read' all the cards three hours after their first introduction in the classroom—which probably doubled his sight vocabulary.

Perhaps the most significant point, however, is that, whereas it is relatively easy for a teacher to equip herself with a rudimentary Anglo-Romany *vocabulary*, understanding and participating in a conversation is another matter, for the language is spoken with such rapidity and rich supportive gesture that it becomes totally indecipherable to someone with only a few Anglo-Romany words culled from a word list or from children.

Many other experiences elsewhere reveal that this is tricky territory to enter. In one on-site educational unit the travellers were taught an international Romany movement's national anthem. They quickly mastered it and sang it every day for two weeks or more. But later, when there was a request by the children to sing it again, it was, 'Can we's sing that French song again, Miss?' Much depends upon whether it is a traveller-only or a mixed class situation and upon whether the travellers approve of cultural exposure. It was concluded ultimately that in only exceptional situations should Anglo-Romany or Shelta words be used in the classroom, and then only if the children volunteered to do so. Teachers are advised to inform parents about any use they may wish to make of the secret languages. It was also thought that the use of Anglo-Romany (or Shelta, for that matter) should be limited to a vocabulary of about thirty or so of the most common words (see Appendix A).

Vocational aspects

There is some debate within gauje Gypsy support groups as to whether there is an urgent need for a programme of industrial retraining and vocational guidance for travellers. Those who believe that there is point to signs that the scrap market may collapse, to the take-over of the fruit-producing farms by the big companies and the resulting decline in casual picking opportunities for travellers, and to the existence, especially on some of the well-established local authority sites, of families 'on the welfare'. Those who oppose such a course suggest that the survival of the traveller has been due to his ability to turn his hand to anything, to respond to the needs of the host society for some service (very often not recognized as a service at all but as 'parasitical scavenging') and to their family-oriented economic system. Certainly all would admit the almost complete failure of attempts to settle travellers in regular employment other than casual labouring where there is a great deal of individual freedom—logging or even gardening.

The dilemma is whether or not to make vocational training an important part of the later secondary school years. On present evidence and in view of the present attitude amongst the travellers, any such training should be limited to equipping travellers with skills—perhaps welding, vehicle maintenance (linked to the literacy of vehicle maintenance manuals) or metalwork and so on. It is clear that any attempt to determine employment would fail because it is anathema to travelling society, for that society thrives basically on its talent for discovering the host society's need for casual and mobile work. To interfere in vocational matters would be in direct conflict with the travellers' ethos of making their own way by their wits and their strength.

The solution to this dilemma is a logical one: day- or block-release of the child into the care of his parents for educative industrial training. Such a system may require LEA discretion under section 56 of the 1944 Act, but it is perhaps the only valid answer to secondary withdrawal. In order to work, such a system would require the release of a teacher to conduct intensive tuition during evening sessions or summer schools. But until the time when educated travellers can become teachers there is probably no substitute.

The whole concept may have increasing appeal at a time when secondary truancy and internal discipline problems are beginning to cause deep professional concern. Certainly curriculum and organizational innovation created for travellers' children may have application to other groups of children in the future.

Teaching the nomad

The second chapter of this report (see page 9) pointed to a widespread notion that education and nomadism were incompatible. It is hoped that it has been established that such a notion is ill-founded. 'Regular school attendance is incompatible with nomadism' might be a better formulation.

Of all the problems raised by the education of travelling children, their mobility presents the teacher and the educational administrator with the hardest task. Practicability apart, there are still major hurdles: whether the profession would accept the need for a common curriculum and common teaching materials, whether there would be sufficient personnel to fill the posts created (which would entail high mobility and sub-standard, possibly harsh, work environments).

Various suggestions can be made for the education of nomadic families' children:

(a) The establishment of designated special traveller units, possibly attached to existing schools, in places where it is known that nomadic groups regularly turn up; these may need to be linked to an as yet non-existent network of transit camps or authorized halts.

(b) The setting up of regional, even national co-ordinating bodies which would oversee the liaison between such units and maintained schools affected by nomadic attenders. Perhaps the most important role for such co-ordinating bodies is to establish a system of common record keeping and to establish an efficient means of record transfers. Such a system is already in preparation in trial form in the West Midlands education authorities, further information being obtainable from the Wolverhampton Education Offices.

(c) The development of teaching materials which are both suitable for common use in these designated educational establishments and also adaptable for outdoor use and for use in small mobile classrooms (e.g., mini-buses), and which have a strong self-teaching component to enable travellers to continue learning literacy skills without teacher supervision when they are on the road and far from the designated centres. Such a component could be linked to a television literacy programme or to cassette programmed instruction tapes.

(d) The creation of a teaching force, trained and equipped with resources of transport and communication, capable of maintaining such a programme.

Until an adequate network of sites has been provided, and special provision for nomadic families made, it is difficult to see how such suggestions could be implemented successfully. However, that should not prevent the establishment of a few pilot projects with nomadic children.

Notes and references

1 David Mackay and Brian Thompson, *The Initial Teaching of Reading and Writing*, Schools Council Programme in Linguistics and English Teaching, Paper 3 (University College, London/Longmans Green, 1968), pp. 9, 33.

2 Ibid., p. 9.

3 Ibid., p. 33.

4 Paul Widlake, *Literacy in the Secondary School* (National Association for Remedial Education, 1972), pp. 4–5. Obtainable from NARE, 20 Hanbury Crescent, Penn, Wolverhampton.

5 Maria Montessori, *The Montessori Method* (Heinemann, 1914); Sylvia Ashton-Warner, *Teacher* (Penguin Books, 1966; first published by Secker & Warburg, 1963); H. Kohl, *36 Children* (Penguin Education, 1972); Erik Erikson, *Childhood and Society* (Hogarth Press, 1964; also Penguin Books, 1969); Rachel Scott, *A Wedding Man Is Nicer than Cats, Miss* (David & Charles, 1971).

6 Donald Moyle, *The Teaching of Reading* (Ward Lock Educational, 1968); James Webster, *Practical Reading* (Evans, 1965); Fred J. Schonell, *Backwardness in the Basic Subjects* (Oliver & Boyd, 1948) and *Psychology and the Teaching of Reading* (Oliver & Boyd, 1961); A. E. Tansley, *Reading and Remedial Reading* (Routledge & Kegan Paul, 1967); M. D. Vernon, *Reading and Its Difficulties* (Cambridge University Press, 1971); J. C. Daniels and H. Diack, *The Phonic Word Method of Teaching Reading* (Chatto & Windus, 1957) and *The Standard Reading Tests* (Chatto & Windus, 1960); H. Diack, *Reading and the Psychology of Perception* (R. Palmer, 1960); Jessie Reid, ed., *Reading: Problems and Practices* (Ward Lock Educational, 1972); Alec Williams, *Basic Subjects for the Slow Learner* (Methuen Educational, 1970); Paul Widake, *Literacy in the Secondary School* (see n. 4); David Mackay, Brian Thompson and Pamela Schaub, *Breakthrough to Literacy*, Teacher's Manual (Longman, 1971).

7 Acknowledgement is due to John Wallbridge for help in drafting 'the five stages of literacy'; since writing this our attention has been drawn to a similar five-stage model of reading acquisition in J. L. Presland, 'A psychologist's approach to backward readers', *Remedial Education*, vol. 5, nos. 1, 2, and 3/4 (1970), pp. 5–9, 52–6, 145–7. A much more detailed account of the whole development of reading skills can be found in Ruth Strang, *The Improvement of Reading*, 4th edn (New York: McGraw-Hill, 1967). A readily available reprint of the relevant section of this appears in *Reading: Today and Tomorrow*, ed. Amelia Melnik and John Merritt (University of London Press/Open University Press, 1972), pp. 255–64. Also useful here is *Literacy at All Levels*, ed. Vera Southgate (Ward Lock Educational, 1972). The Schools Council's Project on Extending Beginning Reading, based at Manchester University

and under the direction of Vera Southgate, will shortly add to the knowledge and published material concerned with this neglected area of reading.

8   *The Shadow on the Cheese*, ed. J. Wallbridge (NGEC, 1972), p. 13.

9   See *The Standard Reading Tests* (see n. 6).

10   *The Montessori Method* (see n. 5), pp. 287–90.

11   George Smith of Coalville, Appendix to the Report of the Select Committee on Canals (1883), p. 312.

12   Clifford Parfitt, 'Photography with less able pupils', *Remedial Education*, vol. 4, no. 2 (1969), pp. 89–91.

13   Ewan McColl, Charles Parker and Peggy Seeger, *The Travelling People*, Argo, DA 133 (recording of BBC programme).

14   See also Bibliography.

15   There are as many versions as there are travellers, but the tune remains basically the same. Teachers will soon discover, however, that Gypsies have more than just a 'public-house' singing style: the quavering can be found to relate to Hungarian Gypsy singers and was once accompanied with the Gypsy fiddle ('faking the bosh').

16   *The Shadow on the Cheese* (see n. 8), p. 8.

17   Ibid., p. 11.

18   *Education in the Middle Years*, Schools Council Working Paper 42 (Evans/ Methuen Educational, 1972), p. 96.

7 Conclusions and recommendations

Although this project was established primarily to help classroom teachers, the main need at the present time is for an administrative and organizational response to the widespread non-attendance and educational privation that dominates the traveller community. The following is therefore addressed primarily to LEA officers and other administrators; it is hoped that the previous chapter will provide individual teachers with the advice and information they need.

In order to present the conclusions and recommendations of this project in a compact form yet with sufficient logic and detail to be comprehensive, a flow chart summary has been designed. The remainder of the chapter develops point by point the ideas in the flow chart, and indicates where further information can be found in earlier sections of this report.

It might appear that what has been attempted is a complete answer to all the problems of traveller education; but this is far from the case and recommendations made are of a very tentative nature. The major hypothesis behind them is that it is far too early to attempt anything other than as wide a range of pragmatic responses as can be devised, to evaluate them during and after a trial five-year period, and only then to develop a coordinated and uniform policy, if it is desirable.

The second main hypothesis is that experience to date, except with very recently established projects in both maintained and voluntary sectors, has been with an atypical, more settled and 'accommodating' group of families; and that successful assimilation into normal schools, where it has been achieved at secondary as well as primary level, will not necessarily be effective or desirable for the less settled families whose social and educational problems are more intransigent.

Current state of traveller education

As was suggested in Chapter 2, the once difficult educational problems of the bargees and the fairground children have been wholly or at least partially overcome: the bargees, as a group, have virtually ceased to exist, and the fair-

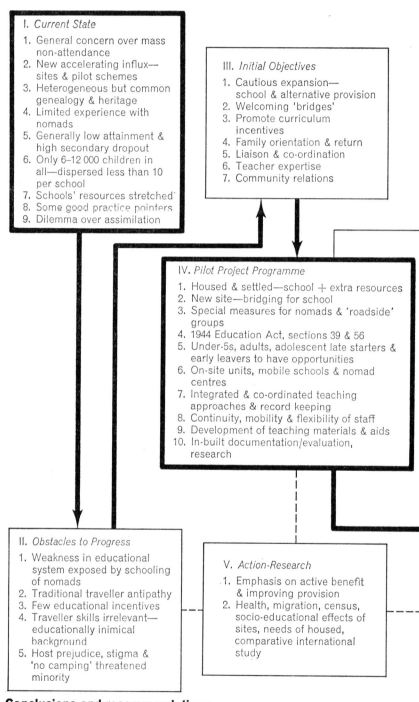

I. *Current State*

1. General concern over mass non-attendance
2. New accelerating influx—sites & pilot schemes
3. Heterogeneous but common genealogy & heritage
4. Limited experience with nomads
5. Generally low attainment & high secondary dropout
6. Only 6–12 000 children in all—dispersed less than 10 per school
7. Schools' resources stretched
8. Some good practice pointers
9. Dilemma over assimilation

III. *Initial Objectives*

1. Cautious expansion—school & alternative provision
2. Welcoming 'bridges'
3. Promote curriculum incentives
4. Family orientation & return
5. Liaison & co-ordination
6. Teacher expertise
7. Community relations

IV. *Pilot Project Programme*

1. Housed & settled—school + extra resources
2. New site—bridging for school
3. Special measures for nomads & 'roadside' groups
4. 1944 Education Act, sections 39 & 56
5. Under-5s, adults, adolescent late starters & early leavers to have opportunities
6. On-site units, mobile schools & nomad centres
7. Integrated & co-ordinated teaching approaches & record keeping
8. Continuity, mobility & flexibility of staff
9. Development of teaching materials & aids
10. In-built documentation/evaluation, research

II. *Obstacles to Progress*

1. Weakness in educational system exposed by schooling of nomads
2. Traditional traveller antipathy
3. Few educational incentives
4. Traveller skills irrelevant—educationally inimical background
5. Host prejudice, stigma & 'no camping' threatened minority

V. *Action-Research*

1. Emphasis on active benefit & improving provision
2. Health, migration, census, socio-educational effects of sites, needs of housed, comparative international study

Conclusions and recommendations

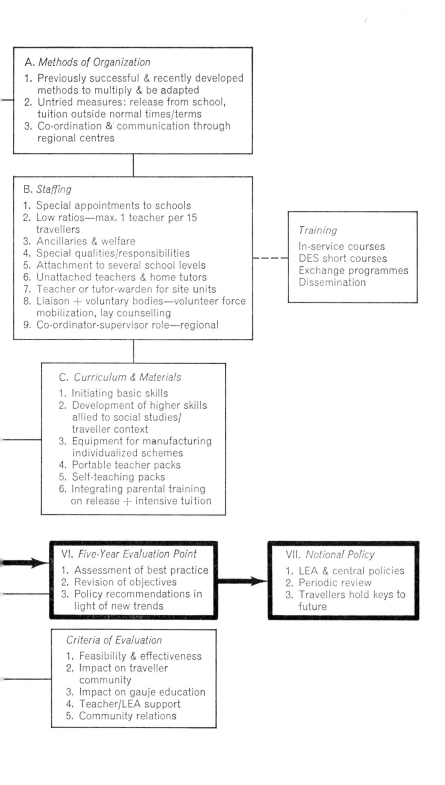

A. *Methods of Organization*
1. Previously successful & recently developed methods to multiply & be adapted
2. Untried measures: release from school, tuition outside normal times/terms
3. Co-ordination & communication through regional centres

B. *Staffing*
1. Special appointments to schools
2. Low ratios—max. 1 teacher per 15 travellers
3. Ancillaries & welfare
4. Special qualities/responsibilities
5. Attachment to several school levels
6. Unattached teachers & home tutors
7. Teacher or tutor-warden for site units
8. Liaison + voluntary bodies—volunteer force mobilization, lay counselling
9. Co-ordinator-supervisor role—regional

Training
In-service courses
DES short courses
Exchange programmes
Dissemination

C. *Curriculum & Materials*
1. Initiating basic skills
2. Development of higher skills allied to social studies/traveller context
3. Equipment for manufacturing individualized schemes
4. Portable teacher packs
5. Self-teaching packs
6. Integrating parental training on release + intensive tuition

VI. *Five-Year Evaluation Point*
1. Assessment of best practice
2. Revision of objectives
3. Policy recommendations in light of new trends

VII. *Notional Policy*
1. LEA & central policies
2. Periodic review
3. Travellers hold keys to future

Criteria of Evaluation
1. Feasibility & effectiveness
2. Impact on traveller community
3. Impact on gauje education
4. Teacher/LEA support
5. Community relations

ground and circus children attend for most of the year when they are in permanent quarters and receive spasmodic education when 'on the circuit'. Although LEAs and schools could develop better communication and common teaching approaches for multiple attendance by fairground children, there is nothing like the critical situation that affects the travellers. For this latter group the main problem is mass non-attendance—anywhere between 75 and 90% are not in school—a phenomenon that once characterized the education of bargees and fairground children but is only just beginning to change for the travellers after one hundred years of compulsory schooling in England and Wales which has been implemented for the rest of society.

The main reasons for this change, which will obviously accelerate as there is a corresponding acceleration in the opening of permanent local authority sites under the 1968 Caravan Sites Act, is the post-Plowden concern of teachers, LEAs, the DES, voluntary bodies and the public. In addition, more travellers than ever before are beginning to seek education and schooling, and are less likely to resist friendly gestures by educationists. If in 1969–70 at least 1500 travellers were known to be on school rolls (see pages 19–22), the situation in 1973 is almost certainly much better, and over the next five years will improve further. Perhaps the only way to trace the gradual growth of attendance would be for travellers to be a distinct category of the annual DES Form 7 returns.

It is impossible to be precise about the total number of traveller children (see pages 21–2 and 65–7), but there may be at least 6000 or as many as 12 000 school-aged travellers. However, they are widely dispersed throughout England and Wales, near host population centres. Unless near an exceptionally large site, a local school will rarely have more than ten on the roll at any one time (a fifteen-trailer site will be unlikely to produce more than thirty potential attenders divided equally between the three age-level schools—see pages 24–5. In certain cases housed families in the neighbourhood may swell numbers a little, and there are indications that the housed exhibit similar educational difficulties, though not so severe, to the caravan-dwelling families to whom they are closely related.

Contrary to the views of some teachers and local authority observers the travellers are a highly distinctive social group with a complex but recognizably ancient heritage. It is a myth that they are merely 'itinerant scrap dealers' or society's drop-outs. It is also a myth that they wish to abandon their life style and settle. Rather, they are facing a crisis inevitably brought about by suburban development, shortage of wasteland, and post-war legislation of planning and site licensing. Though genetically mixed, they are genealogically a close-knit and well-defined group with a unique life style and value system. The majority (perhaps 80%) are English or Welsh with a Romany-oriented cultural heritage; under 15% are Irish Tinkers, found mainly in the North and Midlands, and the remainder are either Scottish (3 to 4%) or of mixed ancestry. However, each of these three groups is intermarried and shares to a varying degree Romany and indigenous nomadic origins (see pages 55–60). The existence of a significant proportion of travelling families of neither Tinker nor Gypsy origin was not confirmed during the project. Yet they are heterogeneous in terms of degree of nomadism (see categorization on pages 63–4), habitation (tents, wagons, but mostly trailer-caravans), legality and security of camping site, previous educational experience and social acceptability to and desire to conform with the host population.

A small minority of settled families have attended local schools for generations; and more recently schools serving sites established in the early 1960s have succeeded in establishing regular attendance, though this is less true at secondary level where premature adult status and early economic roles within the family conflict with schooling.

Projects started during and after this Schools Council study within both maintained and independent sectors have generally revealed that the more nomadic children—those from the unauthorized encampments and those whose families have had little contact with settled communities and school—do not initially thrive in normal classes but require alternative preparatory provision. Even permanent site children may need special measures in the early stages. The problem is exacerbated by the fact that it is not only the rising five-year-olds who need preparation for school; traveller children of all ages may be totally unschooled, and the older the child, the less feasible normal school assimilation can be. There may even be a threshold age at which education in school should not be insisted upon unless there is a genuine desire to attend. This age may be around thirteen.

It must also be stated that attendance regularity declines sharply with advancing age once the secondary stage has been reached, yet the desire for continued education, particularly literacy, may remain strong. Participation by such adolescents in summer school programmes and in late afternoon and evening classes on sites suggests that release from compulsory term and day-time attendance could increase rather than decrease educational contact if opportunities for home and site tuition are available.

Headteachers were unanimous in believing that the attendance of even a small number of travellers requires additional resources in terms of staff, accommodation and capitation allowance. Three factors are basic to successful teaching of travellers: a friendly and welcoming atmosphere in the classroom, extensive site visiting by school staff and plentiful small group and individual tuition. The ability of a school to provide these three ingredients depends upon LEA generosity in addition to teacher dedication.

There is a genuine dilemma over assimilation or pluralism. Many traveller parents desire attendance by their children in the normal way and no obvious differentiation in treatment. Sometimes such parents may need to be persuaded that a transition of preparation or 'bridging' into school is in their best interests. Generally speaking, the decision over the need for special measures is not one that should result from the socio-educational predilections of teachers or administrators, but should be a pragmatic response to a particular situation.

Major obstacles to progress

Several weaknesses of the maintained system are exposed by the special demands of traveller education: the system is neither designed nor geared for a nomadic people with the characteristic mass abstention, late starting, irregularity of attendance, seasonal comings and goings, multiple attendance at several schools during the same academic year and premature withdrawal to participate in the family economy. Indeed, though there is no absolute conflict between nomadism and education, regular school attendance and nomadism are to an extent incompatible.

Schools have rigid term times and operating hours, the clock and the calendar; and they, like the host society generally, operate through systems of postponed rewards and future time orientation. The traveller is oriented to the present and the immediate reward and therefore may be disappointed when he presents his child at school in August only to find the school closed.

There is insufficient liaison among individual schools and among LEAs in ensuring continuity of teaching approaches; record transfers are undeveloped, as are systems of dealing with 'pool' children moving from one school catchment area to another (especially if this also means mobility between local authorities). The present system deals with children individually, not with families and kinship groups, and travellers neither understand the philosophy behind this nor are prepared to see siblings and cousins so dispersed.

If these mechanical problems were all, they could be solved administratively with little difficulty; but such problems are relatively minor when compared to the travellers' traditional antipathy to education and the results of their academically inimical backgrounds. The travellers are proud to be a society apart, not bound by the restrictions and regulations which affect the sedentary house dweller. They also take great pride in 'getting on' independently without education, literacy and received knowledge. Many base their economies on the gullibility and naïvety of gaujes; they have a living proof that education in schools is of little worth in such matters—indeed, that some of their strategies may succeed precisely because education puts blinkers on to the individual. Many, who have a superficial level of literacy and education, will exaggerate their illiteracy and lack of education when they face officialdom or forms.

In many cases the traveller superiority complex is a defence mechanism. They know that there is little likelihood that their children will shine in school, and that actually there is real danger that they will be classified as gnorant, illiterate, even ineducable. They may even fear that their children will be categorized ESN or 'mental'. Attendance at school also exposes their children to host community prejudice, abuse and, on playgrounds, assault—and they may have hurtful experience of this themselves to remember and to embellish in the retelling.

Schooling may be feared because it can be used to indoctrinate and to erode culture; more simply, it may result in softening the child and lowering his resistance to the physical rigours of travelling life. For older children, every hour at school may be an equivalent loss of valuable training and experience within the family economy and the struggle for survival.

Most schools operate on the proposition that education is a major force of upward social mobility through educational attainment and qualification. Schools thus offer an escape route out of the lower socio-economic strata of society. Travellers who are not part of any supposed hierarchical structure view this as anathema, for family and group solidarity and loyalty have priority in their value system.

The problem is therefore not merely one of accessibility of school in practicable terms, but an absence of incentive to take advantage of what it has to offer. School curriculum offers little to the traveller except training in the basic skills of literacy and numeracy, and even in these there is much evidence that few schools are successful in raising standards amongst traveller children to a sufficient level for their educational advantage.

The socialization of the traveller child is almost exclusively within the family and kin-group situation. The child therefore moves only in an illiterate and uneducated circle. He meets few strangers who are interested in helping him to master reading and writing, and certainly his companions are unable to assist. What schooling he does receive is his *only* opportunity to master literacy. Absence of card and board games, writing implements, colouring books, jigsaws and other educationally beneficial games and toys is explicable, for they serve little purpose for traveller life. The skills that the child does develop—which include child minding, collection and classification of metal and other waste products of the gauje world, but also social responsibility to the family by avoiding giving information to outsiders (even to the extent of feigning inarticulacy)—are of little positive value at school. For the same purposes, traveller children also tend to hide their culture and traveller language. From the gauje point of view, the language some do display appears grossly restricted, as indeed it may be if the criteria are elaborated codes and 'intellectual' vocabulary. Teachers can certainly under-estimate their traveller pupils, and this is quickly communicated to the children themselves whose powers of sizing up adults and situations have been specifically encouraged by their parents. The solution to this problem must obviously involve adaptation by both parties, but the initial burden of responsibility for change lies with schools and teachers—the professionals in the situation.

Unfortunately the whole position is complicated and prejudiced by the social tensions that affect travellers at school. This is not merely feelings of claustrophobia in large buildings and unfamiliarity with operating in large peer groups; it is also a question of the travellers' social stigma, the host community's denigration and hostility towards them and the actual insecurity and threatened predicament of the traveller. Unauthorized encampment, harassment, eviction and feelings of being legally outlawed dominate the lives of most travellers and they cannot be ignored in the school setting. Not only can they deprive the school of its traveller pupils overnight, but they also cause the traveller to erect a united defensive attitude and potentially hostile approach to gaujes.

The obstacles that must be overcome if traveller education is to develop successfully are therefore not limited to the practicalities of schooling a group of nomads. They include the factors already mentioned above and the whole situation of site provision and local authority policy (including the ways in which designation orders under the 1968 Act are handled), forces over which teachers and educationists have no direct control.

Initial objectives

The ensuing objectives follow logically from the review of current traveller education and the delineation of the major obstacles to be overcome. The first and major objective must surely be the sustained expansion of schooling and alternative educational provision for traveller children. In order to achieve this it will be necessary to promote greater incentives for travellers to take advantage of places available to their children in maintained schools, to institute a more welcoming and encouraging attitude on the part of EWOs, teachers and headteachers and to continue to expand the special educational provision that is being created for those for whom normal school attendance is difficult and, perhaps, not in their best interests.

It seems important to bear in mind the family-oriented ideals of the travellers, this time for purely educational motives: the unschooled are of all ages, and it seems important to use adults and children as mutual teachers. Moreover, a family approach is most likely to avoid placing the traveller pupil in a situation where the needs of his education are in conflict with those of his family.

Travellers' education will benefit from the flexibility not only of teaching approaches but also of the actual mobility of teaching staff, in the places and times at which they can teach (i.e., teaching anywhere and at any time—not merely when it conveniently fits into existing school terms and times) and the varying roles which they can fill. Because travellers may move from catchment area to catchment area—frequently from one LEA area to another—liaison between appropriate schools and authorities facilitates the entire undertaking.

Additionally, the effectiveness of the learning situation will take precedence over abstract notions about the value of integration and social mixing between traveller and gauje.

It is now possible to envisage greater expertise in teaching travellers. With such an educationally inimical background sustained educational contact alone may be insufficient to achieve satisfactory progress. Intensive, small group or individual attention from a sympathetic and specially trained teacher may be necessary to compensate for that background. The dissemination of information and advice to teachers and administrators is therefore crucial. Besides improving methods of teaching, it may be necessary to devise more suitable teaching materials and curriculum which have a traveller frame of reference, and are more in tune with traveller aspirations.

The last major objective must be improved community relations; and here, although the teacher has an important role, those outside the profession have the major responsibilities: site managers, social service workers, politicians and local residents.

Five-year pilot project programme

The achievement of the foregoing objectives can best be met by a five-year programme of pilot projects which would concentrate on flexibility and variety, pragmatic solutions to particular situations.

For families who are housed or who are settled on sites and who have previous experience of schooling, the allocation of normal places in classes in maintained schools is clearly the most satisfactory response. Methods of organizing withdrawal group tuition for those traveller children who remain well below gauje norms of attainment in the basic skills are already well tried and, given the generosity of LEAs in providing the necessary resources of accommodation and staff, should be sufficient in cases where primary education has been continuous. At secondary level it will be important to keep the children's attendance and progress under close observation, for evidence suggests that premature withdrawal will be common and cannot be prevented by a punitive policy of instituting compulsory attendance orders.

For children on new sites who have virtually no previous educational experience but whose families intend to live a relatively settled life, the main aim should be a bridging or preparatory operation to enable them to take advantage of normal schooling. A variety of measures have already been tried and could be duplicated elsewhere (see Chapter 5).

For nomadic children from both official and unofficial sites, whose social and educational alienation is likely to be more severe, special measures will be needed. These can be developed from the range of provision possible under clauses 39 and 56 of the 1944 Education Act, which were also discussed in Chapter 5, and on page 158.

The important points to note are that it is legally necessary only to ensure that travellers receive 200 teaching sessions a year, possibly composed of five tuition sessions per week for forty weeks in the year, and that these can be outside a school and outside normal school hours and terms. Alternatively this can be arranged so that the child receives some education within a maintained school and some through home tuition from a qualified teacher, and that parental training of the child in traveller trades and family roles can be considered as an integral part of that child's educative experience. However, under strict application of the law, section 39 only operates for a child of compulsory school age who is already registered at a school. Home tuition would therefore only act as a mitigating circumstance to such a child whose parents are prosecuted under this section for failure to see that their child attends for 200 sessions. Moreover, in the case of a child not registered at a school, the 200 sessions per year dispensation does not apply, though the definition of 'efficient full-time education' is vague, if it can indeed be said to exist at all.

The suggestions for some education outside the school are by no means as radical as they first appear, for in most cases this is precisely what is taking place now: attendance at school is frequently limited to 200 sessions, recent pilot projects involving on-site units provide up to five sessions weekly under a qualified teacher, and the children do receive educative upbringing and industrial training from their parents. Ideally, the mere satisfaction of minimum legal requirements is not a very laudable motive: 200 sessions a year may be educationally inadequate, and the real aim is to provide the best and most effective learning. But what is important is that LEAs can legally justify a wide range of experimental practice. Such experiments will not only be appropriate for nomadic children but also for semi-settled travellers who are starting their schooling so late that they will never be able to develop their full potential and catch up with their gauje peers in a conventional school setting. By providing an alternative method of education 'premature withdrawal from school' becomes a well-organized transition to continued education in the home and by parents.

These measures are obviously more feasible on official sites, where special accommodation in the form of a purpose-built community education centre can be provided, possibly through joint financing by the LEA and the other department of the authority concerned with the development and management of the site. Yet it is most important that the illegally encamped should not be neglected. In some cases, mobile units can be used, for there are many ways in which the laws of obstruction and trespass can be avoided and permission granted; alternatively the children can be transported to a local school or a rented hall, which can be used as a classroom.

The teaching of nomadic children is not just a question of providing temporary or mobile classroom accommodation but must include continuity of teaching approaches, and, where practicable, teaching staff. If the families concerned are middle- or long-distance travellers (see pages 61–5), it may be more feasible to transfer to a different staff and there must be considerable communication and liaison and a system of regionally centred record keeping such as that proposed at Wolverhampton. The numbers of children involved are quite small and would involve only a small number of full- or part-time teachers and the services of H.M. or local inspectors to coordinate provision. The idea (see recommendations of the report from Eire discussed on pages 61–2) of establishing nomad education centres, or of designating schools in areas traditionally frequented by such groups as centres, is probably a very sensible one, but it implies that when there are no travellers in the area there would be a problem of redundant staff. However, the service of an additional teacher whose main task is to provide tuition to nomads can easily be transferred to a school receiving settled travellers to assist in withdrawal group teaching. Similarly, an occasion may arise when an on-site unit becomes unnecessary because all the children from a site have been absorbed into local schools, but it would be unwise to close the unit in view of the fact that the teacher attached to the unit could easily turn her concentration to adult or pre-school work and might be needed anyway if a new family moves to the site with no previous schooling.

Especially in large county areas, LEAs already have peripatetic remedial staff and unattached teachers who can, as in Somerset and Cambridgeshire, be sent to relieve pressures on schools receiving a sudden traveller influx; but wherever possible special teachers dealing almost exclusively with travellers are preferable. The Schools Psychological Services and such peripatetic experts can be used to advise and assist but their other responsibilities are often so great that full involvement would be difficult.

During the five years it is hoped that materials and curriculum would be developed which will be more effective than existing ones, and that there would be a genuine attempt to provide a traveller frame of reference in them. Gradually it will become possible for teachers throughout the country to have access to such materials, and the problems travellers face when changing schools (with different reading schemes and approaches) will be eliminated. The adoption of common schemes may be strongly resisted by schools, especially when it would mean that gauje children would be on totally different ones, but this is again a question of the relative importance of the needs of children and the need of teachers to devise methods which make *their* job easier. In this instance, it would seem incontrovertible that the children should be put first.

Perhaps the most essential component of the five-year project programme is built-in evaluation and documentation. One of this project's main conclusions was that it was far too early, and at present too difficult, to attempt an objective assessment of individual methods of organization. There are far too many variables: the age, expertise and approach of the teacher, the social atmosphere in the locality of the site, the wide range of children, the near impossibility of finding appropriate control groups, the limited number of projects and their relative youth. However, as more and more projects are set up, evaluation will become easier, and even the documentation of projects that have been abandoned or expanded becomes illuminating.

At this stage it would be advisable to look specifically at the type of organization and the staff and teaching approaches needed.

METHODS OF ORGANIZATION

From the range of organization described in detail in Chapter 5, it is possible to select several methods which have already indicated a degree of success.

(a) Various strategies for partial class dispersal and withdrawal groups. Delayed transfer into normal classes after a traveller-only reception class, possibly for all ages.

(b) The use of a parked caravan classroom in the school grounds which is not only cheap and potentially mobile, but also provides a secure home-from-home atmosphere.

(c) The totally separate traveller unit in rented accommodation near a site or circuit of encampments to which the children are transported for special inductive education.

(d) The on-site supportive and family education unit—an extension class-room administratively attached to a local school, and with easy access to it.

(e) The 'school on wheels' used to visit unauthorized camps subject to periodic evictions, and isolated families who cannot otherwise go to school.

(f) The nomad education centre discussed earlier in this chapter, which is probably best if based at a maintained school.

(g) The roving teacher equipped with a 'classroom in a suitcase' (or portable teaching equipment that can easily be transported in cars).

(h) Special measures as yet untried, enabling older secondary-age travellers, who have had some previous education or for whom it is now too late to start schooling, to be released from compulsory school attendance fully or partially (session, day or even block release) so that they can receive educative training with parents or other adult travellers, with special tuition for up to five sessions a week in the basic skills, particularly in literacy, with a qualified teacher.

(i) Intensive summer schools (or at other times of the year) in addition to schooling or, in exceptional cases when families are accessible only for short durations, as an alternative to normal term times. The development of a four-term year for nomads.

TEACHING AND ALLIED STAFF NEEDED

It is important to remember that above all else traveller children need a teacher who is friendly and sympathetic and who is prepared to devote a great deal of time to talking and listening to her pupils. Oracy and trust do not necessarily develop in the best accommodation, indeed traveller children will talk most freely in familiar surroundings: their own trailers and the camp site, during private sessions, for instance, in the headteacher's office, and during outside visits. The appointment of teachers with special responsibility for the traveller children is therefore critical to successful practice. Such teachers need freedom from the restrictions of a timetable and travelling allowances to make the essential home and site visits that have been so strongly recommended. Headteachers almost unanimously claimed that the minimum ratio for efficiency was one teacher to every fifteen travellers.

The need for ancillary helpers in addition to extra professional staff is not a luxury, but in situations where it is impossible for financial reasons to appoint a teacher, lay helpers can be of great value in solving the initial social problems during the first stage of regular attendance and in acting as a go-between with school and site managers and wardens.

It is not easy to isolate the qualities required for such appointments, though familiarity with infant methods and pre-reading activities, or alternatively remedial experience seems advisable. Such work is very demanding, and physical stamina and resilience are useful. More important still, it is a great advantage if the teacher is married and has children. This gives travellers a sense of security and a common point of conversation. Furthermore, in units operating outside schools it enables an initial social contact between traveller and gauje children if the teacher is prepared to take her own children to the site.

Several interesting possibilities can be developed. A teacher may be appointed not merely to one school but also to the infant, junior and secondary (or first, middle and senior) schools receiving the children from the same site. The teacher can be responsible for conducting withdrawal group classes in each of the schools and can help to create a family-oriented situation.

The use of peripatetic or otherwise unattached teachers or home tutors has an obvious relevance to traveller education over the next five years. One of the drawbacks of the old attendance officer or school board man was that he appeared to be a law enforcement officer rather than an educationist. The EWO of today has tended to move more into the social welfare role. There is surely great scope for an appointment which involves both roles but has a primary purpose in promoting education actively by initiating children to elementary education during home visits, acting as a homework supervisor and coach, and helping to develop pre-schooling and adult education. The voluntary support groups have proved that especially amongst young people and students there is a large pool of potential helpers. Moreover, LEAs can add to that pool by releasing teachers in ordinary schools which are shortly to receive a traveller influx to participate in home- and site-based teaching as useful in-service training. Colleges of education are a further source of man-power, and as more and more courses are being run on minority group education and as the emphasis is increasingly to place value on the practical experience in training, student teachers are ideal sources of one-to-one intensive teaching.

When a site unit is established it is obviously essential that it be run by a competent full-time teacher, and possibly also an ancillary helper. LEAs may deem it advisable to work closely with whichever department manages the site (usually Social Services) by appointing jointly a tutor-warden. Such appointments are obviously economical in terms of available funds but may also have many advantages in a branch of education in which it is often not possible to dissociate the social from the educational role.

Traveller education may also need fully mobile or roving teachers equipped with mobile accommodation and portable teaching materials in areas where there are numerous transient encampments and isolated families. The type of education they can offer such families cannot of course be full-time, for one teacher cannot be at four or five locations at the same time, but methods of self-teaching and homework can be developed to compensate for this, and anyway, in the very early stages, especially with travellers without previous educational experience, full-time education may be inappropriate.

The demands of co-ordination and liaison in regions of high traveller density (in large conurbations where there are several sites and unauthorized encampments) can be met by the appointment of an LEA officer, preferably at adviser or inspector level, to supervise the education of travellers and to indicate what resources are needed. This appointment might be by several LEAs jointly and financed, as in the West Midlands, partly through an Urban Aid Programme grant. Such appointments could result in a network of central record keeping. Teachers would be able to acquire individual children's records and thus some of the problems of continuity of teaching approaches could be overcome. Traveller parents would almost certainly see such a system as threatening their existence and would therefore have to be reassured and convinced that only teachers and education officers would have access to any data. (See Appendix B.)

TEACHING METHODS, MATERIALS AND CURRICULUM

A detailed consideration of appropriate teaching methods, materials and curriculum has been presented in Chapter 6.

Various materials can be developed individually by teachers, and these may well have an advantage over commercially produced schemes before the eventual development of special traveller teaching aids. In general teachers of travellers may find that equipment such as tape recorders, duplicators, cheap cameras and large-faced typewriters are more effective than printed material, which puts a more passive emphasis on learning and may conflict with the traveller child's often urgent desire to create tangible artefacts of his own.

There is certainly room for the development of teachers' portable packs, capable of being carried in cars and used for teaching in trailers or classrooms. Such packs should contain educationally beneficial games and activities, the raw materials for drawing and writing (teacher's demonstration version and pupil's exercise and homework books), and a variety of aids and reading materials.

The equipment of the child with self-teaching and homework facilities and an educationally acquisitive attitude cannot be over-emphasized. Here the production of cheaply duplicated workbooks and programmed learning apparatus, which can be distributed to children receiving only intermittent teacher contact, must be put high on the list of priorities. Such materials should be suitable for adults, adolescents and much younger children, for there is a strong possibility that they will be used by all members of the family.

Areas for action-research

It is hard for the effects of any inquiry not to be beneficial, for it stimulates greater effort and tends to promote innovation. However, travellers need to be reassured that the purpose of research is to improve methods and provision and not merely go over ground already extensively covered.

Several areas where information is still needed have already been suggested:

(a) Traveller health and medical provision.
(b) Patterns of nomadism and migration of fairground as well as traveller families.
(c) A more accurate census of travellers, which will result in a more realistic assessment of the number of families requiring pitches on permanent and transit sites.
(d) An analysis of the impact of official sites, not least upon the cognitive experience of children and the morale of family life.
(e) The size and educational needs of the housed Gypsy and Tinker population.
(f) A comparative study of traveller education in other countries which might indicate educational practice that could be profitably employed here.

But the most important area must be the analysis of actual teaching methods and provision leading to more effective and efficient education. The least satisfactory area is further research into the travellers themselves, not only because of the obvious question of privacy involved, but because this is now something which has been exhaustively covered.

Particularly to be avoided is the indiscriminate use of psychological and educational tests on traveller children. It is now known that the results of such tests give a misleading and, for travellers, a somewhat insulting indication of intellectual potential. Diagnostic tests, on the other hand, which direct the attention of a teacher to specific areas where skills must be taught and developed have greater justification, though teachers may feel that the questions listed on pages 134–5 of this report are an adequate substitute to actual testing.

Evaluation of five-year pilot project programme

The whole purpose of the five-year programme would be to assess the best measures of dealing with traveller children, and to this end it would be necessary to establish a team of evaluators, centrally co-ordinated, possibly under the aegis of the Schools Council or the National Foundation for Educational Research. Such a team could also undertake the role of ensuring continued teacher dialogue and communication and consultation with traveller organizations. Objectives might need revision and clarification, and it would obviously be necessary to make eventual policy recommendations in the light of the most successful pilot projects and the changing trends that are likely to influence future needs.

Though evaluation would necessarily be a continuous process, there would be a need for a full report to be prepared at the end of the five-year period.

CRITERIA FOR EVALUATION

The criteria which such a team might consider in evaluating the five-year programme might include these main factors:

(a) The feasibility of special measures in terms of available resources, duration of educational contact established, and effectiveness of learning situations measured by progress in the basic skills and academic attainment.

(b) The quality of the over-all impact of the pilot project programme upon the traveller community; whether traditional antipathy towards education has been lessened by the provision of greater incentives and more relevant curriculum.

(c) The characteristics of the response of teachers and administrators, e.g., quality of staff attracted to traveller education, their morale and turnover, the nature of LEA financial and administrative support for them, and so on.

(d) The degree of conflict with or interference in the education of gauje children and the possibilities of using special traveller measures with other groups of children.

(e) The degree to which travellers were able to participate and influence the education of their children, and the extent to which adult education and community development has been achieved.

(f) The effect of the whole programme upon community relations generally.

Notional policy for traveller education

The eventual outcome of the five-year pilot project programme should be the delineation of a policy on traveller education that can be adopted by the LEAs, but possibly also by some form of central agency, which would be established to supervise and co-ordinate nomadic programmes. Obviously educational policy is constantly evolving, and it would be necessary for periodic reviews and changes to be made.

It must also be borne in mind that the whole concept of a definite policy for a minority group directed through a central body is to some extent foreign to the educational system of England and Wales (see note 2, pages 16–17), and it might, of course, not be recommended by the evaluation team. Nevertheless there are indications—for instance, from the centralization of the armed forces' educational system for overseas personnel—that such measures are necessary when dealing with a highly mobile section of the population.

There has been sufficient experience of traveller education to establish the necessity of certain positive discriminatory practices: special methods of organization that are designed to end the mass non-attendance that has dominated the past and results from the unique life style of the travellers, their traditional antipathy towards schooling, and the lack of incentives for them to take advantage of educational opportunities. Specific LEA generosity in providing extra resources to school and other educational units in terms of staffing, accommodation, ancillary and administrative help, travelling allowances for teachers to maintain home–school links, favourable capitation allowances, extra transport facilities for the children to reach school, a generally welcoming and promoting rather than punitive approach on attendance, and allied social and medical services have been proved to be essential. Special grants have already been forthcoming from large charitable foundations, the DES, Urban Aid and from the valuable work of voluntary support groups in raising money from private donations. Such supplementary financing must continue and may well increase, but the main source of funds is obviously the LEAs themselves. Indeed, if as much as is spent per capita on gauje children were to be made available for the education of those travellers at the present time receiving little or no education, the whole situation would be radically changed.

The role of voluntary bodies in leading the way towards special measures (summer schools, teacher training sessions, conferences, pilot innovatory practice in the form of on-site pre-schooling and adult tuition, liaising with and instigating LEA action) must already be recognized and should continue to have a salutary effect.

Finally, however, it is the travellers themselves who hold the key to the success of future traveller education. This report must end on an optimistic note, because the most lasting impression gained of the traveller community is one that has inspired admiration and respect. Teachers in general would reinforce the claim that there is perhaps more hospitality, affection and toleration of the foibles and prejudice of the host community than could possibly be expected from a group which has had less than fair treatment at the hands of the majority.

Though many travellers will not respond favourably to a programme of promotional education, there will be many who do and they will have much to contribute to the variety and colour of our society. This is illustrated by a final anecdote.

The scene is laid, in 1971, in a small branch library a mile from a Gypsy site. It was summer and a hot day. The assistant librarian and two other staff had taken lunch and were waiting for closing time. There were few customers for it was the industrial holiday. Six children entered. They seemed unfamiliar with the surroundings and one member of the library staff had to show them where the children's books were. Ten minutes later the six children came to the counter and tried to offer money for the books. The assistant librarian explained that they didn't have to pay, but that they could join, get tickets and take the books out free, but they must return them. The children said they wanted to be members and a local student-teacher who happened to come by volunteered to sign them in. They handed over their books, had them stamped and waited. When they had had their books returned they just stood there. After an embarrassingly long pause the branch assistant librarian said that that was it—they could go now with their books. Still there was no movement. Eventually the oldest child said: 'Miss, we'm Gypsies. We can't read so 'ere's no point taking these books back home. You's goin' to have to teach us to read 'em ain't you, Miss ?'

Appendices

Appendix A Anglo-Romany and Shelta

Most traveller children can speak at least one of the secret travelling languages —Anglo-Romany, Shelta, Gammon (the cant form of Shelta) or Scottish Tinkers' cant (closely linked to Shelta). The great majority, however, speak Anglo-Romany—*rokker Romanes*. Many teachers will have little evidence that they can do so, even though such languages may be the dominant home speech. It is not really a question of whether the children have two languages and which of them is their first, because there is little evidence that Anglo-Romany as it is now spoken is anything but a vocabulary that can be substituted for English words within a normal English sentence; in other words, Anglo-Romany is only a lexical language and has lost its syntactical structure.[1] Even the Anglo-Romany words are declined and conjugated as English words. This is only a hypothesis because it may be that many families are still able to slip back into the 'deeper' inflected forms so that the gauje visitor who knows many individual words cannot understand. Yet there is no doubt that Shelta and Scottish Tinkers' cant have very ancient origins and that Anglo-Romany has retained its northern Indian roots. Well over 50% of the words in the following list were read in a Bengali restaurant in 1973, and the waiters were able to translate them into English and give a close Bengali equivalent.

Just like Yiddish, which is similar in many ways to Anglo-Romany, these languages have been dismissed as debased: 'Purists deride Yiddish for its "bastard" origin, its "vulgar" idioms, its "hybrid" vocabulary. Hebraicists called it "uncivilized cant". Germans called it "barbarous argot", a "piggish jargon". . . .'[2] The travellers' languages have a much longer history than Yiddish, which appears to be a relatively recent creation from German and Hebrew. The view that living languages *can* be 'bastardized' is based upon a misconception: that a supposed 'pure' form exists (perhaps only Hebrew comes close to this, though that is a sacred liturgical language kept 'pure' by scholars and rabbis). If today's Anglo-Romany is a debased form, then present-day English is a hybrid form of Chaucerian. Languages are constantly evolving and changing, and when they belong to a nomadic people they evolve with greater speed. If they are secret languages of a minority group surrounded by a hostile community then, unless they are also written languages and reserved for some sacred function, they tend to adopt the syntactical and grammatical rules and forms of the native language. Thus both Yiddish and Romanes differ widely when spoken, say, in New York, France, Russia and Sweden. Romanes itself was probably never a 'pure' language, for it is more than probable that the nomadic tribes which left India spoke several languages. Certainly the tribes trekked westwards along different routes and therefore 'borrowed' many different root words according to which countries were passed through and how long was spent in each. In spite of these differences, the common bases of Romanes as spoken today in European countries enables an international conference of Gypsies to communicate effectively (though slowly).

The present controversies over whether Anglo-Romany is a 'creolized' or 'pidginized' language are largely academic socio-linguistic considerations which do not directly concern teachers—or, for that matter, the travellers themselves.[3] A language continues to be virile and 'pure' if it is still evolving and functional. The cry, often heard, that Gypsies no longer speak 'the deep Romanes' can also be found throughout the literature in the last century, yet Anglo-Romany is still used today; and Shelta and Scottish Tinkers' cant are no less alive.

One of the problems of compiling a word list is the wide regional and family variations in pronunciation and vocabulary. The word list that follows is based upon Smart and Crofton for the Anglo-Romany and upon a Shelta list made by the Irish traveller Johnny Connors, checked against MacAlister.[4] Although it has been possible to check some of the words against current usage, teachers may find that many of the words which their children use are different from those given here.*

The main problem in transcribing a language such as Anglo-Romany is whether to adopt a phonology and orthography which will not be too inconsistent with common English spellings and yet will not cause confusion with English words which sound almost the same but mean something totally different, or to use a system that accentuates the 'foreign' etymology and nature of the language. It is the latter course which has been adopted in the word list. If teachers feel that they would prefer to adopt a spelling system which more closely resembles English words, then they can easily do so.

Readers may notice that a proportion of the words in the list are borrowed from non-Romanes and non-Shelta origins. There has been a corresponding export of traveller words into the host community language, though some

* Dr Kenrick and Thomas Acton have kindly suggested changes to the original word lists and have offered additional variations. In the list, the following abbreviations are used to signify main sources: (C) stands for Connors, (M) for MacAlister, (A) for Acton and (K) for Kenrick. Anglo-Romany words which are uncited have been taken from Smart and Crofton and updated by consultation with several travellers.

apparent borrowings are due to more recent Indian influences during the imperialist period.

There is much disagreement among travellers about the use of these languages in the normal classroom, but most would agree that their use should be limited and that teachers who are not themselves of traveller stock cannot be expected to be able to teach a language they do not know and are to a large extent forbidden to know. Nevertheless certain circumstances do exist where the use of Anglo-Romany or Shelta can be justified in the classroom: when traveller children volunteer words, or ask for them to be spelt, when traveller parents have given the go-ahead. *On no account should teachers be the first to introduce Anglo-Romany.* The purpose here is to forewarn the teacher about the kind of words that may be offered.

Word list

(*For teachers' information only*. On no account should any of these words be introduced by teachers.)

ENGLISH	ANGLO-ROMANY	SHELTA/GAMMON
bad	wafedi	ruliah, nays-stach (C)
		gami (M)
beer	lush	gat (C)
	levinor	
	gatter	
chicken	kani	cathlier (C)
		kamag, gretin (M)
children	chavvies	soublics (C)
	tiknies (babies)	gal-yas (C)
		gatrins (M)
		sulans (babies)
cut	chin	shark (M)
dirty	chikli	
dog	jukel	comrah (C)
		komra (A)
eye	yok	gloker, ogler (C)
		lurk (M)
fight	kor (hit)	corbe (C)
	pogger (break)	corib (A)
		lober (M)
go	jav	cruch (C)
	shav	misli, donadu (M)
	jel	
good	kushti	mon-ya (C)
		muni, bonar (M)

hedgehog	hotchi-witchi	
horse	grai	cuie (C)
		kora (A)
		kuri (M)
look, see, watch	dik	gloke, ogle, stach (C)
		suni (M)
mad, silly (insult)	divvi	ruliah (C)
man	mush	fein (C)
		glok (M)
		feen (A)
no	kek, kekka	nays (C)
oh dear! good God! well!	dordi, dordi, dordi!	git galune, galune! (C)
non-traveller(s)	gauje(s)	buffer(s) (C)
'country people'	gorgio(s)	flattie(s) (Scottish and fairground)
one, two, three	yek, dui, trin	
people	foki	foki
		liten (M)
policeman	gavver	wob, sher (C)
	gavengro	shade, shedog (A)
	mushgero	shadog (K)
	muskro	muskro (M)
prison	stirapen	kouay (C)
	stir (also prison slang)	bludunk, rispun (M)
rabbit	shushi	squalor (C)
	morgan (A)	morgin (M)
road	drom	tober
	tober (K. cant)	lanach (M)
steal	chor	nouke, bouge (C)
stop talking	kekka rokker	git (C)
swop/trade	chop	
talk	rokker	tari (M)
wagon	vardo	rogah (C)
		rawg (M)
water	pani	scusick (C)
		skai (M)
		skuck (A)
woman	juvel, rakli (girl)	boure (C)
		buer (A)
		lackeen (C)

Notes and references

1   T. F. Hancock, 'Comment on Dr Kenrick's Anglo-Romany Today' in Proceedings of NGEC Conference 1971, ed. T. A. Acton, p. 15.

2   Leo Rosten, *The Joys of Yiddish* (W. H. Allen, 1970), p. xviii. (Also Penguin Books, 1971.)

3   See Hancock, op. cit., and Dr D. Kenrick, 'Anglo-Romany Today' in Proceedings of NGEC Conference, 1971, pp. 5–14. See also Bibliography.

4   B. C. Smart and H. J. Crofton, *The Dialect of the English Gypsies* (Asher, 1875; reprinted by Gale Research Co., Detroit, 1968); and R. A. Stewart MacAlister, *The Secret Languages of Ireland* (Cambridge University Press, 1937).

Appendix B   A regional scheme for centralization of educational records for Gypsy children

by C. A. Beresford-Webb, Supervisor of Gypsy Education in the West Midlands*

The greatest handicap faced by a child who is forced to travel is that of not being able to maintain constant educational progress. To assist in providing an educational system for the Gypsy or itinerant child it has been proposed that all educational records appertaining to these children in the new Metropolitan County area of the West Midlands, Staffordshire, Shropshire, Warwickshire and the new Worcestershire and Herefordshire County be maintained at a single central office in Wolverhampton. The purpose is to assist in making available to each school that the children attend up-to-date accurate educational information so that their programme of educational study will be disturbed as little as possible.

Experience has shown that the Gypsy child is all too eager to declare himself a non-reader when entering a new school, when in fact he is probably capable of reading quite well. The reasons for this are quite understandable, as to the Gypsy child entry to a new school and the prospect of facing the unknown is always daunting and by claiming to be illiterate he can be sure of being taken over safe and known ground.

The system adopted is an adapted version of the one at present in use by the Forces Educational Services. The basis of the scheme is in two parts: the main educational record folder for the child, and an educational record card carried by the child.

The main educational record

This record has been designed to meet the very complex needs of a child whose education is constantly being disturbed through movement. It will be appreciated that it is more difficult to assess progress in attainments or development skills for a child who is as unsettled as this. For this reason part of the record is devoted to the development of communication skills chart, based on several well-used progress charts, which has been drafted into a tick-off form of chart which will enable class teachers to know exactly how

* This system is already in operation. Further details can be obtained from the Wolverhampton Education Offices.

far the child has developed in any particular skill, what work is likely to be needed to help the child and for the teacher in turn to bring the record up to date showing new skills taught and mastered. This chart is reproduced below. (Other charts cover progress in numeracy, etc.) In addition to this information the record folder will contain full details regarding the child's academic progress. It will note exactly how far the child has progressed in reading skills. It will contain examples of his writing, drawing and number work and information relating to the child's experience with number bonds and mathematical skills. It will also record any serious defects either physical, mental or environmental that the child has which could affect his education.

Photostat copies of these records will be sent immediately to any school taking in one of these children. The school is then responsible for maintaining these records. In this way we must ask for the full co-operation of the schools as some of the information needed is in very minute detail – for example, what reading book the child was last on, which page he was reading and what word or words he was having difficulty with. Information as minute as this may appear irrelevant but in fact can play a very large part in enabling a child suffering from turbulence to settle. The magic of a teacher you have never met before knowing not only which book you were reading but which page you were on and which words you were having difficulty with is sufficient to break down a very large number of the fears and trepidations found in a new environment. When the child leaves the school the completed record is immediately returned to the office in Wolverhampton so that the master copy kept in the office can be brought up to date. The child who is moving takes with him the Educational Record Card (reproduced on page 190) which he presents at the next school he attends. This new school immediately telephones Wolverhampton and obtains over the telephone up-to-date educational information regarding the child, while the office at Wolverhampton sends a photostat copy of the child's records to the new school.

Simplicity of organization is considered to be the key to efficiency, and the scheme has been designed to enable the records centre and the school to operate with the minimum of fuss and bother. By sending photostat copies of the child's records and maintaining the master copy within the office we obliterate the possibility of children's records being lost in the post. In order to assist a record system like this it will be important for copies of end-of-term reports and other relevant information to be sent to the office for inclusion on the child's records. The scheme has been designed to operate on a regional basis and yet it will be possible for it to be co-ordinated on a national level. The main concern at the moment is to ensure that no school has to incur crippling costs in long-distance telephone calls in order to obtain records. It has therefore been decided to use Wolverhampton as a centre as this appears to be almost directly central for the West Midlands area.

PLEASE MAINTAIN THIS RECORD OF THE CHILD'S PROGRESS.

NAME.................

Development of Communication Skills

Developmental Profile

...pleted — a b c d e

	A Date Initials	B Date Initials	C Date Initials	D Date Initials	E Date Initials
Readiness / Sight	**A1** Matches pairs a) pictures b) words. Using letters copies words	**B1** Has sight vocabulary of 12, 50, 100 words	**C1** Words sounded, practised and committed to sight vocabulary	**D1** New words recorded, learnt and remembered. Reads phrases at a glance	**E1** Capable of extending own sight vocabulary
Sound	**A2** Copies sounds made by teacher. Recognises spoken words as a) different b) same	**B2** Recognises sounds as a) different b) same. Letter sounds known ( ) a b c d e f g h i j k l m n o p q r s t u v w x y z	**C2** Sounds phonograms 1. in, an, on 2. ee, oo, ou 3. st, th, tr, sh etc. sounds words 1. monosyllabic 2. polysyllabic Uses phonic conventions listed in append. 2 & 3	**D2** Uses phonic techniques as normal method of reading unfamiliar words	**E2** Sounds new words checking pronunciation with dictionary
Writing	**A3** Traces letters. Copies words	**B3** Copies sentences. Writes own simple sentences	**C3** Writes words spelt orally. Writes own individual record of	**D3** Writes personal and business letters. Writes reports of work	**E3** Makes notes on a) lessons b) information from

	4	**5**	**6**	**7**
Comprehension	**A4** Follows simple oral instructions	**A5** Names objects in pictures. Talks about pictures	**A6** Listens to stories told by teacher	**A7** Shows interest in pictures and wall displays
Information	**B4** Relates text read to accompanying pictures	**B5** Uses picture dictionary (can be of own making)	**B6** Listens to radio, T.V. and teacher's stories. Listens for 5, 10, 20 mins.	**B7** Keeps a diary or personal record of some kind
Stories	**C4** Understands and follows written instructions. Uses workbooks and instruction cards with little help	**C5** Finds information when directed to appropriate book and page	**C6** Reads simple short stories for pleasure. Listens to traditional short stories	**C7** Finds items for wall newspaper. Pursues a personal interest
Events	**D4** Reads school books RA 9 yrs accurately with understanding. Answers questions on above	**D5** Finds information from school library without direction to appropriate book	**D6** Reads own book for pleasure. Listens to full-length books	**D7** Reads a) daily papers b) T.V. papers c) magazines d) official letters
	E4 Takes in what he reads	**E5** Uses reference books in a) school library b) public library	**E6** Enjoys reading full-length books	**E7** Quotes from papers, magazines, etc.

Development of communication skills chart

The educational record card

Each child will be issued with one of these cards which he or she carries on to the next school. The card contains only the minimum of information as the Gypsy is quite naturally very opposed to any form of identity card; and great care should be taken to explain its purpose to parents, that it deals only with educational matters, and is in confidence.

```
EDUCATIONAL RECORD CARD

NAME   [                              ]

DATE OF BIRTH   [                  ]

Educational details concerning this child are available from:
      THE SUPERVISOR OF GYPSY EDUCATION,
      WEST MIDLANDS EDUCATION AUTHORITIES,
      EDUCATION OFFICES,
      ST. JOHN'S SQUARE,
      WOLVERHAMPTON, WV2 4DB.
      Telephone: Wolverhampton 27811 Ext:...............

PLEASE QUOTE REF No   [                ]
```

Upon arriving at a school the Gypsy presents the card and the school contacts the address on the card quoting the reference number given. The office will then supply full information concerning the child's educational attainments both over the telephone and by a photostat copy of the main records sent to the school. Details concerning the child's family will not be included, unless some particular item is considered a major contributing force in the child's education.

Bibliography

General

Acton, T. A., ed. *Current Changes Amongst British Gypsies and Their Place in International Patterns of Development*, Proceedings of the NGEC Conference, St Peter's College, Oxford, 1971.
———. Unpublished thesis—'A Sociological Analysis of the Changing Place of Gypsies etc.', Nuffield College, Oxford, 1972.
———. *NGEC Bibliography on Gypsies*, April 1970.
Adler, M. *My Life with the Gypsies*. Souvenir Press, 1960.
Bercovici, Konrad. *The Story of the Gypsies*. Cape, 1928.
Block, Martin. *Gypsies*. London, 1938.
Borrow, George. *Romano Lavo-Lil*. 1874.
———. *The Romany Rye*. 1857.
———. *Lavengro*. 1851.
———. *The Bible in Spain*. 1842.
———. *The Gypsies of Spain*. 1841.
———. *Wild Wales*. 1862.
Boswell, Silvester Gordon. *The Book of Boswell: Story of a Gypsy Man*. John Seymour. Gollancz, 1970.
Central Advisory Council for Education (England). *Children and Their Primary Schools*. HMSO, 1967. 2 vols. (Plowden Report.)
Centre for Environmental Studies, major sociological report in preparation.
Clébert, Jean-Paul. *The Gypsies*. trans. Charles Duff. Penguin, 1967.
Cowles, Frederick. *Gypsy Caravan*. Hale, 1948.
Croft-Cooke, Rupert. *The Moon in my Pocket: Life with the Romanies*. Sampson, Low & Marston, 1948.
———. *A Few Gipsies*. Putnam, 1955.
Dallas, Duncan. *The Travelling People*. Macmillan, 1971.
Dodds, Norman. *Gypsies, Didikois and Other Travellers*. Johnson, 1966.
Educational Facilities for the Children of Itinerants. Stationery Office, Dublin, 1970.
Evens, E. *Through the Years with Romany*. University of London Press, 1944.
Groome, F. H. *In Gypsy Tents*. 1880.
Hall, Rev. John. *The Gypsy's Parson*. Sampson, Low & Marston, 1894.
Halsey, A. H. *Educational Priority*, vol. 1: *EPA Problems and Policies*. HMSO, 1972.

Hancock, I. F. 'Is Anglo-Romani a Creole?' *JGLS*, 1970 (1–2).

———. 'Comment', *Proceedings of NGEC Conference*, 1971, ed. T. A. Acton.

Hoyland, John. *A Historical Survey of the Customs, Habits and Present State of the Gypsies*. York: Wm. Alexander, 1816.

Ivatts, Arthur. 'Problems of educational policy, design and implementation for a cultural minority—Gypsies.' (Paper 10, Nuffield Teacher Enquiry Conference, *Social Deprivation and Educational Change, April 1972*.) Obtainable from The Secretary, NTE, University of York, York, YO1 5DD.

———. *Report on NGEC Summer Schools*, 1971.

———. Unpublished thesis, *Gypsies*. Department of Social Administration, University of Hull.

Kenrick, D. 'The Sociolinguistics of Anglo-Romani'—(paper delivered to British Association for the Advancement of Science, AGM 1971, Section H). Similar to article in *Proceedings of NGEC Conference*, 1971, ed. T. A. Acton.

Kenrick, D. and Puxon, Grattan. *The Destiny of Europe's Gypsies*. Sussex University Press/Chatto-Heinemann, 1972.

King, Charles. *Men of the Road*. Frederick Muller, 1972.

Leek, Sybil. *A Fool and a Tree*. Lombarde, 1964.

Leland, C. G. *The English Gypsies and Their Language*. 1873.

Levy, Juliette de Baïracli. *As Gypsies Wander*. Faber, 1953.

———. *A Gypsy in New York*. Faber, 1962.

Lyster, M. Gleen. *The Gypsy Life in Betsy Wood*. Dent, 1926.

MacAlister, R. A. Stewart. *The Secret Languages of Ireland*. Cambridge University Press, 1937.

McCormick, A. *The Tinkler-Gypsies*. 1907.

McDowell, Bart. *Gypsies: Wanderers of the World*. National Geographic Society, 1970.

Ministry of Housing and Local Government, and Welsh Office. *Gypsies and Other Travellers*. HMSO, 1967.

O'Connor, John. *Canals, Barges and People*. Art & Technic, 1950.

Petulengro, Gipsy. *A Romany Life*. Methuen, 1935.

Phelan, Jim. *Waggon Wheels*. Harrap, 1915.

Plowden Report, see Central Advisory Council for Education (England).

Puxon, Grattan. *On the Road*. NCCL, 1967.

Reeve, Dominic. *No Place Like Home*. Phoenix, 1960.

———. *Smoke in the Lanes*. Phoenix, 1958.

———. *Whichever Way We Turn*. Baker, 1964.

Rehfisch, Farnham. 'Marriage and the elementary family among Scottish tinkers.' *Scottish Studies*. vol. v, no 2 (1961), pp. 121–48.

Report of the Commission on Itinerancy. Stationery Office, Dublin, 1963.

Sampson, John. *The Wind on the Heath*. Chatto & Windus, 1929.

———. *The Dialect of the Gypsies of Wales*. Oxford University Press, 1926, reprinted 1968.

Sandford, Jeremy. *Gypsies*. Secker & Warburg, 1973.

Scottish Development Department. *Scotland's Travelling People: Problems and Solutions*. HMSO, 1971.

Simson, W. *A History of the Gypsies*. Sampson, Low & Marston, 1865.

Smart, B. C. and Crofton, H. J. *The Dialect of the English Gypsies*. Asher, 1875 (republished by Gale Research Co., Detroit, 1968).

Smith of Coalville, George. *Gypsy Life*. 1880.

Smith, Rodney 'Gypsy'. *Gypsy Smith: His Life and Work*. 1905.

Stancu, Z. *The Gypsy Tribe* (trans. Roy MacGregor Hastie). Abelard-Schumann, 1973.

Starkie, Walter. *Raggle-Taggle*. Murray, 1947.

———. *In Sara's Tents*. Murray, 1954.

———. *Don Gypsy*. Murray, 1937.

Vesey-Fitzgerald, Brian. *Gypsies of Britain*. Chapman & Hall, 1944.

Wallbridge, John, ed. *The Shadow on the Cheese*. NGEC, 1972.

Webb, G. C. E. *Gypsies: the Secret People*. Jenkins, 1960.

Wood, Manfri Frederick. *In the Life of a Romany Gypsy*. Routledge & Kegan Paul, 1973.

Yates, Dora. *My Gypsy Days: Recollections of a Romanie Ranie*. Phoenix, 1953.

———. *A Book of Gypsy Folk-tales*. London, 1948.

Yoors, Jan. *The Gypsies*. Allen & Unwin, 1967.

York Support Group. 'Till doomsday in the afternoon?' 1973 Summer School Report (c/o York Community Council, 10 Priory Street, York).

Books for travellers in the classroom

(Although most of the above books are unsuitable for classroom use, many have stimulating photographs)

Acton, T. A., ed. *The Romano Drom Songbook No. 1*. Romanestan Publications, 1971. (Rather ambitious anthology of Romany/English songs and scores.)

———. *Mo Romano Lil*. Romanestan Publications, 1971. (Amateurish dual Anglo-Romany/English text with anti-gauje tone.)

Adamson, Gareth. *Wheels of the Road*. Dent, 1972. (History of carts and wagons.)

Bibby, Violet. *Sarranne*. Longman Young Books, 1969. (Junior story of nineteenth-century bargee girl in Midlands.)

———. *The Wildling*. Longmans, 1971. (Story of boy with gauje father and Gypsy mother set in reign of James I.)

Cockett, Mary. *Boat Girl*. Chatto-Boyd & Oliver, 1972. (Bargee.)

Flowerdew, Phyllis. *Gypsy Boy*. Flamingo Books. Oliver & Boyd. 1969.

George, S. C. *Barge Boy*. Oliver & Boyd, 1968.

Godden, Rumer. *The Diddakoi*. Macmillan, 1972. (Junior/secondary.)

Gypsies and Nomads. Macdonald First Library. Macdonald Educational, 1973.

Hollowood, Jane. Maggie Storybooks. Chatto & Windus, 1967.

Hornby, John. *Gypsies*. Oliver & Boyd, 1965. (Children's history of the Gypsies and their origins—good but weak on present day. Junior/secondary.)

Horses and Ponies. Macdonald First Library. Macdonald Educational, 1973.

Kaye, Geraldine. *Nowhere to Stop*. Leicester: Brockhampton Press, 1972. (Very realistic and up to date. Junior/secondary.)

———. *Nowhere to Go.* New Oxford Supplementary Readers. Oxford University Press, 1971. (As above.)

———. *Tawno, Gypsy Boy.* Leicester: Brockhampton Press, 1968. (As above.)

———. *Runaway Boy.* Heinemann, 1971. (Main character gauje, but meeting with Gypsy girl.)

King, Charles. *Men of the Road.* Frederick Muller, 1972.

Manning-Saunders, Ruth. *The Red King and the Witch.* Oxford University Press, 1972. (Twenty-four traditional Gypsy tales from Europe. Upper junior/secondary.)

Porter, Sheena. *The Bronze Chrysanthemum.* Oxford University Press, 1973. (Junior/secondary.)

Pullein-Thompson, Christine. *The Gypsy Children.* Reindeer Books, Hamish Hamilton, 1968.

Sinclair, Olgar. *Gypsies.* Basil Blackwell, 1967. (Children's history of the Gypsies and their origins—good but weak on present day. Junior/secondary.)

Smith, John. *The Broken Fiddlestick.* Longman, 1971. (Junior/secondary.)

Trevino, Elizabeth Borton de. *Turi's Papa.* Gollancz, 1969. (Poor Hungarian violinist and son meet Gypsies en route to Cremona.)

Vavra, Robert. *Milane: the Story of a Hungarian Gypsy Boy.* Collins Panorama Book, Collins 1969. (Suitable for all ages, including 5-year-olds, for it contains beautiful colour photographs on every page.)

Zimnik, Reiner. *The Bear and the People.* Leicester: Brockhampton Press, 1973. (Infants' storybook, European setting, Gypsies and performing bear.)

Reading schemes

Crawford, Sheila. *Joe.* Windrush Series, Oxford University Press, 1967. (Junior/secondary. Realistic.)

Goring, D. and Gale, B. *Essex Traveller Reading Scheme.* (Readers and back-up games.) Available soon from 10 Garynesford, Basildon, Essex.

Walsh, J. H. *Gypsy Hill.* Windrush Series. Oxford University Press, 1963. (Junior/secondary. Realistic.)

West Midlands Travellers School. *Traveller Reading Scheme.* (Still in trial stages.) Initial sight vocabulary 100 words—carefully graded readers based on amended Wolverhampton Remedial Services system. Word cards, supplementary readers and phonic kit. Obtainable from Hon. Secretary, WMTS, 204B Lichfield Road, Walsall, Staffs.)

York Gypsy Education Project (Caroline Moseley), *Basic Adult Reading Scheme.* Available from York Community Council, 10 Priory Street, York.

Organizations and further sources

The Advisory Committee on the Education of Romanies and other Travellers (ACERT): The Secretary, 204 Church Road, Hanwell, London W7.

Chaired by Lady Plowden, ACERT consists mainly of former NGEC members. ACERT employs a full-time field development officer whose primary function is to liaise with and advise LEAs. The Committee publishes newsletters, holds teachers' seminars, conferences, and runs summer programmes. Travellers have a controlling vote on all issues including membership. ACERT is non-political, and is grant-aided by the Department of Education and Science.

The National Gypsy Education Council (NGEC): The Hon. Secretary, 61 Blenheim Crescent, London W11.

The NGEC, the first national voluntary body to work for the advancement of traveller education, has had a somewhat turbulent history, losing many of its gauje and traveller members when ACERT was formed in 1973. The NGEC tends to be more radical in its approach and has been less prepared than ACERT to work through the maintained system, stressing instead the importance of preserving traveller culture and promoting educational initiatives which are culturally oriented.

The Gypsy Council (sometimes known as the National Gypsy Council): 18 Poyntz Road, London SW11 or 25 Grasmere Place, Leeds 12.

Established in the late sixties, the Gypsy Council has also had a turbulent history, none more so than at the present time. The primary aim of this political pressure group has been to campaign for caravan sites and the end of discrimination and harassment, but it also undertakes legal and welfare work with travellers.

The Romany Guild: The Organizing Secretary, The Caravan Site, Folly Lane, Walthamstow, London E4.

The newly formed traveller-only body created initially by travellers resigning from the Gypsy Council, but now claiming a substantial traveller membership in the south-east. The Romany Guild remains similar to the Gypsy Council in aims and basic programme, and is a political pressure group. (There is at the present time a move to unite the Gypsy Council and the Romany Guild, possibly under the title of National Gypsy Council, but it is too early yet to judge whether genuine unity has been achieved.)

The Gypsy Lore Society (which publishes the *Journal of the Gypsy Lore Society*)

The society has just lost its dominant organizer through the death of Dora Yates, who has been its driving force for half a century. It is not clear at the time of writing who will take over the running of the society and the editing of the journal. However, back issues and any subsequent issues of the journal can be obtained in any library with a large periodical holding. The society, as its name suggests, is interested in folklore and travellers generally and does not take an active part politically or educationally.

Romano Drom (formerly edited by Jeremy Sandford)

Romano Drom, the Gypsy's newspaper, has not been issued recently and there is some dispute about its ownership, which may not be solved until other differences have been settled within the traveller organizations. No address is available at this time.

The National Book League's Reference Library of Children's Books: 7 Albemarle Street, London W1.

The NBL possesses an exhibition of books on travellers and their education which includes books suitable for the classroom. Loan of the exhibition on application to the NBL.

BBC and ITV (regions)

BBC television and ITV have old films and documentaries which can be hired by schools or groups.

Records

Ewan McColl, Peggy Seeger and Charles Parker, *The Travelling People* (Argo, DA 133). Gauje folk songs with edited conversation interspersed, from travellers and anti-Gypsy militants.
David Blagrove, *Narrow Boats* (BBC REB 56M). Nostalgic record with songs and memories of the old days of the canals.

Acknowledgements

To schools

Teesside
St Mary's R.C. Primary, Stockton
Woodmansey Special Class

York
St Lawrence Primary
Fishergate Primary
Danesmead Secondary

Kingston-upon-Hull
Paisley Primary

Leeds
Ingram Road Infants and Juniors
Matthew Murray Comprehensive

West Riding
Ferniehurst County Primary,
    Baildon
Glenaire County Primary
Baildon Secondary

Rochdale
St Joseph's R.C. High
St John's R.C. Primary
St Peter's C.E. Junior

Wigan
St Thomas C.E. Primary

Manchester
St Luke's R.C. Secondary
St Anne's Infants and Juniors
St Francis R.C. Junior

St Patrick's R.C. Infants
St Francis Secondary

Leicestershire
Lutterworth Sherrier Junior
Manorfield C.E. Primary, Leicester
Stoke Golding C.E. Primary
Mellor Infants and Juniors

Staffordshire
Landywood Junior

Walsall
St Peter's R.C. Primary
Green Rock Junior and Mixed
    Infants

Coventry
Grangehurst Junior and Mixed
    Infants

Warwickshire
Dunnington C.E.

Worcestershire
Norton & Lenchwick C.E. School
Droitwich High
Stourminster Day Special
Ombersley Endowed First
Woodrush County Secondary,
    Wythall

Bedfordshire
Slip End County Primary
Kensworth Primary

Berkshire

Garland Junior
Blands County Infants
Burghfield C.E. Junior
Willink County Secondary
East Challow C.E. Junior

Buckinghamshire

White Spire Special School
Marsworth County Primary
The Grange County Secondary
Parlaunt Park Infant, Slough
Parlaunt Park Junior, Slough
Horton School, Slough
Holmewood County Secondary
Churchmead County Secondary

Hertfordshire

John F. Kennedy Comprehensive
Countess Anne County Primary
Blessed Cuthbert Mayne R.C.
    Junior and Mixed Infants
Cheshunt Boneygrove Infants
Cheshunt Boneygrove Junior
Holdbrook Junior and Mixed Infants
Much Hadham Junior and Mixed
    Infants
Hadham Hall Secondary
Little Hadham Primary
Kings Road County Primary
Gills Hill County Primary Infants
Gascoyne Cecil Junior Mixed

Hampshire

Shepherds Spring County Infant
    School
Shepherds Spring County Junior
Andover C.E. Primary Infants and
    Junior Schools
Andover Harrow Way Secondary
Hook County Primary

Kent

Alkham C.E. Primary
Cuxton County Infants and Junior
    Schools

Holmesdale Secondary
Edenbridge County Primary
Edenbridge Secondary
Great Chart County Primary
Ashford South Secondary
West Malling C.E. Primary
Clare Park Secondary
Bower Grove Special
Cornwallis Secondary
Marden County Primary
Chiddingstone C.E. Primary

Surrey

Horley County Secondary
Outwood County Primary
Salfords County Primary
St John's County Junior
St John's County Infants
Greystones ESN
Ambleside County First
Ambleside County Middle
Riverview County Primary

ILEA

Boxgrove Primary
Abbey Wood Secondary

London Boroughs

North Cray Infants, Bexley
North Cray Junior, Bexley
Kevington County Primary, Bromley
John Bramston Infant School,
    Redbridge
John Bramston Junior School,
    Redbridge
Carshalton Primary, Sutton

Somerset

Rockwell Green C.E. Primary
Court Fields Secondary
Berkeley C.E. VC Primary
Beckington County Primary
Parson St. Primary, Bristol
Selwood County Secondary
Ilton County Primary

Devon
Kingsteignton C.E. Primary

Monmouthshire
Nantyglo Junior and Mixed Infants

Cardiff
Ninian Park Primary

Carmarthenshire
Morfa Infants and Nursery School

Several educational units in the voluntary sector were seen:

The West Midlands Travellers School
Outwood pre-school play group
Redbridge Gypsy School
Three Cherry Trees Site pre-school play group
Bromley and Bexley pre-school play group
Bushey pre-school playgroup
Church of Scotland Socio-Education Project, Perth
West Bromwich Adult Project

A visit was made to Holland, and the Breda Woonwagenkampkinderen and the Groningen school for bargee children were seen.

Acknowledgements to individuals

The following have helped in the project and in the preparation of this report:

	Consultative Committee	*Schools Council*
Thomas Acton	David Lindsay (Chairman)	Helen Carter
Elsie Fisher	Barbara Adams	Phil Clift
Lily Hamblet	David Allen	Ray Donnelly
Arthur Ivatts	C. Beresford-Webb	
Dr D. Kenrick	C. France	
David Morgan	M. J. Gifford	
David Smith	John Russell	
Maree Welch	Norman Thomas, HMI	
	John Wallbridge	
	J. Wight	